Global Marshall Plan

Global Marshall Plan

Theory and Evidence

James A. Yunker

LEXINGTON BOOKS
Lanham • Boulder • New York • London

Published by Lexington Books
An imprint of The Rowman & Littlefield Publishing Group, Inc.
4501 Forbes Boulevard, Suite 200, Lanham, Maryland 20706
www.rowman.com

16 Carlisle Street, London W1D 3BT, United Kingdom

British Library Cataloguing in Publication Information Available

Library of Congress Cataloging-in-Publication Data
Yunker, James A.
Global Marshall plan : theory and evidence / James A. Yunker.
pages cm
Includes bibliographical references and index.
ISBN 978-0-7391-9230-6 (cloth) -- ISBN 978-0-7391-9231-3 (electronic)
1. Economic assistance. 2. Equality. 3. Globalization--Economic aspects. I. Title.
HC60.Y86 2014
338.91--dc23
2014020489

™ The paper used in this publication meets the minimum requirements of American National Standard for Information Sciences—Permanence of Paper for Printed Library Materials, ANSI/NISO Z39.48-1992.

Contents

Tables

Figures

1

Global Economic Inequality

The Marshall Plan of 1948 to 1951, which helped to rebuild Europe in the aftermath of World War II, still stands as perhaps the single most dramatic example in the history of human civilization of noble altruism combined with enlightened self-interest. During the decades following the original Marshall Plan, various visionaries have suggested that perhaps what the world needs now to overcome the problem of global economic inequality is a new Marshall Plan, far more ambitious than the original both financially and geographically, something aptly described as a *Global* Marshall Plan. Basically this new Global Marshall Plan ("GMP" for short) would be implemented through a dramatic expansion of existing foreign development assistance programs, in conjunction with their rationalization and coordination at the global level, carried out under the auspices of a United Nations specialized agency, perhaps designated the "World Development Authority."

Contemporary mainstream opinion, both at the professional and the popular level, basically dismisses the idea of a Global Marshall Plan. Today, "foreign aid" is much maligned as both needless and useless. It is needless because it is no longer necessary to counter the threat of communist expansion. It is useless because it has little or no beneficial effect on the economic progress of the recipient nations. Given the prevalence of these attitudes, most people deem proposals for anything like a Global Marshall Plan to be utopian pipe dreams.

By far the largest amount of foreign aid provided to the developing nations between the early 1950s and the present time consisted of assistance provided by economically advanced capitalist nations to non-communist Third World nations. The major motivation for this assistance was the Cold War purpose of containing communist expansion. With the collapse of the Soviet Union in the early 1990s, the Cold War has receded into an insignificant factor in international affairs. And with it, the containment motivation to foreign aid has receded into insignificance. Closely allied to the idea that foreign aid is needless is the idea that foreign aid is useless. Horror stories abound of enormous wastage caused by incompetence and graft. Critics point out that despite the huge sums invested in foreign aid over the last several decades, much of the world remains mired in poverty. Of course, proponents of foreign aid can argue that the "huge sums" were not so huge after all, in relation to the need, and further that foreign aid may well have been an important factor in the undeniable progress that has been made by many less developed countries (LDCs).

Although the future is uncertain, so far foreign aid, while in retreat, has not become extinct. There were always economic and humanitarian motivations for foreign aid aside from its being an instrument for the containment of communism. Foreign aid has been a recurrent item in national government budgets for long enough to have become institutionally entrenched. While it must be conceded that the economic progress of most LDCs since World War II has been disappointing, a plausible case may be made that foreign aid has been an important factor in determining whatever economic progress has actually been attained. The demise of the Cold War led to reductions in the military budgets of the richest nations, and at least potentially, some of the so-called "peace dividend" might have been allocated to increased foreign aid.

Little evidence exists that any of the peace dividend was utilized for this purpose. How much of the national budget will be devoted to foreign aid depends, of course, on the perceived effectiveness of foreign aid as an instrument for economic progress among poorer nations. The consensus opinion today, among economists, intellectuals, political leaders, and rank-and-file citizens, is that the effect of foreign aid on economic development, while perhaps not negligible, is at best rather slight. To some extent, this judgment is the result of the extremely large economic gap which exists between the living standards of the richest nations and those of the poorest. This extremely high level of global economic inequality naturally engenders attitudes of despair regarding the possibilities for significantly reducing this inequality within the foreseeable future.

Nevertheless, in full recognition that I am swimming against the contemporary tide, I intend to put forward in this book a case for a Global Marshall Plan (GMP). This program would transfer a tremendous quantity of resources from rich nations to poor nations. The scale of the program would dwarf that of all historical foreign aid programs of the post-

World War II era. Yet the scale of the proposed contributions by the donor nations would not be completely unmanageable, especially when viewed in light of the program's potential benefits. The richest nations would contribute amounts ranging from 2 to 4 percent of their national incomes. These resources would be used to augment the generalized capital stocks of the recipient nations, which in turn would permit them to raise their domestic production levels. The program would involve no transfers of consumption commodities; thus it would not involve "redistribution" as that term is usually understood by economists. The transfers would be used exclusively to purchase and install productive capacity (plant and equipment), to augment human capital by means of education and training, and to deepen social infrastructure capital such as roads, railroads, harbors, airports, schools, hospitals, and so on. All three purposes are encompassed by the term *generalized* capital.

Computer simulations of a model of the proposed Global Marshall Plan show the possibility of a tremendous rise in the living standards of the poor nations, while at the same time the living standards of the rich nations continue to rise at rates comparable to historical rates. A diminution of the growth rates of living standards in the rich nations does in fact occur, but it is a very minor diminution. In fact, the diminution could well be described as virtually unnoticeable. The basic idea of the GMP is that living standards in all nations of the world will continue to advance, but the living standards in the rich nations will rise at a very slightly diminished rate in order that the living standards in the poor nations rise at a greatly accelerated rate.

This basic idea must be clearly differentiated from the basic idea of simple redistribution, defined as transferring *consumption* commodities from rich nations to poor nations, or what is the same thing, of utilizing financial transfers from rich nations to poor nations to purchase consumption commodities. Assuming that simple redistribution is implemented at anything beyond token levels, any sort of significant rise in the living standards of the populations of the poor nations would be at the cost of significant falls in the living standards of the rich nations. Beyond that, this kind of redistribution would do nothing, in and of itself, to raise the productive capacities of the poor nations. The intolerable prospect arises of a permanent international dole, of a perpetual condition of dependency of the poor nations on the charity of the rich nations. It is safe to say that such a prospect would be unacceptable, both to the citizens of the donor nations and to the citizens of the recipient nations.

It would be useless to deny that the author of this book believes that the initiation of a real-world Global Marshall Plan would be a good thing. After all, professional economists such as myself rarely devote serious study to major policy innovations that are not currently on the real-world political agenda, unless they strongly suspect that such innovations would be beneficial. They undertake study in hopes of finding evidence that supports their positive view of the proposed innovation. On the other hand, economists will sometimes undertake serious study of policy innovations with which they disagree—but only if such innovations are definitely on the political agenda and seem likely to be implemented in the real world within the relatively near future. Then it becomes important to find evidence *against* the proposed innovation. But whether they are predisposed for or against a certain policy innovation, economists are obliged to follow certain professional standards of objectivity in conducting research on the question. If they uncover evidence that does not fully support their preconceived preference, they are expected to report this evidence.

In keeping with this expectation, I must state firmly at the outset that the research reported here that studies the potential performance of an actual Global Marshall Plan *does not* categorically and definitively support the proposition that a real-world GMP would be effective. To begin with, the computer simulations utilize an economic model that some would deem over-simplified and misleading, as not realistically incorporating the institutional impediments to achieving significant economic benefits through foreign aid. Moreover, even if, for the sake of argument, the model itself is deemed a reasonable approximation to reality, it will be shown that if certain model parameters take on sufficiently adverse values, then computer simulations indicate that a real-world GMP would be an unmitigated failure. From a purely objective point of view, therefore, the central implication of this research is that the success or failure of a real-world Global Marshall Plan is *an empirical question and not a theoretical question*. An economically reasonable model of the international economy shows the possibility of spectacular success that might be achieved by a GMP—but it also shows the possibility of spectacular failure. Contrary to prevalent opinion, however, there is nothing in today's formal economic theory that necessarily leans toward the ineffectiveness of a real-world GMP.

What is highly significant is the strong indication from the research that even if the Global Marshall Plan is an abject failure from the standpoint of the poor nations, in that it would do little or nothing to raise their level of economic prosperity—nevertheless this unfortunate outcome would not significantly diminish the economic prosperity of the rich nations. The evidence strongly suggests that undertaking a Global Marshall Plan would not be a serious burden on the rich nations, regardless of whether or not it benefits the poor nations.

In pondering whether or not to undertake a proposed policy innovation, we consider benefits and costs. Since neither the benefits nor the costs can be predicted with certainty, we are necessarily dealing with a problem in "decision-making under uncertainty." Decision-making under uncertainty is a well-studied area of analysis, but whatever the formal decision-making principle applied, it is necessary to make various assumptions about likely benefits and costs. It is commonly assumed that a real-world GMP would impose a very heavy economic burden on the rich nations, while having little beneficial effect on the poor nations. The research reported here supports neither of these assumptions.

Excessive confidence is generally frowned upon in scientific circles, especially when it comes to a highly controversial proposition or policy proposal. One can never be absolutely sure how a given experiment will turn out. We are all familiar with the "law of unintended consequences" and all that. And professional economists are all very much aware of the possibility that the models that they construct may fall far short of being reasonable approximations to reality. Model forecasts may bear little or no resemblance to what actually happens in the real world.

I should emphasize, therefore, that while I personally strongly believe that a Global Marshall Plan should be implemented in the real world, I also strongly believe that it should be implemented on a *tentative and provisional basis*. It should be clearly recognized and agreed upon by all those involved in the project directly or indirectly, that if the indications from a fair trial period, of perhaps 10 to 15 years, are unfavorable, that the GMP will be phased out and shut down. I am not so confident of the success of the project that I envision its undertaking to be irrevocable and irreversible. Although it is hardly customary at the present time, policy innovations should properly be regarded as *experiments*: if they are successful, all well and good, but if they are unsuccessful they should be abandoned. This crucial attitude should always be kept in mind as the reader evaluates the evidence described in this book.

IS IT A PROBLEM?

Economic inequality has been a fact of life throughout the entire history of humanity. Attitudes toward this inequality cover a wide spectrum. At one end of the spectrum is the view, common during the medieval era, that since economic inequality is God's will, it must be a good thing. At the other end of the spectrum is the view, adopted throughout history by a small minority of radical egalitarians, that economic inequality is a dire evil that could and should be extirpated by any and all means possible.

Somewhere in the middle is the conventional mainstream view that economic inequality is indeed a corrosive and divisive force that weakens society by fostering envy, jealousy, alienation, hostility, and conflict—but which nevertheless serves certain higher purposes of societal welfare. According to this mainstream view, while it is desirable to undertake a certain amount of interventionist social policy for the purpose of mitigating the degree of inequality and alleviating its worst consequences, these measures cannot be pressed too far lest their consequences become seriously dysfunctional in terms of overall social welfare. In other words, economic inequality is in fact an evil, but to some extent it is a *necessary* evil.

Almost all contemporary nations have accepted the welfare state principle that there should be a certain amount of redistribution through public support of a social safety net, financed through progressive taxation of some kind. But while this principle is widely accepted, intense political controversy surrounds the issue of proper implementation of the principle. At the conservative end of the spectrum is the viewpoint that since economic incentives to effort are necessary to economic prosperity, the social safety net should not be too generous, and the degree of progressivity in the tax system should be modest. At the progressive end of the spectrum is the viewpoint that the adverse economic effects of redistribution on effort incentives are often exaggerated, and that taking into account the paramount importance of the human virtues of compassion and charity, the social safety net should be relatively generous, and the degree of progressivity in the tax system should be substantial. Although economists have devoted, and continue to devote, a great deal of effort to constructing models the purpose of which is the estimation of the effects of various aspects of redistribution policy, none of these models is so compelling as to be widely accepted as an objective means of calculating the optimal amount of redistribution. Thus the controversy continues to be fuelled mainly by preconceived notions, with both sides citing evidence consistent with their preconceptions, while disparaging or ignoring inconsistent evidence.

Human personality exhibits conflicting tendencies. Owing to our fundamental psychology, as determined by the inexorable workings of evolution, we are naturally prone to hostility, competition, and conflict with one another. But at the same time we are naturally prone to friendliness, cooperation, and mutual endeavor with one another. Whereas everyone agrees that there is a happy medium on the spectrum between extreme competition and extreme cooperation, conservatives tend to put the optimum more toward the competitive end of the spectrum, while progressives tend to put it more toward the cooperative end. A basic purpose of any politically organized human society is to establish and maintain a framework within society that favors the principle of peaceful cooperation over the principle of competitive conflict.

As global human society has advanced from the multitude of independent tribal groupings of prehistoric times to the relatively limited number of nation-states of today, the principle of peaceful cooperation has slowly but steadily eclipsed the principle of competitive conflict. As politically organized human societies have declined in number but increased in size, the cooperative principle has been extended over larger and larger expanses of territory, and over more and more human individuals. Although crime and other forms of civil violence cannot be entirely eliminated in even the most peaceful and civilized of nations, the safety and security of the typical individual today is vastly superior to that of the typical individual in prehistoric times.

While national governments exert every effort to foster and facilitate the cooperative principle within nations, the same principle is not nearly as important in dealings among nations. The sovereign nation-state system of today is essentially a form of organized anarchy. Of course, this is not to imply that contemporary nations do not cooperate. They cooperate in a wide variety of ways, from the activities of the United Nations down to bilateral trade agreements. But relative to relations among individuals within the typical nation-state of today, relations among nations are not guided, to nearly the same extent, by ingrained habits of friendliness and cooperation inculcated by many decades of rigorous national government enforcement of a wide variety of laws, regulations, and social standards. Relations among nations are guided far more by calculations of short-term national self-interest, and far less by calculations of long-term global benefits to all humanity.

One implication of this situation is that the redistributive principle is far less honored at the international level than it is within nations. Citizens of a specific nation are educated and trained from an early age to feel a sense of responsibility and concern for other citizens of the same nation, even if those other citizens happen to live hundreds or even thousands of miles away. This sense of responsibility and concern is radically diminished in the case of citizens of other nations. Of course there are many cases of family relationships and friendships that cross national boundaries. But as a general rule, any given citizen of any specific nation feels rather little concern and responsibility for people of other nations, especially if these other nations are geographically distant and culturally dissimilar. Thus the foreign aid expenditures of the wealthy nations today are considerably lower than their expenditures on domestic social welfare programs.

To that minority among contemporary humanity who have been blessed with economic affluence, it is very difficult to confront the fact of massive poverty throughout the contemporary world. This fact is so overwhelming and seemingly immutable that it is difficult to grasp. Psychologists agree that when it comes to disturbing realities, a mentally healthy individual will not dwell upon them, and will, in fact, put them out of mind to the maximum extent possible. For example, a mentally healthy person does not reflect at length about his or her own death. The thing is that global poverty is not like personal death: it is not necessarily inevitable and unavoidable. This is a problem that may have a solution—a "cure." As will be shown by this research, that cure may be a Global Marshall Plan. Global poverty is analogous to a cancer in the human body. Cancers may be and often are fatal. But in many cases, proper medical treatment will cure cancer and enable the patient to survive and thrive for many years to come. A Global Marshall Plan is a possible cure for the economic inequality cancer that is now eating away at global human civilization.

Let us consider the global economic inequality situation as it exists today.[1] Applying the proverbial "good news-bad news" dichotomy, let us first look at the "good news," the economically favorable aspects of the contemporary human condition, before proceeding onward to look at the "bad news."

The principal item of good news is that economic living standards, as measured in the authoritative World Development Indicators database maintained by the World Bank, are rising virtually everywhere in the world, and have been doing so for a long time, with the single significant exception of several nations in sub-Saharan Africa.[2] Even relatively poor nations, by the per capita income criterion used by the World Bank, manifest striking evidence of economic prosperity. No longer are huge skyscrapers, lavish shopping malls, and immense traffic jams confined to the wealthy nations—they are now to be found everywhere in the world. Moreover, there are economic elites in virtually every nation of the world whose day-to-day living standards match those of the economic elites in the wealthy nations. Nor is economic progress confined to the highly affluent. At the other end of the economic spectrum, for any arbitrarily specified "poverty line," in most nations the proportion of the national population below this line has been gradually diminishing.[3] Furthermore, this broad-based rise in per capita income has been achieved in the face of relatively rapid population growth around the world—higher in some nations and lower in others—but appreciable even in the slowest-growing nations. The pessimistic prognostications of Parson Malthus in the early part of the nineteenth century, based on the proposition that there is a chronic tendency for population growth to outrun productive capacity growth, may eventually be borne out (as was widely feared during the "great over-population scare" of the mid-twentieth century), but apparently that day is not yet at hand.

Of course there are costs involved in economic growth and rising living standards. It is not only enthusiastic environmentalists who are concerned about the increasing pressure being placed on the natural resource base by the combination of increasing population with increasing average living standards. And skeptical questions could also be raised that the World Bank statistics on per capita income might be exaggerating the actual amount of economic progress. As development proceeds in traditional societies, more and more economic activity becomes monetized, and the World Bank statistics measure monetized economic activity, not total economic activity. Total economic activity and consequent production output may not be rising by as much as the statistics suggest. Thus the "good news" embodied in World Bank statistics on per capita income growth may not be as good as one might hope.

But it is when we turn to the "bad news" that we perceive a problem that is possibly fraught with ominous implications. Although it is true that average living standards, as measured by per capita income, are rising in almost all the nations of the world, the fact remains that the absolute distance (the "gap") between average living standards in the advanced industrialized nations and those in the developing nations has reached alarming proportions, and is continuing to grow. Both the good news and the bad news are illustrated by the numerical information contained in Table 1.1. This information is plotted graphically in the accompanying Figure 1.1.

Figure 1.1 is a plot of Gross National Income (GNI) per capita, using the Purchasing Power Parity (PPP) method of computation, in current international dollars, from 1980 (when the World Bank commenced providing PPP estimates of national income) up through 2010, for four nations: China, India, the United States, and Japan. PPP is a newer estimation method for national output that endeavors to take better account of differences between the actual purchasing power of the various national currencies. It is believed by most economists familiar with the issue that PPP estimates provide more accurate information on relative living standards than the older computations using official exchange rates between currencies. PPP estimates also show smaller differences in living standards than those indicated by the exchange rate method.

The upper panel of Figure 1.1 is in effect a graphical depiction of the "good news" concerning the current economic status of humanity. Between them, China and India account for nearly 40 percent of the human

Table 1.1
Per Capita Income (PCY) Growth, 1980-2010
United States, Japan, China, India

year	U.S	Japan	China	India
1980	25,408	17,843	524	883
1981	25,872	18,423	544	913
1982	25,396	18,956	586	920
1983	25,951	19,421	642	965
1984	27,712	20,175	731	978
1985	28,455	21,359	816	1,008
1986	28,939	21,825	872	1,032
1987	29,832	22,660	957	1,049
1988	31,065	24,181	1,049	1,122
1989	31,497	25,397	1,077	1,163
1990	31,646	26,709	1,104	1,201
1991	31,195	27,520	1,188	1,187
1992	31,753	27,726	1,338	1,228
1993	32,142	27,713	1,503	1,264
1994	33,201	27,835	1,682	1,324
1995	33,865	28,315	1,818	1,401
1996	34,922	29,055	1,983	1,483
1997	36,141	29,480	2,151	1,517
1998	37,463	28,829	2,285	1,583
1999	38,796	28,699	2,438	1,690
2000	40,232	29,321	2,634	1,723
2001	40,187	29,416	2,826	1,782
2002	40,205	29,419	3,076	1,826
2003	40,795	29,862	3,381	1,939
2004	42,032	30,618	3,711	2,060
2005	43,167	31,151	4,085	2,218
2006	44,249	31,836	4,602	2,388
2007	44,058	32,689	5,249	2,595
2008	43,583	32,338	5,732	2,656
2009	41,441	30,438	6,214	2,844
2010	42,541	31,846	6,791	3,088

Source: World Development Indicators

population of the world, and as can be seen both countries are experiencing very healthy economic growth. Since the early 1990s, China's economy has been the more dynamic of the two, but Indian economic growth has also been quite impressive. The average annual growth rate for India from 1980 through 2010 was 4.26 percent, while that for China was 8.91 percent. Both of these growth rates are far superior to the 1.73 percent and 1.96 percent maintained respectively by the United States and Japan over the same period of time. Looking at the upper panel of Figure 1.1,

Figure 1. 1.
Per Capita Income (PCY) Growth, 1980-2010
United States, Japan, China, India

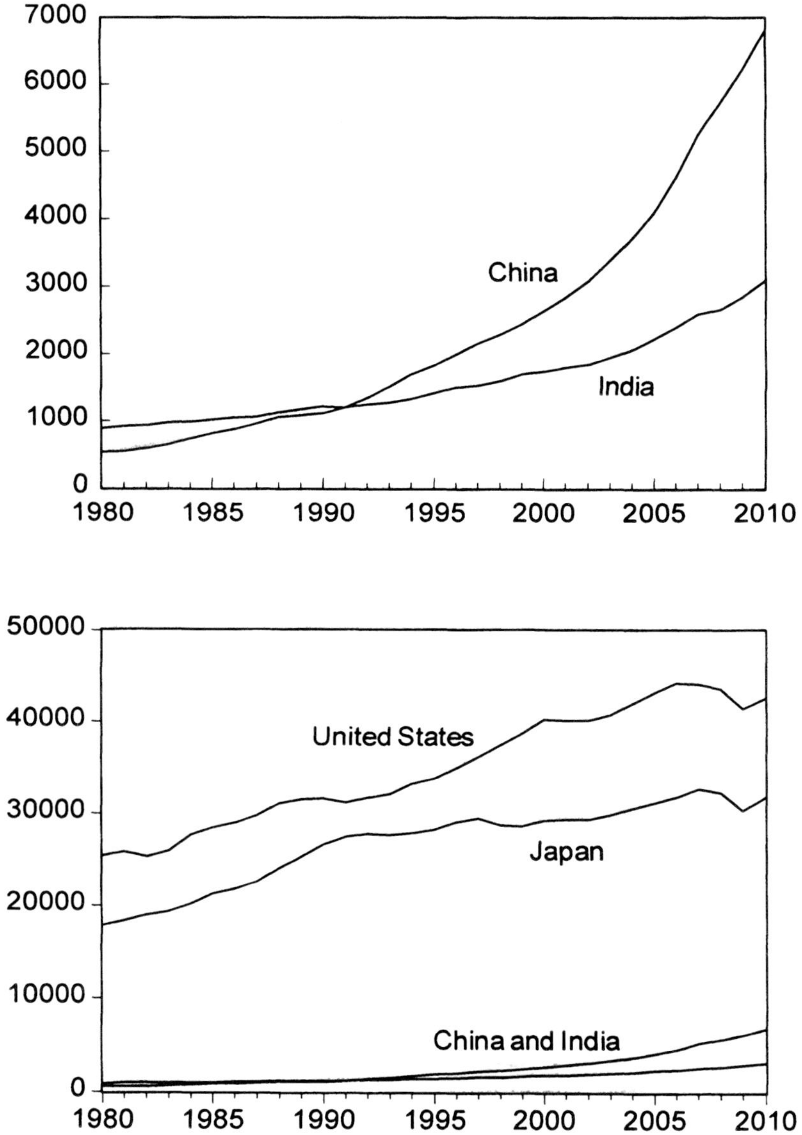

the average person might easily conclude that all this fuss about global economic inequality, world poverty, and so on and so forth, is much exaggerated. Unless the World Bank is very seriously in error regarding the economic condition of these two countries, it would appear that they are progressing very nicely in terms of their average living standards.

The lower panel of Figure 1.1 is in effect a graphical depiction of the "bad news" concerning the current economic status of humanity. It puts the "healthy economic growth" in China and India into proper perspective by adding to the graph two additional plots for the advanced industrial nations of the United States and Japan. Note the difference in scaling on the vertical axis: in the upper panel the range is between 0 and 7,000, while in the lower panel the range is between 0 and 50,000. The economic growth of China and India is indeed very healthy, but the economic growth of the United States and Japan is also fairly healthy, and the latter two countries started from a much higher base in 1980. Despite the considerably higher growth rates of China and India relative to those of the United States and Japan, therefore, there is still, as of 2010, a very substantial absolute gap in average living standards as measured by per capita income.

If one makes the somewhat radical simplifying assumption that two nations are growing according to constant annual geometric growth, and that the poorer nation is growing at a faster rate than the richer nation, one can mathematically determine, on the basis of the initial gap in per capita income, how long it will take the poorer nation to catch up with the richer nation in terms of per capita income. For example, given the relative per capita incomes of the United States and India in 2010, if the Indian economy continues to grow at exactly the 1980-2010 rate of 4.26 percent per year while the U.S. economy continues to grow at the 1980-2010 rate of 1.73 percent per year, it will require 106 years for India to catch up with the United States.

This same exercise applied to China and Japan indicates China catching up with Japan in terms of per capita income in a mere 23 years. While this is a possibility, I suspect most economists would agree that the extraordinarily rapid growth of the Chinese economy over the last 30 years is unlikely to be sustained over a substantial period into the future, and thus it is implausible that China will catch up to Japan in 23 years in terms of per capita income. At one time the Japanese economy was expanding at a breakneck clip, but in more recent decades Japanese growth has been at a more modest pace. From 1980 through 2010, Japan experienced an average annual growth rate of 1.96 percent in per capita income, only slightly above the 1.73 percent of the U.S. economy. The slowing rate of PCY growth for advanced nations such as the U.S. and

Japan is clearly visible in Figure 1.1. Most likely the growth rates of developing countries such as China and India will also slow down at some point. Will these two countries achieve PCY parity with countries such as the United States and Japan before this point is reached? This is clearly possible, but not at all certain.

The unreality of such arithmetical exercises as these, based as on constant-rate geometric growth, need not be belabored. Constant-rate geometric growth may be a reasonable approximation to reality only over the briefest time periods. In the real world over any appreciable length of time, economic growth rates of various nations fluctuate widely in response to a number of factors. What seems clear, however, is that over an extended period of time into the indeterminate future, there will exist very substantial differences in the average living standards of the various nations. Some might argue, on the basis of speculations such as "asymptotic upper limits" on economic productivity within the rich nations, that "sooner or later" the poor nations are bound to catch up to the rich nations in terms of average living standards. I would respond to this argument that there is no guarantee of such a thing happening, and even if it does, it will likely happen later rather than sooner. We will probably have to live with severe economic inequality for a very long time—perhaps forever. That is, of course, unless humanity decides to do something about it.

Should humanity "do something about it"? That is, should humanity organize a Global Marshall Plan in the hope of being able to close the presently existing economic gap within a reasonably abbreviated period of historical time, say between 50 and 100 years? The answer to this question depends on the potential benefits of a GMP relative to its potential costs. Obviously, any such estimation of benefits versus costs must be highly uncertain. We are faced here with a classic problem in "decision-making under uncertainty"—in this case, a great deal of uncertainty. Nevertheless, to have any opinion on the matter, we are obliged to make these estimates. When some people glance at the current global economic inequality situation and then make the snap judgment that anything like the proposed GMP in the real world would inevitably be an exercise in futility, they are basing this verdict on a very rough, quasi-instinctive benefit-cost analysis. Snap judgments are quite often incorrect judgments.

In Chapters 3 and 4 below, I will discuss evidence from a computer simulation experiment that suggests that a Global Marshall Plan of sufficient scope and scale could result in a dramatic increase in the economic growth rates of the poor nations at the cost of a very minor reduction of the economic growth rates of the rich nations. As will be discussed, this remarkable indication is explained by one of the most fundamental principles of neoclassical economic theory: diminishing marginal productivity of a factor of production, specifically in this case, diminishing marginal productivity of capital. The economic benefit to the populations of the developing countries would be tremendous relative to the economic cost to the populations of the advanced nations. Although this evidence, derived from computer simulations, deserves to be taken seriously, I do not claim that it is by any means conclusive. Everyone knows the old computer adage: "garbage in—garbage out." Although arithmetical computations done by a computer are virtually immune from error, if the assumptions and/or the data on which they are based are invalid or inaccurate, then the computational results will almost certainly be incorrect. It must be left to the judgment of the reader to what extent the inputs into the GMP computer simulations are plausible, and consequently the degree of consideration that should be given to the simulation output.

But even if the typical citizen of a rich nation—that is, a nation that would have to contribute some of its national output into the transfer fund—were prepared to give full credence to the "best-case scenario" GMP simulation results, that citizen might still be tempted to question whether a real-world GMP should be initiated, on the basis of the traditional egoistic question: "What's in it for us?" After all, even the best-case scenario simulations show that if a real-world GMP is undertaken, there would be some slowing in the rate of per capita income increase in the rich donor nations. True, it would be a very slight slowing, but it would still be a slowing. Given the prevalence of nationalistic, us-versus-them attitudes in today's world, some citizens of the rich nations might be tempted to ask: "Why should we make any sacrifices whatsoever for the benefit of foreigners?"

I will refrain at this stage from appeal to human morality, higher ethical values, sensitivity, compassion, common decency, and so on and so forth. Not that such an appeal is irrelevant and unimportant. In a larger sense, the proposal for a Global Marshall Plan must be based, at least partially, upon just such an appeal. But the hard fact remains that at root, concern for our fellow man is based on concern for ourselves. According to the Biblical injunction, "Do unto others as you would have them do unto you." In practice, we behave considerately toward others in the hope—frequently disappointed—that they will do likewise toward us. As small children, we are "socialized" by our parents, teachers, and peers to respect the interests of others. Eventually, our inherent tendencies toward cooperative and considerate behavior toward others become internalized, and we unthinkingly "do the right thing" not in the conscious hope of reward or fear of punishment, but simply because it is the right thing to do. These tendencies are "inherent" in humans because natural selection tends to weed out of the population those with genetic propensities toward unduly self-centered behavior.

Our tendencies toward considerate, cooperative, and caring behavior are strongest toward others close to use—family and friends. They become steadily weaker as the others become more distant: people in the same local community, the same state or province, the same nation, and finally, in the same world. Other human beings living on the same planet as ourselves, but outside our own nation, are at a disadvantage in terms of meriting consideration from us, not only because they tend to be more physically distant, but because of two additional factors, among others: (1) there is little effective law at the international level because of the absence of an effective international authority; (2) every national population nurtures various historical grievances against other nations. Thus nations, with the approval of their respective populations, behave far more inconsiderately and less cooperatively toward other nations than do properly socialized human individuals toward other people in their close vicinity.

So, against this hard-nosed background, why might the populations of the rich nations take a sufficiently helpful attitude toward the populations of the poor nations to consider participating in a Global Marshall Plan? They should do so because of both tangible and psychic benefits to themselves and their descendents from living in a more secure and harmonious world. The economic gap as it exists today constitutes a serious impediment to international harmony and cooperation, and thereby represents a serious threat to long-term peace and prosperity.[4]

Since the economic gap appears to be an impermeable problem, and since there is a natural aversion to acknowledging and appraising such problems realistically, it is difficult for many people today to grasp this "inconvenient truth." Thus, many historians and international relations specialists will argue that although existing global economic inequality is regrettable, it does not represent a significant hazard to the future prospects of human civilization. Various evidence might be cited in support of this proposition. In the first place, people who are truly mired in deepest poverty possess neither the physical nor the psychological means with which to make trouble for the more affluent. Applying this insight to international relations, the poorest nations of the world actually represent the least threat to the wealthy nations. Secondly, history provides an abundance of examples of warfare among peoples and nations that were quite homogeneous in terms of economic circumstances. For example, at the outbreak of World War I, living standards in the contesting nations of France and Germany were quite comparable. Indeed, the example of

World War I, among others, suggests that geographical contiguity is a far more significant factor in the outbreak of warfare than economic inequality. Other factors that have contributed to hostility and warfare in the past include racial differences, religious differences, ideological differences, and cultural differences.

Clearly this argument possesses some merit, in that it makes us aware that economic inequality is only one of several contributory factors to international tension, hostility, conflict, and warfare. On the other hand, the fact that economic inequality is only one of several factors does not translate into the proposition that economic inequality is an unimportant factor. History is full of plundering expeditions by poorer peoples desirous of appropriating the material possessions of richer peoples. One thinks of the barbarian invasions of the Roman empire, of the Viking depredations of the coastal areas of Britain and other European nations, of the Mongol invasions of China and Russia.

Nor is the economic incentive to aggressive warfare exclusively confined to the earlier periods of human history. The critical catalytic factor in the two world wars of the twentieth century was Germany's self-perception as a "have-not" nation. The critical factor in the buildup of tension that culminated in World War I was Germany's desire to possess an overseas colonial empire equivalent to that of Britain and France. The critical factor in the buildup of tension that culminated in World War II was Germany's desire to carve a huge land empire out of Eastern Europe and the Soviet Union, an empire which would have been equivalent to the overseas colonial empires of Britain and France. Living standards in Germany just prior to both World War I and World War II were equivalent to those in Britain and France, and they were certainly higher than those in Eastern Europe and the Soviet Union. This did not prevent Germany from considering itself a "have-not" nation relative to Britain and France, and consequently from inculcating such hostility toward these latter nations as ultimately to precipitate total war.

Historians and social analysts inclined to deprecate the role of economic inequality in generating international instability might acknowledge the significance in past history of plundering expeditions by poorer societies against richer societies, but they will argue that such expeditions are no longer feasible in the contemporary world owing to technological developments in weaponry. These developments have endowed the military forces of the rich nations with tremendous superiority over those of the poor nations. The Persian Gulf War of January-February 1991 might be cited—in which the technically superior and better trained forces of the U.S.-led coalition slaughtered Iraqi forces with impunity—as an example of what would assuredly happen if a poor nation were ever imprudent enough to invade a rich nation.

Even assuming that this is true at the present time, and without commenting on the morality (or lack thereof) of this somewhat arrogant attitude, there are at least two important counterpoints to be made. First, this attitude neglects the continuing financial costs of supporting a military establishment sufficiently strong to deter aggression by poor nations for a prolonged period stretching into the indefinite future. Military expenditures by the rich nations have indeed declined significantly since the demise of the Cold War, but they have not declined as much as would have been possible in the absence of the large economic gap. If all or most nations had roughly equivalent per capita income, and thus the tendency toward economically inspired aggression were much lower, it might become possible for the rich nations to reduce military expenditure to only 1 or 2 percent of Gross National Income.

The second point is that it is imprudent to assume that the military situation that holds today will persist indefinitely into the future. It is not impossible that a relatively poor nation will become a military superpower in the future. Indeed, the People's Republic of China is an obvious candidate for this status. There are some interesting parallels between the P.R.C. and Japan. When Japan joined the Axis in the 1930s and embarked upon its career of aggressive expansion that contributed to World War II, it was an "up and coming" nation that deemed itself, despite its ever-increasing material prosperity, a "have-not" nation. The fateful "Greater East-Asia Co-Prosperity Sphere" represented an effort by Japan to escape what it considered to be economic subservience to foreign interests. Should the P.R.C. determine to pursue its economically defined national interests more aggressively in the future, history might repeat itself, with far worse consequences.

In current discussions of the threat to worldwide security and equity represented by the relative poverty of such a large proportion of the world population, the possibility of armed aggression by the poorest nations against the richest nations is rarely considered, owing to the fact that the implicit time horizons of these discussions are very short, and do not allow for significant changes in current conditions. To the extent that all-out nuclear world war is envisioned, it is in the context of the poorer regions of the world generating localized wars in which the superpowers might become embroiled.

An example of what might eventually happen in the future is suggested by the Persian Gulf War of 1991. Iraq, under the oppressive dictatorship of Saddam Hussein, lusted for the lucrative oil wells of Kuwait. Less generously endowed with oil resources than Kuwait, Iraq's 1990 per capita income in current U.S. dollars (according to World Bank data) was $2,170, relative to Kuwait's per capita income of $12,590. On the pretext of a long-defunct historical claim, Iraq invaded Kuwait in the modern equivalent to a plundering expedition. Clearly the motivation in this case was entirely economic. The United States and its allies came to the rescue of Kuwait, and expelled the Iraqi forces in a "short, victorious war." But let us imagine that in 1991 Iraq had had a military alliance with the Soviet Union analogous to the military alliance that Serbia had with Russia in 1914, an alliance that turned out to be one of the critical linchpins into World War I. Let us further imagine that in 1991 the Soviet Union was not on the verge of dissolution, but was still very much the same as it had been in 1970 or 1980. In that case, the Soviet Union might well have accepted the Iraqi historic claim to Kuwait, have taken the position that the Iraqi invasion of Kuwait was an "internal matter," and have demanded that the United States and its allies desist from their intervention. Ultimatums may well have ensued. The outcome could have been nuclear world war. Persistent inequality among nations might generate analogous situations in the future.

Another potential source of disaster is terrorism. Terrorist outrages on the scale of the 9/11 attack might precipitate confrontations between nuclear superpowers. In response to 9/11, the United States mounted a military expedition into Afghanistan in an effort to bring the Al-Qaeda planners of the attack to justice—an expedition that most assuredly did not have the authorization of the Taliban-controlled sovereign government of Afghanistan at that time. Consider the potential parallel between the 9/11 outrage and the 1914 assassination that led to World War I. On June 28, 1914, Archduke Francis Ferdinand, heir to the throne of the Austro-Hungarian empire, was assassinated in Sarajevo by Serbian nationalists desirous of expanding Serbian sovereignty at the expense of Austria. Austria demanded that Serbia allow Austrian police into its territory to hunt for those responsible for planning the assassination. Serbia, with the backing of its ally Russia, refused. Ultimatums were issued, and within a month Europe was embroiled in World War I.

Had the Soviet Union still existed in 2001, and had it been persisting in its traditional ideologically motivated opposition to the foreign policy of such "imperialist capitalist powers" as the United States, the stage might have been set for World War III. When the government of Afghanistan declined to allow the United States access to its territory to hunt for the Al Qaeda leaders, had the Afghan government had a military alliance with the Soviet Union, and had the Soviet Union backed Afghanistan in the same way that Russia backed Serbia in 1914, the outcome might have been similar to the outcome in 1914—disaster.

Obviously, the Islamic militants involved in the 9/11 attack did not have uppermost in their conscious thoughts that the United States enjoyed higher per capita income than the nations of the Middle East—even oil-rich Mideast nations such as Saudi Arabia, of which most of the hijackers were citizens. But the fact of economic inequality certainly augmented their hostility toward the United States. Poverty, whether actual or merely perceived, provides rich soil for the cultivation of emotions of resentment and hostility—emotions that nourish fanaticism of all sorts. Given conducive conditions, one single terrorist action might light the fuse on nuclear Armageddon.

Leaving aside apocalyptic visions, humanity confronts very serious threats aside from nuclear disaster. The population explosion throughout the world over the last century is putting ever-greater pressure on both the natural resource base and the purity of the natural environment. The AIDS crisis has reminded us of our potential vulnerability to catastrophic epidemics of contagious diseases. Drug abuse has become a major contributor to crime and a major threat to the social fabric. These are global problems in that they have important ramifications in almost every nation on the planet. The extent to which humanity will be able to cope effectively with these problems is critically affected by the predisposition among nations toward mutual respect, trust and cooperation. The economic gap may be seriously reducing this predisposition. The wide gulf between living standards in the rich nations and those in the poor nations naturally generates a certain amount of hostility and resentment in the latter against the former. This in turn creates a reluctance in the poor nations to do "favors" for the rich nations.

The United States wants Mexico to exert more effort to stem the flow of illegal migration from Mexico to the U.S. But to Mexico this migration reduces its own unemployment problems, and brings into Mexico a considerable amount of U.S. currency from illegal aliens in the U.S. to their families in Mexico. It might seem to the Mexicans rather selfish of the U.S. to want to keep out Mexican migrants, when U.S. per capita income is approximately six times that of Mexico. The United States also wants Colombia to exert more effort to curtail the flow of illegal drugs from Colombia to the U.S. But to Colombia this traffic provides a substantial amount of both domestic employment and foreign exchange. It might seem to the Colombians rather selfish of the U.S. to be so insistent on Colombian assistance in fighting the U.S. drug war, when U.S. per capita income is approximately eighteen times that of Colombia. Many rich nations throughout the world want Indonesia to exert more effort to suppress slash and burn methods among its subsistence farmers, because these methods result in augmented atmospheric pollution. One major constraint on the Indonesians in acceding willingly to this desire, however, is the low per capita income of Indonesia.

To some extent it is a problem of lack of resources. It requires police resources for Mexico to impede the flow of its migrants into the United States, for Colombia to suppress drug production and marketing, for Indonesia to deter its subsistence farmers from engaging in slash and burn agriculture. But also to some extent it is a problem of lack of will. It is perhaps not unreasonable for a poor population, with an average standard of living that would be considered grinding poverty in the rich nations, to be reluctant to commit significant resources to policies the major benefits of which accrue to the populations of the rich nations, who are already enjoying lavish living standards. It is perhaps not unreasonable that these populations, and their political leaders, experience a strong temptation to rebuff representatives from the rich nations who come to them with transparently self-serving advice and recommendations. The rich nations are generally uninterested in various proposals put forward by the poor nations toward reducing the economic gap. It is perhaps unfair, therefore, to expect the poor countries to happily embrace policies that are more obviously beneficial to the rich nations than they are to the poor nations.

Were the nations of the world to have relatively comparable average living standards, it would be easier for them to reach various compromises, accommodations, and agreements on how to deal with the larger global problems that threaten humanity. A successful Global Marshall Plan might be instrumental to significant improvement in international relations, and to more effective global governance.

OUTLINE OF THE STUDY

The research described in this book might be described as fairly demanding. It deals with the controversial topic of foreign aid, utilizes analytical methodology, and arrives at decidedly unconventional conclusions. Unfamiliar territory requires a good map. It is hoped that the strain on the reader's patience will be somewhat alleviated by providing at this point a brief narrative outline of the remainder of the book. This outline will list the chapter and section titles, and provide for each a brief summary of contents.

Chapter 2: Foreign Aid: History and Evaluation. This chapter contains a selective review of statistical information, analysis, and controversy pertaining to foreign aid, as a means of assessing the potential success or failure of the proposed Global Marshall Plan. Admittedly, the relevance of the reviewed evidence is indirect, since no prior experience exists with foreign aid on the scale envisioned by the GMP. But indirect evidence is better than no evidence at all. The chapter commences with a general discussion of definitions, types, and motivations of foreign aid.

Six Decades of Foreign Aid. This section discusses the evolution of foreign aid since its inception with the Marshall Plan in the immediate aftermath of World War II up to the present day. Just as a major motivation for postwar U.S. Marshall Plan assistance to Western Europe was containment of communist expansion, so too this was a major motivation for the extension of foreign aid to the LDCs of the Third World from the 1950s through the 1980s. The collapse of the Soviet Union in the early 1990s virtually eliminated the communist menace, but other motivations to foreign aid remain important, from economic motivations (for example, desire for stronger trading partners among the LDCs) to security motivations (for example, abatement of terrorist tendencies within the LDCs), to basic humanitarian motivations (concern for others). Total foreign aid provided by the member nations of the Development Assistance Committee (DAC) of the Organization for Economic Cooperation and Development (OECD) has expanded greatly from 1960 to 2010 in current dollar terms. But when adjusted for inflation it is seen to have risen far less. When further adjusted for growth in the recipient population of the low and medium income nations, it is seen to have remained relatively flat from 1960 to 2010 in terms of real per capita foreign aid receipts. Although the relative importance of the United States in aid provision has declined since the early 1960s, it remains the largest single provider. For the United States and all other donor nations, the percentage of national income devoted to foreign aid remains quite small, in recent years mostly in the vicinity of one-quarter of 1 percent. Among DAC donor nations, the U.S. supports the largest military establishment. As a percentage of Gross Domestic Product in 2010, United States expenditures on defense were 24 times expenditures on foreign aid.

Research on Foreign Aid. Some foreign aid recipient nations, such as Taiwan and South Korea, appear to have been benefited considerably from the aid, while others, especially the sub-Saharan African nations, do not seem to have been benefited at all. Various efforts have been made, using statistical data over a range of nations and time periods, to ascertain where the "preponderance of evidence" lies with respect to the effect of foreign aid on the economic growth of recipient nations. While a well-known early econometric study by Gustav Papanek (1973) indicated a statistically significant positive effect of foreign aid on economic growth, later work has shown this result to be non-robust. For example, another well-known econometric study by Paul Mosley, John Hudson, and Sara Horrell (1987) showed no statistically significant effect of foreign aid on growth. On the other hand, there have also been several more recent studies which do find a positive effect of foreign aid on growth. One of the best known of these is a study done by Craig Burnside and David Dollar and described in an article that appeared in the *American Economic Review* in September, 2000. The Burnside-Dollar research was soon challenged by a number of other economists, including William Easterly, who is perhaps the most prominent critic of foreign aid on the contemporary scene. Judging from the large number of economic studies that have been done over the last several decades. it seems rather unlikely that the discipline of economics will provide truly compelling evidence on the effect of foreign aid on economic growth within the foreseeable future. This does not prove that foreign aid has been ineffective in the past or will remain ineffective in the future. It is certainly arguable that various data and estimation problems (including the problem of relatively small quantities of aid for most LDCs) are obscuring a positive relationship between aid and growth that is actually quite strong.

Viewpoints on Foreign Aid. Foreign aid contributions to the economic development of the LDCs clearly did not duplicate the success of the Marshall Plan. By the end of the four-year Marshall Plan period, the Western European nations were well on the road, not only to economic recovery from World War II, but to the high level of prosperity they exhibit today. By contrast, after five decades of foreign aid between the early 1960s and latter 2000s, most of the recipient Third World nations remain poor. Although considerable progress has been made by many of these nations, and although a few of them have exhibited remarkable growth (for example, the "Asian tiger" nations), on the whole results have been disappointing. To critics of foreign aid, this situation is attributable to the inherent ineffectiveness of foreign aid in the promotion of economic progress. To defenders of foreign aid, it is attributable both to the relatively limited scale of foreign aid, and to the fact that throughout the Cold War and beyond, it has been allocated mostly on political criteria rather than economic. This section briefly describes major arguments made by opponents and proponents of foreign aid.

GMP Aspirations. Although hardly enjoying mainstream support, the basic notion of a Global Marshall Plan has been in limited circulation for a considerable length of time. In fact, antecedents of the idea can traced back to the "big push" concept developed by Paul N. Rosenstein-Rodan in a seminal article published in the *Economic Journal* in 1943. The idea was inspired by the Soviet experience of rapid industrialization during the 1920s and 1930s. Mustering the means necessary for rapid industrialization almost entirely from internal resources meant that the living conditions of the Soviet people had been reduced to subsistence levels, resulting in severe social and political stresses as manifested by the oppressive Stalin dictatorship. But if the means of industrialization could be provided from external resources, rapid growth could be achieved without imposing impossibly harsh conditions on the populations of the developing nations. This section describes contributions bearing upon this concept by several individuals including Stringfellow Barr, Seymour Melman, and George J. Church. A recent invocation of the Global Marshall Plan term was by Al Gore in his 1992 book *Earth in the Balance*. Although more concerned with environmental issues than with economic progress per se, Gore's proposals do envision coordinated global action on an unprecedented scale.

Chapter 3: A Global Marshall Plan Model. The purpose of this research is to develop formal scientific evidence on the potential performance of a very large-scale economic development assistance program termed the Global Marshall Plan (GMP). A model of the world economy is specified with nations as economic units and years as time periods. Key elements of the model are the production function, the consumption function, the transfer allocation function determining each nation's foreign aid contribution, and the share function determining each nation's foreign aid receipts. Owing to the model's tight focus on foreign aid, the single model link between the national economies consists of transfers of generalized capital through the GMP. An informal overview of the GMP model is provided in this introductory section to Chapter 3, with special emphasis on the production function.

The GMP model production function is a Cobb-Douglas form in generalized capital and labor. Generalized capital represents all factor inputs into the productive process aside from raw labor. Raw labor is proxied in the model by population. Generalized capital, for which no empirical measures are currently available, is the value of all physical capital (plant and equipment) utilized in production, plus the value of all education and training inputs into the population, plus the value of all social infrastructure physical capital such as roads and schools. For any nation at any point in time, output Y is a Cobb-Douglas function of population P (a proxy for productive labor), generalized capital K, the total factor productivity coefficient A, and the parameters α and β, representing respectively the output elasticity of generalized capital K and the output elasticity of population/labor P. Of these determinants, only α and β are assumed always invariant across nations.

The proposed GMP is based on the hypothesis that most of the observed differences in output per capita ($y = Y/P$) across nations are the result of K differentials rather than A differentials. The program aims at influencing the future development of national K stocks: the K stocks of rich nations will grow at a slower rate in order that the K stocks of poor nations grow at a faster rate. According to conservative critics of foreign aid, the main reason for observed differences in per capita output are total factor productivity differentials: these tend to be low for poor nations because of imbedded political and cultural conditions. To the extent that this conservative hypothesis is true, it is intuitively evident that the GMP will have limited impact on the global inequality problem. The parameter utilized in the GMP model to gauge the extent to which current per capita output differentials are the result of A differentials rather than K differentials is ξ.

Theoretical Specification. This section contains the analytical exposition of the GMP model. The discussion of the production function is mostly concerned with the specification of the role of the ξ parameter in the empirical determination for each nation of the initial values of generalized capital stock K and total factor productivity coefficient A on the basis of observed initial period data on per capita output y and population P. Once output Y in a certain nation at a certain time period is produced, it is allocated to four uses: military expenditure M, consumption C, gross transfer T, and domestic investment I. Military expenditure is assumed to be a fixed proportion of total output. Consumption is derived from a linear function of "disposable income," defined as total output less military expenditure. The gross transfer T is a proportion λ of the nation's "residual," defined as total output less military expenditure and consumption. The remainder $(1 - \lambda)$ of the nation's residual goes to domestic investment I. The proportion λ for a particular nation is determined by that nation's "ratio," defined as the ratio of that nation's per capita consumption to maximum per capita consumption (i.e., per capita consumption of the richest nation in the world). The "transfer allocation function" is designed so that richer nations have larger proportions of their residuals going into the total transfer fund. Another formula is derived to determine the share of each nation in the total transfer fund. The share of each particular nation is determined by two factors: its population and its "difference," the latter defined as the difference between the per capita consumption of the richest nation in the world and the per capita consumption of that particular nation. Transfer amounts and share amounts of each nation are computed separately. The net transfer is the difference between the transfer amount and the share amount. This amount will be positive for rich nations and negative for poor nations. Positive net transfers are foreign aid donations; negative net transfers are foreign aid receipts.

The model is completed by a set of equations representing transition from period t to period $t + 1$. These latter equations introduce a number of additional parameters. One of these, χ (the "conversion effectiveness coefficient"), represents the proportion of each recipient nation's net share that is actually transformed into effective generalized capital. According to conservative critics of foreign aid, the actual value of this parameter is likely to be small, owing to significant administrative costs and/or to the diversion of significant resources to private uses through graft and corruption.

Numerical Implementation. The dataset used for GMP model validation purposes was taken from the World Development Indicators databank. This dataset consists of annual values from 1980 through 2010 (31 years inclusive) for total population P and for four comparable per capita income (PCY) measures for the 146 nations that were listed in the data source as having populations of one million or more in 1980. Coverage of these variables in the source is quite good, so that a relatively small amount of like-case estimation and interpolation has to be used to complete the data set. It was found from experiment that qualitatively the results from the simulations are the same regardless of which particular World Bank measure of per capita income is used. Therefore to streamline the exposition, only results using PCY4 (GNI per capita, Purchasing Power Parity, constant 2005 international $) are reported in this book. This measure of PCY is arguably the most sophisticated, because it takes into account inflationary influences, as well as utilizing the Purchasing Power Parity approach, which most economists believe represents a better measure of relative living standards among nations. For convenience in presenting results, the 146 nations in the full dataset were divided into seven groups according to per capita income: group 1 includes the richest nations and group 7 the poorest nations.

The GMP model contains some 14 parameters whose numerical values must be specified prior to computer simulation of the model. Numerical parameter values are specified on the basis of three criteria: (1) they are consistent with a priori economic theory; (2) they lie within the wide boundaries of plausibility established by impressionistic appreciation of related empirical literature; (3) they produce a reasonably satisfactory fit between the empirical data and the model results over the validation period extending from 1970 through 1995. Conformity with the third criterion is attained by means of trial-and-error simulations of the GMP model over the validation interval. Although the set of parameter values utilized for the benchmark policy simulation satisfy these criteria, the nature of the results obtained might easily engender suspicions that these results are "too good to be true" and are the consequence of "overly optimistic" benchmark parameter values. Therefore, a very important component of the research is to explore the sensitivity of the results to substantial changes in the benchmark parameter values. Results from this aspect of the research are reported in the final section of Chapter 4.

The validation simulation compares the GMP model estimates of per capita income for the 146 nations in the World Bank dataset over the validation interval from 1980 to 2010. Since the actual foreign aid transfers during this period were quite small in relation to those envisioned by the Global Marshall Plan, the GMP model was simulated under the "no-GMP" condition. This is done by setting equal to zero the λ^{max} parameter from the transfer allocation function, the parameter that denotes the maximum proportion of its residual that any specific nation allocates to its own gross transfer into the total transfer fund. When this parameter is zero, nothing goes into the total transfer fund, and there is no GMP in operation. The fit of the model solution in per capita income to empirical per capita income is evaluated by comparison plots of weighted mean PCY for income groups of nations, and by plots of two aggregate inequality measures: Weighted Mean Ratio (WMRatio), and Minimum Ratio (MinRatio). The "ratio" r is defined as the ratio of the per capita income of a specific nation to the per capita income of the richest nation in the dataset for a specific time period. The WMRatio is the population-weighted mean of ratios over all nations in the dataset. MinRatio is the lowest ratio over all nations. It is shown that while the model does not track short-term fluctuations in per capita income, it does track long-term growth patterns quite well. The overall fit of the simulation PCY data to the empirical PCY data is quite close, as measured by two statistics: WMRSQ is the population-weighted mean R-Squared between simulation PCY and empirical PCY for all nations over the 31 years of the validation interval. RSQ30 is the R-Squared between simulation PCY and empirical PCY over all nations for the final period 30 of the validation interval. The values of these two statistics for the benchmark parameter values are WMRSQ = .8351 and RSQ30 = .8744. These figures indicate a respectable fit, taking into account the high degree of simplicity and aggregation of the GMP model.

Chapter 4: Application of the GMP Model. Whereas the validation simulation described at the conclusion of Chapter 3 covers the 31-year interval between 1980 and 2010, the policy simulations described in the present chapter cover the 51-year interval between 2010 and 2060. The fact that the beginning year of the policy simulation interval has already passed into history shows that this is a "what if" experiment, to estimate what might have happened had a Global Marshall plan been commenced in 2010. The benchmark with-GMP policy simulation result presented in this chapter shows the possibility of a dramatic acceleration in the economic growth rates of recipient nations, at the cost of only a very slight retardation in the economic growth rates of donor nations. This latter outcome suggests the political feasibility of a real-world Global Marshall Plan.

However, it also requires emphasis that the non-benchmark with-GMP model results clearly show the possibility of program failure. If certain parameter values are sufficiently adverse, then the recipient nations make little or no progress despite the operation of the Global Marshall Plan. While the possibility of failure shown by certain simulations of the GMP model might be taken, by some, as evidence of the inevitability of failure of a real-world GMP, it may be more reasonable to take these particular results as evidence of the inherent realism of the GMP model, so that the clear possibility of a high level of success shown by the benchmark simulation with-GMP is taken more seriously.

Benchmark Policy Simulation. To provide context for the benchmark with-GMP results for 2010-2060, results are also shown for an extension of the validation simulation interval (1980–2010), described in the last section of Chapter 3, through the remainder of the policy simulation period (2010–2060). The intention is to estimate the likely course of global economic development in the absence of a Global Marshall Plan. This simulation indicates that there will be little change during the 2010-2060 interval in the basic patterns established during the 1980-2010 interval: generally faster growth in the richer nations than in most of the poorer nations, with a rising absolute gap in living standards, and gradually increasing measures of aggregate inequality.

However, the without-GMP model simulation does show an interesting result for the income group 4 nations. This group contains nations in the mid-income level, on the border between the high-income groups 1, 2, and 3, and the low-income groups of 5, 6, and 7. This group of nations shows a sudden, radical acceleration in economic growth, quickly bringing these nations into a pattern of convergence with the richer nations. It is shown that the structure of the GMP model admits of the rapid "takeoffs" hypothesized in Walt Whitman Rostow's "stages of economic growth" theory.

Foreign aid critics might be tempted to cite this result as evidence that massive foreign aid is not, after all, necessary to eventual economic convergence, since if we wait long enough, all or most nations will eventually reach their takeoff points. The problem with this particular argument is that it implicitly concedes that the GMP model is sufficiently realistic for its results to be taken seriously. But if this is indeed the case, then surely the dominant result forthcoming from the benchmark with-

GMP model simulation ought be taken seriously: that dramatic acceleration of the economic growth rates of the poor nations is possible at the cost of a very slight decrease in the economic growth rates of the rich nations, and that a high degree of economic convergence can be achieved within a 50-year period.

To emphasize the difference, some of the tables and figures in this section provide "side-by-side" comparisons of benchmark GMP model simulation results for the "without GMP" case and the "with GMP" case. These exhibits clearly show that at the same time the poor nations are benefiting enormously from the program, the diminishing effect of the program on the economic growth of the rich nations is very slight. To illustrate, for the richest group 1 of nations, weighted mean PCY is estimated to increase from $37,080 in 2010 to $67,292 in 2060 if there is a GMP in operation, relative to an increase from $37,080 in 2010 to $68,246 in 2060 if there is no GMP in operation. The difference between with-without PCY in 2060 is –1.40 percent. Meanwhile, for the poorest group 7 of nations, weighted mean PCY is estimated to increase from $908 in 2010 to $51,331 in 2060 if there is a GMP in operation, relative to an increase from $908 in 2010 to $1,233 in 2060 if there is no GMP in operation. The difference between with-without PCY in 2060 for the poorest group of nations is approximately 4,064 percent.

Of course, to many economists, these remarkable results will not at first be believable. An argument is developed that these results are not at all miraculous but are merely the consequence of one of the most fundamental suppositions of economic thought: the principle of diminishing returns to a factor of production. Generalized capital is a factor of production; the rich nations have much more of it than the poor nations; and consequently the marginal product of new generalized capital resources is much greater in poor nations than in rich nations. In itself, this is not a controversial proposition. What the benchmark GMP model simulation brings to light, however, are the extraordinary potential numerical implications of this proposition.

Burden of the GMP. From the point of view of strict economic logic, the burden of the GMP on the rich donor nations is the reduction in their per capita income growth with the GMP in operation, relative to their per capita income growth without the GMP in operation. In the with-without comparisons discussed in the previous section, it was noted that the reduction in per capita income growth is quite minor for the richest group of nations. This section amplifies this information by showing the percentage reduction in PCY growth for the richest 30 nations in the world in 2010 according to the World Bank's PCY4 measure of per capita income. The percentage difference in projected PCY in 2060 for the U.S.

between the with-GMP and without-GMP situations is –1.400 percent. The percentage differences tend to increase slightly as we go down the list of 30 nations in order of decreasing PCY, but the highest difference on the list is –2.103 percent.

This section also presents estimates of the percentages of national income that would be paid into the GMP total transfer fund by the richest 30 donor nations over the course of the program. As expected, the percentages increase with the per capita income of the donor nation, but even for the richest nations they would remain under 4 percent. For the United States, for example, the estimated percentages are 2.917 in 2020, gradually rising to 3.065 percent in 2010. The modal percentage among the top 30 is around 2 percent. There is no getting around that fact that these percentages are extremely high relative to past history; however they are not completely beyond the pale of feasibility. This is especially true because the true economic cost of the program to the rich nations is in terms of their own reduced economic growth—and the reduction in rich nation growth under the GMP is very modest, as demonstrated by the with-without GMP comparisons. The indication of the benchmark with-GMP simulations is that even though the rich countries would be contributing far more to foreign aid than they ever did in the past, this would still not have an appreciably adverse impact on their own economic growth.

Sensitivity Analysis. This section reports results for a large number of GMP model simulations using alternative numerical parameter values. For most of the 14 parameters of the model, substantial variation in the numerical parameter value around the benchmark value does not materially affect the favorable outcome of the Global Marshall Plan. There are two major exceptions to this rule, exceptions that were not unexpected. One of these relates to ξ, the parameter that determines the extent to which initial differentials in per capita income y are the result of differentials in total factor productivity A as opposed to differentials in generalized capital K. The other relates to χ, the parameter that determines how much of the recipient nation's share in the total transfer fund is effectively converted into generalized capital. The benchmark value of ξ is 0, indicating that all y differentials are the consequence of K differentials rather than A differentials. As ξ increases toward 1, the effectiveness of the GMP in reducing world inequality by raising output in the poor nations steadily diminishes. If $\xi = 1$, indicating all y differentials are the consequence of A differentials rather than K differentials, then the GMP is in fact a complete failure: it has virtually no impact on world inequality. The results are qualitatively analogous for adverse variation in the value of χ.

However, two important points are revealed by the simulations with increasing ξ values. The first is that even if the value of ξ is very much above its optimistic benchmark value of 0, the Global Marshall Plan would still have a major alleviating effect on the global economic inequality situation. For example, if $\xi = 0.5$, the projected WMRatio for 2060 would be 0.3072, which is very much above its 2010 value of 0.1882. The second point is that the cost to the rich nations of the GMP program, in terms of reduced economic growth, is minimal whatever the value of ξ. To illustrate, at the benchmark $\xi = 0$, for the United States (a representative donor nation), U.S. per capita income at the end of the 50-year with-GMP period is projected to be $75,840, relative to $76,484 if $\xi = 1$. In contrast, for Nigeria (a representative recipient nation), at the benchmark $\xi = 0$, Nigerian per capita income at the end of the 50-year with-GMP period is projected to be $51,987, relative to $2,303 if $\xi = 1$. This result exemplifies the indication that higher values of ξ relative to its benchmark value would be very unfortunate from the point of view of the developing nations that would be the beneficiaries of the Global Marshall Plan. But this would have a virtually imperceptible effect on the economic prospects for the rich nations that would be supporting the program. In other words, the cost of a real-world GMP to the rich nations would remain quite minor whatever the value of ξ.

Results for the χ parameter are analogous to those just described for the ξ parameter. The simulations for χ variation show that χ has to take on an extremely adverse value to render the GMP ineffective in raising output in the poor nations and decreasing world inequality. They also show that regardless of the χ value, the cost of a GMP to the rich nations, in terms of reduced growth, would be minimal. On the whole, therefore, the qualitative conclusion that a Global Marshall Plan would be beneficial to humanity is very robust against parametric variation of the GMP model.

Chapter 5: Summary and Conclusion. The introductory section of the final chapter briefly summarizes the purposes, methods, and conclusions of the research. The purpose has been to evaluate the potential performance of a very large-scale economic development assistance effort termed the Global Marshall Plan. The method has been computer simulation of a numerically specified model (termed the GMP model) comprised of 146 nations over the 51-year interval 2010–2060. The model validation phase of the research involved a simulation of the model with benchmark parameter models over the 31-year interval 1980–2010. A good fit was obtained between the model estimates of per capita income and the empirical values of per capita income for the 146 nations over the validation interval. The GMP model with benchmark parameter values was then simulated over the policy interval 2010–2060 for the case in which the GMP was not operating, and for the case in which the GMP was operating. Comparison of the two cases shows that the program could have a tremendous accelerating effect on the living standards of the poor recipient nations, while causing only a very minor reduction in the rate of growth in living standards among the rich donor nations. This result argues toward the implementation of a Global Marshall Plan in the real world.

Evaluating the Research. Given the reigning pessimism with respect to the near-term economic prospects of the LDCs, the immediate reaction of many if not most contemporary economists to the results forthcoming from this research will be that they are simply "too good to be true." This section anticipates and responds to some of the more important objections that could be raised to the research. To the objection that the GMP model benchmark parameter values are over-optimistic, the response is that this possibility was investigated extensively in the sensitivity analysis reported in the last section of Chapter 4. That analysis indicated that with the exception of the two parameters ξ and χ, variation of parameter values within reasonable ranges around the benchmark values does not materially affect the qualitative conclusion that a GMP would be desirable. As for ξ and χ, it requires very substantial variation away from their benchmark values to cause the GMP to be a complete failure, on top of which, even the worst values for these parameters do not materially increase the very minor retarding effect of the GMP on economic growth in the rich nations.

To the objection that the research results are inconsistent with past experience (which suggests a very weak and uncertain effect of foreign aid on the economic growth of the recipient LDCs), the response is that while past aid expenditures may have seemed large in an absolute sense, they were small relative to the need, and did not rise to the level of the critical mass needed to initiate rapid growth in the poor nations. To the objection that the GMP model is an over-simplification of reality and generates some obviously implausible results, the response is that the model is not unduly simple by current standards of economic policy analysis, and in any event simplicity would not necessarily bias the results in favor of GMP effectiveness.

Two additional objections are not so much to the research itself, but to the desirability of economic growth in and of itself, especially very rapid economic growth. Rapid economic growth might exacerbate economic inequality, and it might also have severely adverse effects on the natural environment. While these kinds of problems are certainly very serious, it is questionable that they add up to a sensible case against economic growth. They are more realistically regarded as unfortunate side effects that should be controlled insofar as possible, consistent with the overriding objective of reducing the global inequality problem within a reasonable period of time. Moreover, it might be regarded as rather hypocritical for people living in the richest nations to preach the virtues of slow growth to the impoverished populations of the developing nations, when the former are enjoying the highest living standards ever attained in the history of humanity. The section is concluded with a discussion of the relevance of both the "distributional Kuznets curve" and the "environmental Kuznets curve." The Kuznets curve hypothesis is that while dysfunctional conditions, such as economic inequality and environmental deterioration, tend to rise with per capita income up to a certain point, after that point has been passed, rising per capita income becomes associated with better conditions: less economic inequality and an improved environment.

The Implementation Issue. Still another objection to the research is that it ignores the numerous implementation questions that have been raised in the evaluative and prescriptive literature on foreign aid. While it is true that the present research has nothing substantive to offer on the practical issues concerning how a real-world Global Marshall Plan should be organized, administered, and implemented, this is not a valid objection to the research itself. It is necessary to proceed one step at a time. The purpose of this research is to show that a real-world GMP is not necessarily doomed to failure through the inexorable workings of economic reality. Using a model consistent with accepted economic theory, and using economic data obtained from a reputable source (the World Bank), computer simulations demonstrate the possibility that a tremendous amount of economic equalization among nations might be accomplished without this reducing the economic prosperity of the rich donor nations. Of course, "demonstrating the possibility" is not the same as "proving the likelihood." But in this era of reigning pessimism concerning foreign aid as a means to global economic equalization, it is a necessary first step. That said, some suggestions are offered, based on consensus views among foreign aid authorities, on how best to operate a real-world GMP.

Why a GMP? Some cynics and pessimists would argue that it does not matter how strong a case can be made in favor of a Global Marshall Plan in objective terms, that such a program would never be approved by the populations of the rich nations owing to entrenched prejudices and preconceptions. This argument is rejected, and in its stead is proposed the hypothesis that the populations of the rich nations reject the notion of a major expansion of foreign development assistance on the basis of a fully rational—but incorrect—weighing up of the relative benefits and costs of such an expansion. To some extent they underestimate the benefits, but to a much larger extent they overestimate the costs. Prior to reviewing the benefits and costs, the usual disclaimer is provided: the author recognizes the possibility that the results of this research may be seriously misleading, and therefore reiterates that the proposal is that a Global Marshall Plan be initiated *on a tentative and experimental basis*, with the clear understanding on the part of all participants that the program will be terminated if, after a reasonable trial period, it is not making adequate progress toward its goal. As to the benefits of a world characterized by relatively modest differences in the living standards of the various nations, they include amelioration of anxieties and apprehensions among both rich and poor populations caused by the economic gap, reduction of the likelihood and intensity of armed conflicts within and among nations, and achievement of more effective international cooperation and coordination toward control of the interrelated problems of population growth and environmental degradation.

The book is concluded with an appeal to those higher qualities within humanity that have been responsible for the impressive progress of human civilization throughout history. We owe it to ourselves and our descendants to make a serious effort to overcome the debilitating problem of world inequality by means of initiating a Global Marshall Plan.

2

FOREIGN AID: HISTORY AND EVALUATION

To the dismay of some far-right conservatives in the United States and elsewhere in the economically advanced world, foreign development assistance programs are thoroughly entrenched within the fiscal procedures and administrative structures of the respective national governments. Despite perpetual grumbling by those obsessed with minimizing the tax burden, especially on the affluent, there is little likelihood that foreign development assistance programs (i.e., foreign aid) will be eliminated within the foreseeable future. The United States Agency for International Development (USAID), established in 1961, is still functioning, and there are analogous government agencies in most of the 28 member nations of the Development Assistance Committee (DAC) of the Organization for Economic Cooperation and Development (OECD). The International Bank for Reconstruction and Development, established in 1945 and commonly known as the World Bank, has for many decades operated as a major conduit for multilateral aid flows from the wealthy industrialized nations to the poorer developing nations. For their part, the developing nations possess various government agencies, financial institutions, private business enterprises, and non-governmental organizations (NGOs) for channeling investment resources received from the donor nations into various productive applications. This is a favorable situation because it means that a Global Marshall Plan does not have to be initiated from scratch. The administrative apparatus is already in place and operating smoothly (if not optimally); it just needs to be scaled up and improved.

Nevertheless, at the present time a tremendous expansion of existing foreign development assistance programs of the wealthy nations seems to most people, whether citizens of rich nations or poor nations, veritably unimaginable. A massive "Global Marshall Plan" has been periodically bruited about ever since the original Marshall Plan was completed in 1952. But to date, nothing has come of these grandiose speculations. Among citizens of the richer nations, it is a conventional assumption (and a convenient rationalization) that such a massive international economic development effort would almost certainly be no more than an exercise in futility: despite heavy burdens on the rich nations, the poor nations—owing mostly to graft, corruption, and incompetence—would fail to experience significant economic progress. This assumption is no doubt somewhat less conventional among the citizens of the poor nations, but the latter tend to assume that such a massive international effort is impossible simply because it would be far beyond the bounds of generosity that can reasonably be expected of the citizens of the rich nations. In addition to this, from a psychological point of view it is contrary to the self-respect of the citizens of the poor nations to have to acknowledge that their own economic progress may be significantly dependent on the "charity" of the rich nations.

This chapter provides a selective review of statistical information and professional literature that bears on the potential success or failure of a Global Marshall Plan. Two disclaimers have to be provided at the outset. First, the review provided here is in no sense a comprehensive survey of the literature on the economics of foreign aid. Even in this specialized area within the broader field of economic development, the theoretical and empirical literature has become very substantial, and it would be beyond the scope of this research to try to provide readers with detailed information on it.[1] Second, the relevancy of the reviewed material to the central question tackled by this research is rather more indirect than is normally the case. The central research question herein may be expressed as follows: "How likely is it that a worldwide economic development assistance program on a massive scale (a Global Marshall Plan) would achieve a high level of equalization in living standards across all or most nations within a relatively brief period of historical time?" Owing to the fact that the great majority of economists at the present time assume that such a program would be very unlikely to succeed, or in any case that there is no significant political support for such a program, this question is never addressed in the professional literature, at least in a direct and systematic manner.

The purpose of this research is to present significant evidence to the effect that despite the present strong consensus to the contrary, a worldwide economic development assistance program, on an unprecedentedly massive scale, might indeed achieve a high level of equalization in world living standards across all or most nations within a relatively brief period of historical time. Whether this opinion will become widely shared is a question only time will answer. In light of the reigning pessimism regarding the possibilities for dramatic economic progress throughout the world within the foreseeable future, it seems clearly unlikely that this particular piece of research, or any such piece of research, will inspire sufficient confidence in the potential success of a Global Marshall Plan to form a basis for the actual implementation of such a project. However, for those who may come to believe that such a project ought to be implemented, there exists at least one important ray of hope. That ray of hope is that the *principle* of economic development assistance, in the decades following the end of World War II, has become politically accepted within the rich nations to the point of permanent institutional implementation. At this point, it is not a question of *whether* foreign aid is justified, but rather *how much* foreign aid is justified. In the United States, the Foreign Assistance Act of 1961 authorized the establishment of the Agency for International Development (AID), which carries on today after more than five decades, despite much erosion of optimism and budgetary allocations. USAID represents a working institutional prototype for what may eventually become a major component of a real-world Global Marshall Plan.[2]

Motivations of donor nations, in the provision of foreign aid, may be conveniently classified (with some inevitable degree of overlap) as political, economic, and humanitarian. Politically, foreign aid is intended to keep populations and governments of poorer nations friendly toward donor nations: to keep radical political parties that preach hostility toward rich nations (especially communist parties) out of power in poorer nations, and to dispose the poorer nations to military cooperation with donor nations in the maintenance of strategic security against hostile nations (especially communist nations). Economically, foreign aid is intended (in the short run) to induce poorer nations to follow trading and investment policies (i.e., relatively free trade with minimal tariff and quota restrictions, and receptivity to outside investment by foreign individuals and firms) that foster prosperity in the donor nations, and (in the long run) to enable poorer nations to themselves achieve a higher level of prosperity, that will make them stronger trading partners with the donor nations, and which will further reinforce prosperity in the latter nations. The humanitarian motivation comes from humankind's innate tendencies toward cooperation and assistance, the result of millennia of Darwinian natural selection.

The term "foreign aid" refers to resource flows to poor nations provided by the national governments of rich nations, either bilaterally (from one specific rich nation to one specific poor nation), or multilaterally (involving international financial agencies funded by multiple rich nations that provide resources to multiple poor nations). Resource flows may be in the form of grants, which do not involve repayment obligations, or in the form of loans, which do involve such obligations. Major foreign aid categories include project assistance for both commercial and socioeconomic infrastructure projects, technical assistance (provision of expert advice and planning), military assistance, food aid, debt relief, and humanitarian relief. In addition to foreign aid, resource flows from rich to poor nations occur as a result of profit-seeking investment by business enterprises in the rich nations, and also as a result of charitable activity by foundations and other nongovernmental organizations (NGOs) in the rich nations.

Throughout the second half of the twentieth century, a substantial quantity of economic resources have been transferred via foreign aid from a relatively small number of rich donor nations to a relatively large number of poor recipient nations. In the same period, most of the poor recipient nations have made substantial economic gains. The most important exception to the rule of appreciable economic progress within the poorer nations has been the sub-Saharan African nations. Although most of the poorer nations of the world have registered substantial economic gains over the last few decades, progress has not been as dramatic as had been hoped. On the whole, economic progress in the rich nations has been greater than that in the poor nations, with the result that the absolute gap in living standards has been growing. No doubt a significant drag on individual living standards in the poorer nations has been the relatively high rate of population growth in most of these nations. But differences in population growth rates between rich and poor nations is not the only factor, nor even necessarily the single most important factor, in the persistence of the economic gap.

Opinions on the role and effectiveness of foreign aid cover a wide spectrum. At one extreme are strident denouncers of foreign aid, who argue that foreign aid in the past has not achieved either its political or its economic goals—and moreover, it will not achieve these goals in the future, whatever the scale on which it is provided or the manner in which it is provided. Foreign aid, according to this point of view, not only places a heavy burden on the tax-paying citizens of the rich donor nations, but it is incapable of improving the productive capacity of the poor nations. Within the latter nations, the only parties to benefit from foreign aid are pre-existing wealthy elites and corrupt government bureaucrats entrusted with the management of foreign aid funds. Adherents to this viewpoint often recommend that foreign aid disbursements be terminated quickly and completely.

On the other side, supporters of foreign aid maintain that it has been an important component in whatever economic progress has in fact been achieved by the poor nations. Without the foreign aid of the past, they assert, the present situation would be much worse than it is. The disappointing degree of economic progress in the poor nations they attribute to two factors: (1) foreign aid has not been provided in sufficient abundance to have a dramatic impact on economic progress in these nations; (2) what foreign aid has been provided has incorporated too high a component of relatively unproductive aid forms (e.g., military assistance, debt relief, and food aid rather than project assistance). They argue that foreign aid contributions to the economic development of the poor nations ought to be continued and possibly increased. At the extreme end of the spectrum of opinion on foreign aid are a few individuals (such as this author) who believe that foreign aid should not just be increased—rather it should be tremendously expanded to a level that would justify the term "Global Marshall Plan."

SIX DECADES OF FOREIGN AID

A little over six decades ago, the United States, in cooperation with the Western European nations, planned and implemented what still stands as the largest and most successful single philanthropic endeavor in the history of humanity: the European Recovery Program, commonly known as the Marshall Plan (after George C. Marshall, Secretary of State at the time, and formerly overall U.S. military commander during World War II). Between 1948 and 1952, the United States provided over $13 billion in economic assistance to help the Western European nations recover from the devastating destruction brought about by World War II. The large-scale resources provided by the Marshall Plan dramatically accelerated Western European economic recovery from the war.[3]

Table 2.1 presents basic statistics on the Marshall Plan. The large scale of the economic assistance provided under the Plan is evident both in terms of the donor nation (the United States) and the recipient nations (the Western European nations). Over the four-year period of the Plan's operation, well over 1 percent of U.S. GNP went into Marshall Plan transfers, while these transfers represented well over 2 percent of the combined GNPs of the Western European nations. The largest annual amount was transferred in the first year of the Plan period, with the annual amounts being gradually reduced over the following years.

Table 2.1
Marshall Plan Statistics

Year	(1) Marshall Plan Aid (billions of current U.S. $)	(2) U.S. GNP (billions of current $)	(3) Marshall Plan Aid as % of U.S. GNP	(4) Western European GNP (billions of current U.S. $)	(5) Marshall Plan Aid as % of Western European GNP
1948	5.953	257.6	2.31	131.6	4.50
1949	3.523	256.5	1.37	140.8	2.50
1950	2.406	284.8	0.84	151.4	1.59
1951	1.486	328.4	0.45	158.5	0.94
all	13.368	1127.3	1.18	582.3	2.29

Sources: (1) Herbert Carleton Mayer, *German Recovery and the Marshall Plan: 1948-1952*, Bonn, Brussels and New York: Edition Atlantic Forum, 1969, unnumbered table (page 73): "ECA/MSA—Allotments to All Member Countries between 3 April 1948–31 December 1952"; (2) *Historical Statistics of the United States: Colonial Times to 1970*, Washington D.C.: U.S. Department of Commerce, Bureau of the Census, 1975, Series F 1-5 (page 224): "Gross National Product, Total and Per Capita, in Current and 1958 Prices: 1869 to 1970"; (3) computed from (1) and (2); (4) Imanuel Wexler, *The Marshall Plan Revisited: The European Recovery Program in Economic Perspective*, Westport, CT: Greenwood Press, 1983, Table 26 (page 251): "Western Europe's Gross National Product, 1947-51"; (5) Computed from (1) and (4).

The profound impact of the Marshall Plan on the human imagination is still felt today. It still provides a source of legitimate national pride to Americans, and residual gratitude among Europeans helps to maintain generally friendly and cooperative international relations between the United States and the European nations even to the present day. Still, it would be naive to interpret the Marshall Plan as an exercise in pure and unadulterated altruism. Pure and unadulterated altruism involves significant self-sacrifice with no consideration of either present or future recompense. But the American people during the period of the Marshall Plan had at least two vital motivations of self-interest: economic and political. The economic recovery of Western Europe after World War II would help to assure continued prosperity for the United States by restoring its important prewar trading partners to economic health. The political motivation was even more important. The economic recovery of Western Europe was vital to containing postwar Soviet expansion, which if left unchecked might well have ultimately constituted a direct threat to the two central institutions of the U.S. socioeconomic system: capitalism and democracy. In the absence of these self-interested political and economic motivations, it is doubtful that the United States would have supported anything approaching the scale of the Marshall Plan. No doubt some purely humanitarian aid would have been extended to the suffering people of postwar Europe, but it would have been a small fraction of the actual economic assistance provided under the Marshall Plan. Primarily the Marshall Plan was more of a manifestation of enlightened self-interest than of pure altruism, and its planning and implementation were more testimony to the intelligence and vision of the American people than to their benevolence and compassion. That said, it is also true that benevolence and compassion were factors that helped to swing public opinion in favor of the Plan, thereby reducing the inevitable political opposition against it to a manageable level.

World attention during the 1930s and 1940s was largely focused on the emergent fascist threat, a threat that led up to the cataclysm of World War II from 1939 through 1945. Political and economic recovery from the ravages of World War II were greatly complicated by the emergence of the communist threat. The "grand alliance" between the Soviet Union and the Western Allies broke down almost immediately after the war. To most Western observers, the totalitarian dictatorship of Joseph Stalin appeared almost as socially dysfunctional as the totalitarian dictatorship of Adolf Hitler, and the hegemonic ambitions of the Soviet Union as hardly less dangerous than those of Nazi Germany. Prior to World War II, the Soviet Union was alone in the world in its espousal of worldwide socialist revolution. Within a few years of the end of World War II, communist governments espousing worldwide socialist revolution were in control of several other nations: East Germany, Poland, Hungary, Czechoslovakia, Romania, Bulgaria, Albania, Yugoslavia, North Korea, North Vietnam, and, above all, China, with its large land territory and huge population. Communist parties were active in many noncommunist nations, seeking to gain power through democratic elections if possible, but by revolutionary violence if necessary. It was a time of acute anxiety, as evidenced by the excesses of the House Un-American Activities Committee (HUAC) and Senator Joe McCarthy.

The main elements of the international confrontation between the noncommunist nations and the communist nations were well established by the mid-1950s. The central military aspect of containment was the "balance of terror" created by the nuclear arms competition between the United States and the Soviet Union, in which the initial emphasis on sheer destructiveness (mega-tonnage) of individual bombs was gradually replaced by emphasis on reliable delivery via ballistic missiles. In addition to this central aspect, the Western powers had also given notice of their intention to resist localized communist expansion by military means short of nuclear war: weaponry delivered to the noncommunist Greek government in the latter 1940s had been used to defeat the communist guerillas, and Western armed forces, chiefly American, had been used to oust North Korean and Chinese forces from South Korea—after a long and bloody conflict—in the early 1950s.

The central economic aspect of containment consisted of the effort to raise living standards within the noncommunist less-developed countries (LDCs—the "Third World") of Africa, Asia, and South America, in order to make them more resistant to communist infiltration and takeover. This anti-communist strategic motivation was certainly an important factor—and quite possibly the dominant factor—in the foreign aid programs of the richer Western nations as they developed during the 1950s, 1960s, and beyond. Of its nature, communist ideology seeks support among the poor and oppressed, since they are presumably to be the chief beneficiaries of socialist revolution. The teeming masses of the LDCs provided fertile ground for communist ideology—at least potentially. The rich Western nations reasoned that the less abundant were poor and oppressed people throughout the world, the less dangerous would be the international communist movement.

Developments in economic thought are greatly influenced by crucial real-world events. The Great Depression of the 1930s was the catalyst to Keynesian macroeconomic theory and stabilization policy. The conflict between communist and noncommunist ideologies was a major catalyst to contemporary growth and development theory. While the capitalist economies stagnated during the Great Depression, the socialized, collectivized, planned Soviet economy surged ahead impressively, albeit at a tremendous human cost. Prolonged continuation of the economic growth patterns of the 1930s would have soon led to the Soviet Union surpassing the United States, the wealthiest of the wealthy capitalist nations, a prospect utilized by the communist leadership both to inspire the Soviet people and to proselytize among the populations of the capitalist nations, both developed and developing. But by the mid-1950s, earlier concerns about communist parties gaining power within the wealthy capitalist nations, either by democratic processes or revolutionary means, were rapidly fading. First and foremost, the social and political liabilities of the communist nations, especially the lack of free speech and genuine democracy, greatly reduced the credibility and appeal of communist ideology. In addition to that, the massive destruction of World War II, followed by the heavy military burdens imposed on the communist economies by the Cold War arms competition, greatly reduced economic progress within these nations.

But while communism was a fading threat as far as the populations of the rich nations were concerned, the huge populations of the poor nations were another story. Presumably it is easier for prosperous and well-educated people to perceive the various deficiencies of the communist social system, than it is for impoverished and poorly educated people to do so. Economists in the wealthy capitalist nations did their part to meet the threat by focusing on the determinants of economic progress, and by considering possible policies by which the rate of economic progress might be accelerated. When the noted economic historian Walt Whitman Rostow published his influential *Stages of Economic Growth* in 1960, the work's subtitle (*A Non-Communist Manifesto*) clearly evidenced the fact that a major motivation for concern over the economic development of the LDCs was the perception that poverty in these nations strengthened the communist side in the Cold War confrontation.[4]

Central to Rostow's exposition was the notion of a "take-off into self-sustaining growth." This refers to the critical period during which a national economy raises its level of saving and investment to a point where long-term economic growth becomes permanent. According to Rostow, all of the rich nations of the current period underwent this transition at some point in the past, and presumably (hopefully?) all of the currently poor nations will also undergo it at some point in the future. When all or most of the currently poor nations have finally achieved self-sustaining growth, then the communist strategic threat would wither away. An obvious mechanism for achieving "take-off" conditions within a poor nation would be the provision of generous but temporary foreign aid contributions by wealthy nations, analogous to the Marshall Plan aid contributions that had been instrumental to the postwar recovery of Western Europe. Such was the prevailing vision at the time of the "institutionalization" of foreign aid in the early 1960s, exemplified by the establishment of the United States Agency for International Development (USAID) and various other national foreign aid bureaus, as well as by the formation of the multilateral Organization for Economic Cooperation and Development (OECD). It was anticipated that as more and more countries were "immunized" against communism by rising economic prosperity, the need for further foreign aid would diminish.

But as the years and decades passed after the early 1960s, the relative optimism of that period regarding the prospects for rapid, world-wide economic progress, gradually faded. Although almost all of the poor nations have witnessed some economic progress, and a few of them have indeed experienced dramatic "take-off" transitions, an extremely high level of economic inequality persists, and tremendous numbers of the human population continue to live in conditions of poverty. At the same time, throughout the 1960s, 1970s, and 1980s, concerns about communist expansionism gradually declined. For the most part, the populations of the poor nations remained resistant to communist ideology. Almost all of these nations had small but influential wealthy elites with a strong interest in preserving the capitalist status quo. An important development was the empirical falsification of the "domino theory" in the years following the communist takeover of South Vietnam in 1975, a nation whose abortive defense had cost the United States 60,000 dead and tremendous economic resources. During the 1990s, the collapse of the Soviet Union and ensuing events further reduced concerns over communist expansionism to residual proportions. In short, both the perceived effectiveness of foreign aid, and the perceived necessity for foreign aid, have declined very significantly since the early 1960s.

Tables 2.2 through 2.4, and the accompanying Figures 2.1 through 2.3, provide basic numerical and graphical information on the history of foreign aid from 1960 through 2010. As of the time of writing, some of the data series extend a bit beyond 2010, but for the sake of convenience and consistency with the simulation results discussed in Chapter 4 below, I will use data only up to 2010. For the sake of economy, the numerical data in the tables are at 5-year intervals; however, the figures are based on all 51 years in the range.

Table 2.2 shows the total amount of Official Development Assistance (ODA) expended by member nations of the Development Assistance Committee (DAC) of the Organization for Economic Cooperation and Development (OECD) between 1960 and 2010, along with the percentages of DAC Total ODA provided by the major donor nations: the United States, the United Kingdom, France, Germany, and Japan. Figure 2.1 is a plot of the percentages of DAC Total ODA provided by the United States and Japan, which are the two nations that show the most variability in the range. As is evident from this figure, the U.S. percentage of the total dropped steadily from 60 percent in 1960 to about 10 percent in the mid-1990s, thereafter showing a rise to about 20 percent at the end of the period. Meanwhile, Japan maintained a steady rise from 2 percent to around 20 percent in the mid-1990s. For a time it appeared that Japan was likely to become the single largest provider of foreign aid. But then the combination of slowing growth and the global recession of the 2000s caused Japan's foreign aid generosity to taper off rather quickly. The performance of Germany, the other defeated nation of World War II, has been roughly analogous to that of Japan: a rise followed by a decline. The British and French percentages have not changed as much as the others over the 1960-2010 period.

Table 2.2
Major ODA Donor Nations, 1960-2010, at 5-Year Intervals

Year	Total ODA	Percentage of Total ODA U.S.	U.K.	France	Germany	Japan
1960	4.254	59.02	8.70	17.60	4.79	2.25
1965	6.243	62.00	7.27	11.59	7.03	3.76
1970	6.838	46.97	7.18	10.95	8.92	6.82
1975	18.792	31.39	6.82	11.26	12.74	8.66
1980	34.546	27.25	7.08	11.03	13.62	12.80
1985	32.276	32.91	5.35	10.97	10.30	13.29
1990	58.540	21.51	4.98	13.53	11.93	17.12
1995	59.145	12.50	5.43	14.33	12.77	24.59
2000	49.776	18.42	8.33	7.60	9.31	25.00
2005	108.652	25.80	9.95	9.26	9.31	12.12
2010	131.670	23.53	10.12	10.01	10.07	8.57

Note: Total ODA = Official Development Assistance flows from all Development Assistance Committee (DAC) members, in net terms (new payments less repayments), billions of current U.S. $.
Source: Organization for Economic Cooperation and Development (OECD): OECD StatExtracts.

Figure 2.1
Percentage of Total ODA, United States and Japan, 1960-2010

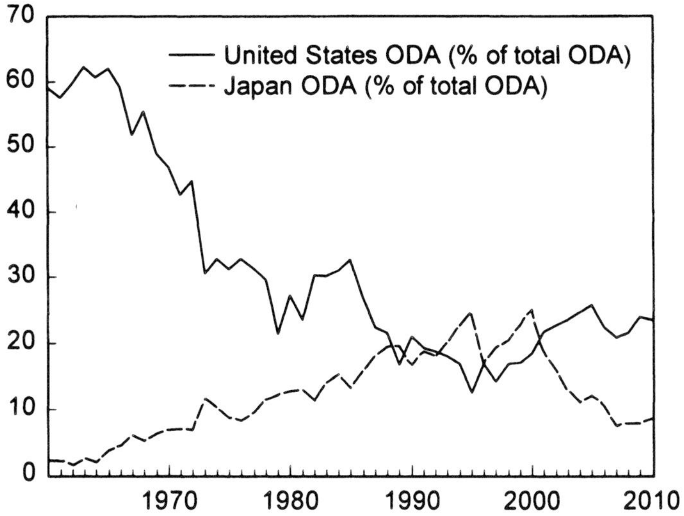

Table 2.2 shows a very substantial increase in Official Development Assistance between 1960 and 2010, from 4.254 billion U.S. dollars at the beginning of the period to 131.670 billion U.S. dollars at the end of the period. These are indeed huge sums: critics of foreign aid like to refer to them as "stupendous" and "staggering." Certainly these sums are indeed stupendous and staggering from the point of view of a typical household or business enterprise. But it is important that they be put into proper perspective. Global human civilization has become very large in the contemporary age, and many raw numbers are extremely large. But when a certain extremely large raw number is divided by another extremely large raw number, the result is not necessarily very large. Table 2.3 provides context for the total ODA figures shown in Table 2.2.

First, it demonstrates that although the raw ODA amounts are quite large in absolute terms, they nevertheless represent a very small fraction of donor economic output. The first three columns of the upper part of the table show respectively total ODA from all donor nations, total GNI for "high-income nations" according to the World Bank's classification (high-income nations being a proxy for donor nations), and total ODA as a percentage of total GNI. The figures in the third column should not be taken for proportions—they are percentages. For example, when the 2010 figure for total ODA (131 billion, 670 million dollars) is divided by total GNI for 2010 (45 trillion, 678 billion, 296 million dollars), and the result expressed in percent terms, it amounts to 0.2883 percent. This is slightly over one-fourth of 1 percent.

Moreover, the raw ODA figures do not take into account either inflation or the increase in the recipient population. The last two columns of the upper part of Table 2.3 show the translation of the current U.S. dollar ODA figures in the first column into constant 1982-1984 U.S. dollars using the Consumer Price Index provided by the Bureau of Labor Statistics. The last column of the upper part of Table 2.3 is the first column in the lower part of the table. The second and third columns in the lower part of the table show respectively the total population in the high-income nations (the donor nations), and the total population in the low and middle income nations (the recipient nations). The fourth column shows ODA expenditures per capita for persons in the high income nations. The fifth column shows ODA expenditures per capita for persons in the low and middle-income nations. In 2010, for example, per capita ODA for the high-income nations was $46.92 in constant 82-84 dollars, and per capita ODA for the low and middle income nations was $10.79 in constant 82-84 dollars. Neither of these numbers are very impressive.

Table 2.3
Total ODA Adjusted for Inflation and Population Growth
1960-2010 at 5-Year Intervals

Year	Total ODA All Donors Bil. Cur. $	Total GNI High-Income Bil. U.S. $	ODA as % of High-Inc Total GNI	U.S. CPI 82-84 = 100	Total ODA All Donors Bil. 82-84 $
1960	4.254	1,043.298	0.4078	29.6	14.374
1965	6.243	1,531.382	0.4077	31.5	19.821
1970	6.838	2,428.464	0.2816	38.8	17.625
1975	18.792	4,771.865	0.3938	53.8	34.930
1980	34.546	9,043.208	0.3820	82.4	41.925
1985	32.276	10,309.526	0.3131	107.6	29.996
1990	58.540	19,002.760	0.3081	130.7	44.789
1995	59.145	25,538.125	0.2316	152.4	38.809
2000	49.776	27,325.427	0.1822	172.2	28.906
2005	108.652	37,562.549	0.2893	195.3	55.633
2010	131.670	45,678.296	0.2883	218.6	60.383

Year	Total ODA All Donors Bil. 82-84 $	Total Population High Income Billions	Total Population Low-Mid Inc Billions	Per Cap ODA High Inc 82-84 $	Per Cap ODA Low-Mid 82-84 $
1960	14.374	0.868	2.168	16.55	6.63
1965	19.821	0.925	2.401	21.41	8.25
1970	17.625	0.970	2.715	18.15	6.49
1975	34.930	1,017	3.048	34.32	11.46
1980	41.925	1.060	3.378	39.54	12.41
1985	29.996	1.099	3.740	27.27	8.02
1990	44.789	1.139	4.139	39.30	10.82
1995	38.809	1.178	4,519	32.94	8.59
2000	28.906	1.210	4.891	23.88	5.91
2005	55.633	1.246	5.244	44.64	10.61
2010	60.383	1.287	5.598	46.92	10.79

Source: ODA, Population, and GNI: World Bank World Development Indicators database; CPI (Consumer Price Index, All Urban Consumers): U.S. Bureau of Labor Statistics.

Some of the above points are illustrated by Figure 2.2. The upper panel of this figure shows considerable growth in total ODA, even in real terms (using constant 1982-1984 dollars). However, the lower panel shows that in terms of percentage of GNI, donor nations' expenditures on ODA have declined very considerably since the 1960s.

Figure 2.2
ODA in Current and Constant 82-84 Dollars,
Total and Percentage of GNI, 1960-2010

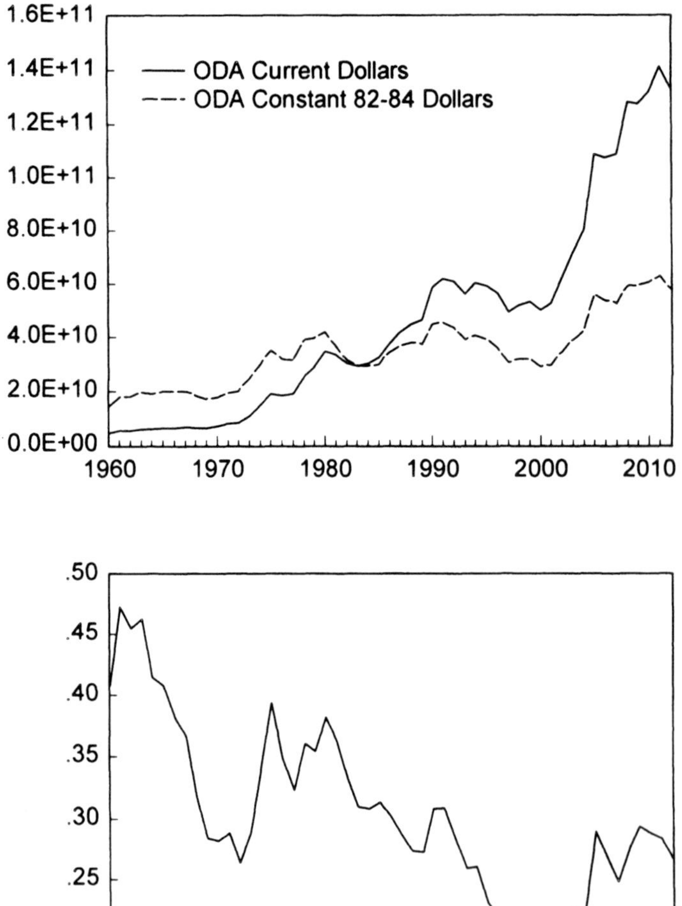

Although the relative importance of the United States as a foreign aid donor nation has declined since the 1960s, the U.S. remains to the present day the largest single provider in both absolute and percentage terms.[5] Table 2.4 compares U.S. foreign aid expenditures to U.S. defense expenditures over the 1960-2010 period, both in absolute terms and as a percentage of Gross Domestic Product (GDP). Figure 2.3 illustrates the percentage figures. Taking the 1960-2010 period as a whole, defense outlays have seen a long-term decline from approximately 10 percent of GDP to approximately 4 percent of GDP, a decline interrupted by the Vietnam involvement in the latter 1960s and the Reagan-era arms buildup of the 1980s. During the same period, ODA has also seen a long-term decline, from approximately 0.6 percent of GDP in 1960 to approximately 0.2 percent of GDP in 2010. These latter figures should not be misinterpreted as proportions. They are in fact percentages: respectively six-tenths of 1 percent and two-tenths of 1 percent. Just how small are U.S. ODA expenditures relative to defense expenditures is particularly evident in Figure 2.3, where the ODA percentage line crawls along just above the lower axis.

Table 2.4
United States Foreign Aid (ODA) Relative to
Defense Expenditures, 1960–2010

Year	ODA (Bil. cur. $)	Defense (Bil. cur. $)	GDP (Bil. cur. $)	Defense (% GDP)	ODA (% GDP)
1960	2.76	48.10	506.32	9.50	0.55
1965	4.02	50.60	674.67	7.50	0.60
1970	3.15	81.70	984.34	8.30	0.32
1975	4.16	86.50	1,517.54	5.70	0.27
1980	7.14	134.00	2,627.45	5.10	0.27
1985	9.40	252.70	3,948.44	6.40	0.24
1990	11.39	299.30	5,441.82	5.50	0.21
1995	7.37	272.10	6,976.92	3.90	0.11
2000	10.00	294.90	9,830.00	3.00	0.10
2005	27.26	495.30	12,382.50	4.00	0.21
2010	30.35	693.60	14,450.00	4.80	0.20

Sources: ODA: Organization for Economic Cooperation and Development, International Development Statistics database; GDP (Gross Domestic Product) and Defense Outlays: United States Statistical Abstract.

Figure 2.3
United States Foreign Aid (ODA) Relative to
Defense Expenditures, 1960–2010

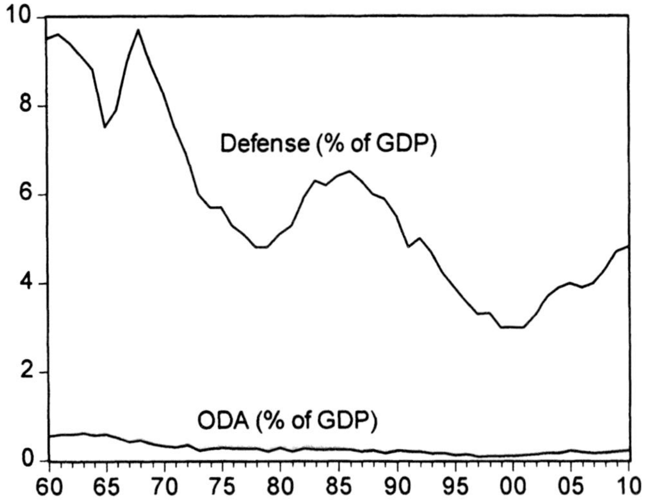

During the period of relatively high aid enthusiasm in the early 1960s, the United Nations proposed a goal of 0.7 percent of national income to be devoted by industrialized nations to foreign development assistance. The United States came close to this goal in the early 1960s but has since gradually diverged from it. In principle, foreign aid and defense spending are competitors for the public budget, but owing to the fact that foreign aid has always been a minor budgetary factor relative to defense spending, there is no obvious relationship between the two. Nevertheless, it is fairly plausible that the heavy budgetary demands imposed by the Vietnam War (as manifested by the spike in defense spending from the mid through the latter 1960s) operated as a strong deterrent to expanding U.S. foreign aid commitments, and served to dampen the relatively optimistic viewpoints of the early 1960s.

As noted in Table 2.1, U.S. Marshall Plan foreign aid expenditures from 1948 through 1951 amounted to somewhat over 1 percent of U.S. GNP. During the relatively optimistic early 1960s, at a time when the basic "swords into plowshares" concept was fairly widely entertained, U.S. foreign aid expenditures were about 0.6 of 1 percent of GDP (a measure of national output closely correlated with GNP—Gross National Product), and defense expenditures were declining sharply. The escalation of the Vietnam involvement during the latter 1960s brought the decline in defense spending to a halt, and commenced a slow but persistent decline in foreign aid spending. To some extent, this decline may be attributed to the politically popular viewpoint that the U.S.'s increasingly prosperous ally nations, in Western Europe and elsewhere in the world, should assume a larger portion of the foreign aid burden. And to some extent, it may be attributed to a fundamental disenchantment with foreign aid, a disenchantment greatly aggravated by the Vietnam experience. Vietnam seemed to demonstrate that not even very large-scale foreign aid would necessarily make a poor nation immune to communism. It also seemed to demonstrate that if the preconditions in a certain poor nation are quite favorable to communism, not even very large-scale military involvement will preserve that nation from communism. The consolation, in the years following the loss of South Vietnam and Cambodia to communism, was the apparent inapplicability of the "domino theory."

The second major increase in U.S. defense spending occurred in the early 1980s, as President Ronald Reagan endeavored to improve the strategic military position of the United States in relation to the international communist threat. By this time, however, foreign aid spending was sufficiently modest that there was no evident decreasing side effect of the military buildup on foreign aid. Whether Reagan's escalation of the Cold War arms competition had anything to do with it continues to be debated by the descendants of "hawks" and "doves," but in any event, as the 1980s progressed, the Soviet people gradually came to the realization that they had had enough of communism and the Cold War. Gorbachev's perestroika and glasnost initiatives escalated into what is probably the single most drastic nonviolent social transition the world has ever seen. As of the early 1990s, Russia, the peripheral republics of the ex-Soviet Union, as well as several Eastern European nations comprising the Soviet Union's erstwhile security buffer, have all become independent nations trying hard to reproduce the capitalist economies and democratic political systems of the wealthy nations of the world. In response to the decline of the international communist threat, U.S. military spending commenced a major decline, from 6.4 percent of GDP in 1985 to 3.0 percent of GDP in 2000. This liberation of 3.4 percent of national output from military uses did not lead to any significant increase in foreign aid, and in fact the percentage of U.S. GDP devoted to foreign aid continued its long-term decline.

Following the 9/11 outrage in 2001, there was a U.S. military response in the form of the 2001 invasion of Afghanistan, followed by the

2003 invasion of Iraq. The "war on terror" has necessitated a military buildup: military spending as a percent of GDP rose from 3.0 percent in 2000 to 4.8 percent in 2010. Meanwhile, foreign aid spending as a percent of GDP rose from 0.10 percent in 2000 to 0.20 percent in 2010. Apparently increased foreign aid spending is also regarded as part of the war on terror. This supports the view that defense spending and foreign aid spending have in common that they are largely motivated by security considerations. During the earlier part of the 1960-2010 time frame, the threat came mostly from international communism; during the later part it came mostly from international terrorism.

RESEARCH ON FOREIGN AID

Has foreign aid had a positive effect on the economic development of the recipient nations? It is widely accepted among development economists that this question cannot be reliably answered on the basis of results from individual projects, even if results from a great many individual projects are examined. For example, when foreign aid is utilized to build a factory, that factory might become highly profitable, or it might become bankrupt. If it is highly profitable, this does not necessarily show that foreign aid is effective, because that factory might have been constructed more economically by private investors. Moreover, the success of the factory might be at the cost of bankrupting other, previously established factories. On the other hand, if the factory built with foreign aid is soon bankrupted, that does not necessarily show that foreign aid is likely to be ineffective. Even in the most prosperous of the wealthy industrial nations, numerous business enterprises established by profit-seeking private investors encounter unanticipated difficulties and end up bankrupt. It is also true that although the factory built with foreign aid eventually failed, while it operated it may have pumped into the economy quite a large quantity of physical and financial resources which benefited other sectors.

When we turn to projects for expanding or deepening social overhead capital, it becomes even more difficult to evaluate relative success or failure, because this cannot be gauged simply on the basis of bottom-line profit. When a road or a school is built, the benefits are widely dispersed and estimates of their financial equivalent are necessarily problematical. Of course, the net returns on social overhead capital projects *must* be estimated lest accountability be lost—but such estimates are obviously subject to a very high degree of uncertainty.

Owing to these problems, therefore, the great majority of serious economic work on aid effectiveness utilizes aggregate statistics rather than enumeration of project results. One could try to estimate the effect of foreign aid on economic growth for one nation over an extended period of time (time series analysis), or the effect of foreign aid on economic growth for a large group of nations at one period of time (cross section analysis), or the effect of foreign aid on economic growth for a large group of nations over an extended period of time (pooled analysis). A large quantity of statistical data has accumulated over time, some issued directly by the national governments, and some collected from the national governments and issued by international agencies such as the United Nations, the Organization for Economic Cooperation and Development, and the World Bank. Although the statistical methodology utilized to examine the data is varied, it also seems safe to say that the multiple regression methodology is dominant.[6]

Over the last several decades, numerous economists have made numerous attempts to estimate the effect of aid on economic growth. These attempts frequently utilize some variant of multiple regression to estimate the effect on some specific growth variable of some specific aid variable, holding other determinants of growth constant. For example, a study might estimate the relationship between the growth rate of GNP per capita and foreign aid as a percentage of GNP, holding other determinants of growth constant. Other determinants of growth might include domestic investment, export growth, population growth, and so on. The estimate would be obtained by regressing the growth rate of GNP per capita on foreign aid as a percentage of GNP, domestic investment, export growth, population growth, and so on.

Emphasis is normally focused on whether or not there is a positive and statistically significant effect of the aid variable on the growth variable. If this is true, the hypothesis that aid increases growth is supported. If it is not true, this hypothesis is not supported. Less attention has been paid to the issue of the *numerical* effect of aid. Conceivably there could be a statistically significant positive effect of aid on growth, but the effect would be of such small magnitude as to be numerically immaterial. On the other hand, it is also conceivable that there could be a numerically material positive effect that is not statistically significant by classical hypothesis testing standards.

On the basis of a large quantity of completed research to date, it would be safe to say that there is no compelling statistical evidence to support the hypothesis that foreign aid has a statistically significant and numerically material positive effect on the economic development of the recipient nations. A very considerable number of statistical investigations have indicated no statistically significant effect at all of aid on growth. These studies are counter-balanced by a very considerable number of statistical investigations that do find a statistically significant positive effect of aid on growth—although, as just mentioned, the investigators rarely discuss the issue of the numerical magnitude of the effect. The "great success stories" of foreign aid, such as South Korea and Taiwan, were mostly completed by the end of the 1960s. Using more recent data, it appears that normally a fairly sophisticated approach to the data is required to obtain the result that aid has a positive effect on growth. Simple inspection of the raw data does not suggest much if any effect of aid on growth. The great abundance of literature on this issue precludes anything more than a cursory review for present purposes. Brief summaries are provided of a few representative studies.

Perhaps the best known of the earlier studies supportive of aid effectiveness is that of Gustav F. Papanek (1973).[7] Papanek's dataset consisted of 85 observations on nations, 34 from the 1950s and 51 from the 1960s. Variables included the dependent variable of average annual growth rate of GDP, and four independent variables: domestic savings, aid receipts, foreign private investment, and other foreign inflows, all taken as percentages of GDP. Equations were estimated using ordinary least squares. In the equation for all observations, using all four independent variables as explanatory variables, the estimated coefficient of the aid variable was 0.39 with a corresponding t-statistic of 5.8 (Papanek, 1973, Table 1). This highly significant result indicates that an increase in 1 percent in the foreign aid percentage of GDP will, other things being equal, lead to a .39 percent increase in the growth rate of GDP. All four explanatory variables in the main equation had the expected positive coefficients, and were significant at the 5 percent level. The numerical value of the estimated coefficient of the aid variable was higher than that of any of the others. Papanek also reported results for Asian countries only ($n = 31$) and countries in the Americas only ($n = 37$): the indication of these latter regression equations being that aid effectiveness had been much greater for Asian countries than for countries in the Americas.

Although fairly strong as econometric evidence goes, Papanek's results did not persuade the growing number of foreign aid skeptics. One of the more plausible arguments put forward by the skeptics has been that foreign aid receipts permit LDC governments to ease up on their own internal development effort, to reduce domestic saving and investment, to lower taxes, and to allocate more public expenditure to wasteful purposes (the "fungibility" hypothesis). To the extent that this is true, and foreign aid merely substitutes external resources for the internal resources that would otherwise have been mustered to achieve the goal level of growth, there should be no relationship between foreign aid and growth. Or if any relationship is found to exist, it would be of an associative rather than a causal nature. Therefore, the question remained as to whether the results obtained by Papanek would hold up using different samples of nations, different time periods, and different equation specifications and/or estimation methods.

Of the several studies that offered a negative answer to this question, one of the most ambitious and influential in its time was that of Paul Mosley, John Hudson, and Sara Horrell (1987).[8] The empirical work of Mosley, Hudson, and Horrell (M-H-H) is based on a theoretical model of utility maximization by government authorities. Maximization occurs subject to a government budget constraint that includes foreign aid receipts as an exogenous source of revenue (along with the endogenous sources tax revenue and borrowings). The model is not fully operational from an estimation point of view, among other reasons because it involves unmeasured goals in the various government decision variables. However, it provides insight into factors that affect the effectiveness of foreign aid as an instrument toward economic growth in a particular nation, as well as a theoretical underpinning for the common perception that the ratios of domestic saving and foreign aid to national output are not only interrelated but also dependent on the growth rate of national output. To the extent that this latter perception is correct, it means that the ordinary least squares estimation technique utilized by Papanek is theoretically inappropriate, and should be replaced by one of the more sophisticated alternative simultaneous equations estimation techniques such as two-stage least squares or three-stage least squares.

Notwithstanding their model, the Table 3 results of M-H-H are obtained from the traditional ordinary least squares estimation method. This technique continues to be frequently applied in many cases where it is theoretically inappropriate, because the method has been found from experience to be quite robust in a wide variety of circumstances. The M-H-H Table 3 reports a number of regression equations similar to those of Papanek, except that two additional control variables are added (growth rate of export values, and growth in the adult literacy rate), and national output growth is measured in GNP terms rather than GDP terms. In addition, the raw data on aid are adjusted to incorporate a lagging process designed to simulate the actual time of impact of aid flows: this lagging process is based on World Bank estimates of the average distribution across years of benefits from aid-financed projects. Separate results are reported for the 1960-1970, 1970-1980, and 1980-1983 time frames, and for all developing countries, poorest countries, middle-income countries, African countries only, Asian countries only, and Latin American countries only. There are a total of 18 estimated equations, and the aid variable is statistically insignificant in all but three. In the three cases of significance, aid is found to be positively related to growth for the Asian countries only in the 1970-1980 and 1980-1983 periods, while it is found to be *negatively* related to growth for all developing countries in the 1960-1970 period. In their Table 4, M-H-H compare ordinary least squares estimates with three-stage least squares estimates (a theoretically appropriate method) for the case of all developing countries, for 1970-1980. Both the OLS and 3SLS estimates indicate an insignificant effect of aid on GNP growth. M-H-H conclude that the main qualitative conclusion from the OLS estimates of Table 3—that there is no robust statistical evidence for a positive effect of foreign aid on growth—is unaffected by a switch to 3SLS estimation.

The M-H-H study is representative of several more recent studies that contradict Papanek's 1973 findings in favor of aid effectiveness. However, there have also been a number of more recent studies which do find a positive effect of foreign aid on growth. One of the best known of these is a study done by Craig Burnside and David Dollar. First issued as a working paper by the World Bank Policy Research Department in June 1997, the study was then expanded in the 1998 World Bank monograph *Assessing Aid: What Works, What Doesn't, and Why* (co-authored by Dollar and Lance Pritchett of the World Bank's Development Research Group), and still later was described in an article by Burnside and Dollar in the *American Economic Review* (September, 2000).[9]

Given the sponsorship of the study, it is perhaps not surprising that its findings are consistent with the "party line" of the World Bank, which says that foreign development assistance is indeed effective in promoting the economic growth of recipient nations—but only if the governments of these nations are implementing "good policy." By "good policy" is meant policy consistent with the so-called "Washington consensus": fiscal discipline to avoid budget deficits and inflation, modest welfare programs, limited business regulation, minimal economic planning, trade liberalization, and openness to foreign investment.[10] Shortly after familiarity with the "consensus" became widespread in the latter 1990s, it suffered a decline in popularity during the global economic crunch of the 2000s. Of course, Washington consensus policies tend to impose various economic hardships on the population. And it appears that under severe recessionary conditions, even the economies of those nations conscientiously practicing "good" policy do not do very well. It becomes doubtful, therefore, whether it is sensible to persist with these policies.

Burnside and Dollar's dataset includes information for six four-year time periods (1970-1973 to 1990-1993) on 56 developing countries. In addition to the usual economic variables, it includes a "political instability" variable based on ethnic fractionalization and assassinations, and an "economic management" or "policy" variable based on four subsidiary indicators: an index of trade openness, the rate of inflation, government surplus or deficit, and an index of "institutional quality." The variable of main interest is foreign aid as a proportion of Gross Domestic Product (GDP). The foreign aid variable is adjusted to include the concessional component of loans as well as grants. In the regression equations, the aid variable is not the observed value of aid (as a proportion of GDP) but rather its "instrumented" value. "Instrumented aid" is the estimated value of aid from a subsidiary regression of aid on such exogenous variables as initial GNP per capita, population, policy, region, and arms imports. Use of instrumented as opposed to observed aid is an effort to evade the statistical problem of feedback causation ("simultaneous equations bias" in the econometric literature). In this context, the problem is as follows: Foreign aid receipts might have a positive effect on economic growth performance—but economic growth performance might have a negative feedback impact on foreign aid receipts. That is to say, foreign aid to countries with strong growth might be reduced because the "need" for aid is smaller. This feedback effect tends to make it difficult to estimate the causative impact of foreign aid on economic growth.

In other words, if there are two causative relationships operating simultaneously, the first a positive causative relation between foreign aid as the independent variable and economic growth as the dependent variable, and the second a negative relation between economic growth as the independent variable and foreign aid as the dependent variable—it is difficult for statistical analysis to separate the first from the second. Econometric theory has produced a standard methodology for dealing with the problem that will definitely be successful in disentangling the two relations—if certain preconditions are met. But it is frequently uncertain whether these preconditions are actually met in any given practical application. Thus there is an additional element of uncertainty regarding the reliability and validity of statistical estimations under feedback causation conditions.

Using standard econometric methodology for dealing with feedback causation, Burnside and Dollar find that the aid variable (the ratio of foreign aid to GDP) has a significant positive effect on the growth rate of per capita GNP—but only when it is combined in a multiplicative fashion with the policy variable (economic management). To be more precise, their variable "aid/GDP" is statistically insignificant in the determination of per capita GNP growth, but their variable "Management x aid/GDP" (the product of the policy variable times the aid variable) does in fact have a positive and statistically significant effect on per capita GNP growth. This result seems fairly robust over a variety of specifications that include or exclude middle-income countries, include or exclude outliers ("unusual" observations), and treat the policy variable as endogenous or exogenous.

Burnside and Dollar define "mediocre policy" as a value of the policy variable of 1.1 and "good policy" as a value of the policy variable of 2.7. With good policy, the mean marginal effect of aid on growth over several specifications is computed as 0.5. This indicates that a unit increase in the aid/GNP percentage—given that policy is "good"—will increase the growth rate of per capita income by 0.5 percent. On the other hand, if policy is "mediocre," the mean marginal effect of aid on growth is computed to be zero. The clear implication of this finding, as expounded thoroughly in *Assessing Aid*, is that if more developing countries would simply follow "good policy," then there would be a substantial and easily verified positive effect of foreign aid on economic growth. There is also an implicit warning to governments of developing countries tempted to persist with "bad policy": "If you do so, your foreign aid may well be curtailed because it is a burden on us and it is not doing you any good."

This result is almost "too good" in the sense of being so precisely in line with the policy preconceptions of the World Bank. One wonders how much data manipulation and specification experimentation were required in order to reach these conclusions. One cannot help but wonder, accordingly, whether similar results would be obtained with different datasets and/or specifications. In fact, the Burnside-Dollar research was soon challenged by a number of economists, including William Easterly, the author of such influential negative appraisals of foreign aid as *The White Man's Burden: Why the West's Effort to Aid the Rest Have Done So Much Ill and So Little Good* (2006).[11] The June 2004 issue of the *American Economic Review* contained an exchange between Easterly (with co-authors Ross Levine and David Roodman) and Burnside-Dollar on the proposition that—assuming the recipient nations are practicing good policy—foreign aid will be effective in promoting economic growth in these nations.[12] The Easterly-Levine-Roodman critique demonstrated that with certain seemingly defensible modifications in the estimation data and methodology, the effect of aid on growth becomes statistically insignificant. Burnside and Dollar responded that these particular modifications are not as "defensible" as Easterly-Levine-Roodman claim.

From a non-specialist's perspective, this particular exchange appears to constitute yet another confirmation that even though data is abundant and estimation methodology sophisticated, it is unlikely that economic research will provide truly compelling evidence, one way or the other, within the foreseeable future, on the effect of foreign aid on the economic growth of recipient nations.

Nevertheless, it seems safe to say that the general tone of the literature on foreign aid during the first years of the twenty-first century has become even more pessimistic than ever before. In principle, foreign aid is supposed to improve the economic welfare of people in the recipient nations, and to strengthen tendencies toward good governance and democratic political conditions. A number of recent studies have posed serious challenges to these expectations.[13] "Corruption" has become an especially popular buzzword among many economists and policy-makers, eclipsing even "incompetence." Corruption refers to the degree to which real-world conditions diverge from political and social ideals: employees pilfering and malingering rather than performing their work honestly, business executives looting their companies rather than managing them honestly, government officials extorting bribes rather than performing their public duties honestly. In other words, many people are pursuing their short-term personal interests, often by illegal and/or unethical means, rather than long-term social interests. A certain amount of serious statistical evidence has accumulated that corruption is a serious problem in many developing nations, and that rather than ameliorating the problem, foreign aid is aggravating it.

Current foreign aid critics such as William Easterly are following a path well trodden by Peter T. Bauer, the twentieth century's leading intellectual champion of pessimism concerning the prospects for economic progress in the Third World. Virulent contempt for the LDCs, their people and their governments, is a pronounced undercurrent throughout Bauer's voluminous work. According to Bauer, the imbedded institutional, cultural, and attitudinal characteristics in many if not most LDCs are such as to pose high and probably insurmountable barriers to significant economic advance. A corollary of this proposition is that economic development assistance from the advanced nations will have either no influence or a perverse influence on the economic condition of the recipient nations. This message was tirelessly reiterated and elaborated in great detail in numerous articles and several books published between 1957 and 1991.[14] Bauer relied upon anecdotal and impressionistic evidence to make his points. What the more recent literature contributed by Easterly and others is doing is backing up Bauer's propositions with statistical evidence. While the statistical evidence against foreign aid effectiveness is hardly conclusive, it must be acknowledged that it is impressive.

VIEWPOINTS ON FOREIGN AID

Given the technical complexity and conflicting findings of the economic literature on foreign aid, it is not surprising that this literature has had little discernible effect on public opinion on the subject. As is usually the case with controversial political issues, opinions on foreign aid cover a wide spectrum. At the extreme negative end of the spectrum is the viewpoint that foreign aid is a total waste of resources that imposes heavy burdens on the taxpayers of the wealthy donor nations while having either no effect at all on the economic growth of the LDCs—or quite possibly a negative effect. At the opposite extreme positive end of the spectrum is the viewpoint that foreign aid could and should be expanded into a Global Marshall Plan. Somewhere in the middle is the widely accepted conventional viewpoint that while the effectiveness of foreign aid might be dubious, it does have at least a few beneficial effects, and so a certain modest allocation of national resources into this avenue is sensible and desirable.

In most of the wealthy nations, including the United States, foreign aid has become institutionally entrenched as a recurrent component of the national government budget. But relative to other recurrent components of the national government budget, such as defense and domestic welfare, its entrenchment is not deep. In the United States, for example, few if any calls are heard for the abolition of the U.S. Department of Defense or the Social Security Administration, and the "zeroing out" of their annual appropriations. The same cannot be said for the U.S. Agency for International Development (USAID), through which United States official foreign aid disbursements are channeled. An example of the extreme negative viewpoint on foreign aid is a 1995 policy paper by Doug Bandow entitled "A New Aid Policy for a New World" which was (and still is) posted on the Web by the Cato Institute, of which its author is a Senior Fellow. In the Executive Summary of this paper, Bandow summarizes the anti-aid viewpoint as follows:

> Since 1945, Washington has disbursed generous amounts of foreign aid in attempts to achieve a variety of foreign policy goals ranging from political influence to economic development. Today, the poor record of foreign assistance programs is widely recognized. Many countries receiving the aid are more impoverished now than when U.S. assistance began; the few that are making progress are doing so in spite of, not because of, foreign aid. . . Some Republican proposals to reform foreign aid are more encouraging [than Clinton's proposals] because they envision cutting programs that have clearly failed or serve no national interest. But the Republican proposals should be viewed only as a starting point. In the

> post-Cold War world, developing countries are moving away from the type of central economic planning that U.S. aid has financed in the past. The United States should encourage that trend by zeroing out foreign aid. That includes foreign aid programs intended to promote free-market reform; even that type of assistance tends to delay, rather than accelerate liberalization. . . Washington can do much to help poor nations by abolishing the U.S. Agency for International Development and most of its functions. Instead of disbursing foreign aid, the United States should open its market to the developing world's goods.

Almost 20 years have passed since "A New Aid Policy for a New World" was written and disseminated—and USAID is still in business. Nevertheless, while Doug Bandow's recommendation that the United States abolish USAID and terminate foreign aid has not yet been implemented, the prevalence of this sort of viewpoint is effective in keeping the agency's budgetary allocations relatively low.

Criticism of foreign aid has been substantial ever since foreign aid spending commenced becoming substantial early in the Cold War era. To some extent, this criticism has been the inevitable consequence of conservative distrust of government and scorn for welfarism in general. But if the beneficiaries of government action and welfare programs are (what conservatives tend to view as) the "undeserving poor" of foreign lands, as opposed to the domestic "undeserving poor," that makes the presumed evil even worse. As the pendulum of public opinion swung slowly but consistently toward the right throughout the 1970s and beyond, criticism of foreign aid became increasingly abundant, more tightly focused, and better presented. The barrage of criticism has been fairly effective, and in the United States especially, it is fair to say that advocates of foreign aid tend to be on the defensive.

Major propositions of the "case against foreign aid" include, but are not confined to, the following: (1) owing to corrupt and/or incompetent administration, planning, and monitoring, aid resources are largely wasted and have little if any beneficial effect on the masses of poor people in the LDCs; (2) the provision of aid resources to LDCs permits their governments to reallocate resources that would otherwise have been invested in social infrastructure into such unproductive ends as high-tech weaponry and presidential palaces; (3) aid resources intended for private enterprises in LDCs are wildly misallocated because aid administrators have no banking or business experience, and no personal financial interest in the outcome of the investments they approve; (4) aid disrupts the economies of the recipient nations and causes numerous bankruptcies among small farmers and businessmen; (5) aid fosters a dependency mentality that hampers the efforts of LDCs to achieve self-sufficient, sustainable economic growth; (6) much aid is used to prop up corrupt, incompetent, and/or oppressive political regimes that would probably collapse in the absence of aid; (7) aid is provided to nations that are following obviously dysfunctional policies such as import substitution, central planning, excessive welfare entitlements, and socio-economic micromanagement; (8) aid benefits mostly if not entirely aid administrators, political authorities, government bureaucrats, and dishonest businessmen rather than the general population of the recipient nations; (9) aid fosters dysfunctional conditions such as economic inequality, corruption, and rent-seeking. The list goes on.

The extreme case against foreign aid sometimes endeavors to evade inferences that this case is based squarely upon crude selfishness, by means of alleging that the termination of foreign aid would be "for their own good"—referring to the general populations of the LDCs. Rarely is the case put forward as a calm balancing of the marginal costs versus the marginal benefits to the U.S. population, with the former being estimated as greater than the latter. Nor is the case expressed in terms of the costs to the populations of the rich nations being numerically greater than the benefits to the poor nations. Rather, the fundamentally implausible argument is routinely put forward that foreign aid not only reduces the welfare of the populations of the rich nations *but it also* reduces the welfare of the populations of the poor nations.

One indication of insincerity with respect to concern for the welfare of the populations of the poor nations is the fact that many of the complaints about foreign aid have to do with potentially correctable errors and deficiencies. If food aid is bankrupting local farmers, this problem could potentially be avoided by providing aid in different forms. If foreign aid is being provided to oppressive regimes with an excessive penchant for presidential palaces, this problem could potentially be avoided by redirecting aid to nations whose leaders are democratically accountable and who content themselves with reasonable living standards. If foreign aid is being extended to LDC governments that are pursuing obviously dysfunctional policies such as protectionism or centralization, this problem could potentially be avoided by making aid conditional upon more sensible economic policies.

That foreign aid has been mishandled in the past does not necessarily imply that it must continue to be mishandled in the future. For example, in their critique of foreign aid programs in sub-Saharan Africa ("Foreign Aid, Institutions, and Governance in Sub-Saharan Africa," *Economic Development and Cultural Change*, 2004), Stephen Knack and Deborah Bräutigam summarize their conclusions as follows:

> We find evidence that higher aid levels are associated with larger declines in the quality of governance, as measured by subjective indicators. We also find higher aid associated with lower tax effort in Africa. The conclusion offers some recommendations for reducing the possible deleterious impact of aid. Paradoxically, our argument is not that aid to Africa needs to be reduced; in many cases, more aid will be better. But aid needs to be delivered more selectively and in ways that reinforce a virtuous cycle of development rather than contributing to a vicious cycle of poor governance and economic decline.

But such reasonable solutions are often ignored in popular discussions in favor of strident calls for the complete abandonment of foreign aid. Open hostility and contempt are frequently expressed toward allegedly corrupt and greedy politicians and government bureaucrats in the LDCs; just beneath the surface one senses an equally virulent hostility and contempt toward the general populations of these nations, who are presumably, for whatever reason, either unwilling or unable to require their authorities to adhere to reasonable standards of civilized behavior. After all, presumably governments reflect peoples—corrupt peoples tend to generate corrupt governments. The possibility that poverty itself may aggravate natural human tendencies toward greed and corruption is generally ignored. And foreign aid critics outraged by Third World self-seeking greed and corruption should perhaps remind themselves that such unseemly conditions are hardly unknown in the First World. Indeed, the era of rapid industrialization in the United States during the latter part of the nineteenth century has been characterized by some historians as the "robber baron" era.

That many expressions of the anti-aid case are overblown will be apparent to most individuals of politically moderate persuasion. Most of the evidence cited in support of the ineffectiveness or perversity of foreign aid is anecdotal in nature and dubiously representative of the overall picture. For example, while much is made of specific failed projects, more balanced appraisals indicate that the rate of return is high on most projects, especially those funded by multilateral agencies such as the World Bank. Inconsistent evidence, such as the fact that South Korea and Taiwan were major aid recipients during the initial phases of their extraordinary growth eras, is either ignored or dismissed with unsupported statements to the effect that aid "had nothing to do" with growth acceleration. Equally unsupportable are dogmatic statements that foreign aid depresses economic growth performance by sapping incentives, encouraging waste, distorting relative prices, and so on. To many thoughtful observers, a more plausible explanation for the disappointing growth rates in many if not most of the LDCs is simply that foreign aid has not been provided in sufficient abundance to make a significant difference.

The pro-aid response centers around the argument that although the strategic political purposes of foreign aid have been greatly downgraded by the conclusion of the Cold War, these purposes have not disappeared altogether, and the economic and humanitarian purposes of foreign aid are just as relevant now as they were during the Cold War. Increasing prosperity among the LDCs would create a more favorable international economic environment for the rich nations. Many individuals in the rich nations continue to perceive a strong moral obligation to provide a reasonable amount of economic assistance to those in need. Although not as dramatic as the Cold War threat of instantaneous nuclear holocaust, the continuing interrelated threats of global environmental degradation and overpopulation could be just as dangerous to the long-run welfare of the populations of the rich nations.

The following excerpts from testimony of Donald F. Gordon, of the Overseas Development Council, given before the House International Relations Committee on February 26, 1997, suggest the flavor of the post-Cold War pro-aid case:

> Under Brian Atwood's energetic and creative leadership, USAID has gone a significant way toward streamlining its bureaucracy and redirecting its operations. Despite these efforts, however, the U.S. foreign aid program remains politically adrift, having lost its Cold War anchor as a tool for containing communist expansion. Foreign assistance has lost its core political constituency and much of its support, and foreign aid levels are in decline. Forced continually to defend its eroding mandate, USAID finds it ever more difficult to undertake effective development work. What is called for is not the end to aid, nor the continued nibbling away of USAID's capacity to undertake its mandate, which will make aid failure a self-fulfilling prophecy. Rather, we need an even more substantial revision of our assistance policies and practices in ways consistent with changing foreign policy purposes and changed realities in the developing world. To do so necessitates better integrating our aid efforts into our foreign policy process.
>
> During the Cold War, the main purpose of aid was to support strategically important regimes regardless of whether the recipient government was following effective development policies or used aid resources efficiently. Some argue that, after the Cold War, there is no longer a foreign policy role for foreign aid. According to this view, eliminating most aid is an appropriate "peace dividend" from the end of the Cold War. While containing a kernel of truth—some types of aid have become passé and some longtime recipients are no longer attractive—this view ignores the

> emerging foreign policy interests of the United States. Today, it is advancing global problem-solving, promoting crucial transitions, and development itself, not the buying of allies, that serve our contemporary foreign policy goals and interests.
>
> In a world no longer dominated by major power conflict, an array of serious global problems (some new, others unattended to in the past) that no nation can handle on its own call for new forms of international cooperation. Among the most important of these are global environmental degradation, international drug trafficking and the spread of infectious diseases. These problems directly affect our quality of life at home and can only be addressed through effective cooperation with developing countries. Absent aid, we would be totally dependent upon persuasion and treaty negotiations for tackling these problems, especially in poor countries that may want to respond but lack the financial and technical wherewithal to do so.

Although the collapse of the Soviet Union and the end of Cold War has significantly reduced the apparent need for foreign aid as an instrument for the containment of communism, at the same time this development has improved the prospects for effective utilization of foreign aid resources. During the height of the Cold War, a disproportionate amount of foreign aid was directed to nations in immediate danger of communist takeovers, to nations ruled by overbearing dictators whose only virtue was their opposition to communism, to "socialist-leaning" nations of geopolitical significance whose governments threatened to become more friendly with the Soviet Union or the People's Republic of China. The bargaining power of recipient LDC nations in foreign aid negotiations was in a long-term state of decline for a prolonged period prior to the termination of the Cold War, but no doubt the termination accelerated the decline. Thus it became easier for donor nations to induce recipient nations to abide more closely to the various precepts of eventually became known as the "Washington consensus."

As mentioned earlier, the "Washington consensus" holds that the prospects for a given nation's economic growth are generally more promising to the extent that the nation: (1) participates more in the world economy by reducing import restrictions and encouraging export growth; (2) reduces direct government participation and intervention in the economy by privatizing public enterprises, minimizing bureaucratic regulation of private enterprise, abolishing institutions and curbing policies that involve any sort of economic planning, and generally increasing the scope of laissez faire in the domestic economic realm; (3) maintains redistributive taxation and social welfare programs at a modest and reasonable level; (4) welcomes foreign private investment and strictly respects the private property rights of foreign investors. Of course, not all of the precepts of the Washington consensus, some of which are directly contrary to propositions which were part of the conventional wisdom of the 1940s and 1950s, are universally applauded. Evidence is far from compelling that LDCs which enthusiastically embrace all or most of the Washington consensus thereupon experience rapid growth. The global economic downturn of the 2000s disrupted the economies even of those developing nations that were seriously committed to this policy direction.

When even professional economists cannot agree on specific policy issues, it is no wonder that ordinary citizens and political authorities cannot agree. In addition, the factor of national pride inevitably enters into economic policy discussions between officials of different national governments. Predictably enough, officials of recipient nations do not relish "being dictated to" by officials of donor nations. No opinions will be offered herein on the overall validity of the Washington consensus. No doubt some of its prescriptions would be more efficient and effective than others—the question is: "which ones?" But what does seem obvious is that now donor nations have more clout in determining the internal economic policies of recipient nations than they had during the Cold War, when LDC governments were able to play off the noncommunist and communist superpowers against one another.

Of course, another major factor in determining the amount of clout possessed by representatives of the donor nations, aside from the presence or absence of superpower confrontations in the global arena, is the amount of foreign aid at stake. Officials of recipient nations who are dubious concerning policy changes proposed by officials of donor nations will be more inclined to acquiesce the larger are the aid donations under consideration. The end of the Cold War in the early 1990s initiated a major downsizing of military expenditures, especially among the wealthy donor nations. It is hardly implausible that this major reduction in the military burden on the economy was a major factor in the successful economic record of the 1990s. Even though military expenditures have increased somewhat in the aftermath of the 9/11 outrage, the wealthy nations of the world are still very rich in terms of both total income and "disposable" income (income left after military obligations have been met). Being richer, they are able to afford more of all goods—and one such good would be a more politically stable, ecologically sound, and morally equitable global environment. "Psychic benefits" may be more difficult to measure, but that does not make them any less real.

GMP ASPIRATIONS

At the extreme positive end of the spectrum of opinion on foreign aid is the view that what would be desirable at this point in history is not merely a modest scaling up of ODA, but rather a quantitatively massive expansion of the existing ODA programs of today into a full-scale Global Marshall Plan (GMP), worthy of both the name and the spirit of the original post-World War II Marshall Plan. Although hardly enjoying mainstream support, the basic notion of a GMP has been in limited circulation for a considerable length of time. In fact, antecedents of the idea can be perceived well before the postwar Marshall Plan.

In early discussions of economic development, an important focus was on the "big push" concept. The major inspiration for the concept, as enunciated in the seminal 1943 article by Paul N. Rosenstein-Rodan entitled "Problems of Industrialization of Eastern and Southeastern Europe," was the Soviet experience of rapid, planned, state-led industrialization in the late 1920s and throughout the 1930s. The basic idea can be illustrated by a physical metaphor: Imagine a large, round rock half-buried on a hillside. In its present situation, it possesses a great deal of inertia. Therefore a substantial amount of effort (a "big push") is needed to dislodge it from its resting place. But once it has been so dislodged and is rolling down the hill, no further special exertion of energy will be needed to keep it going. The economic translation of the metaphor of a rock half-buried on a hillside is the "underdevelopment trap" or "low-level equilibrium trap" as formulated by Harvey Leibenstein and others.[15]

Much of the "big push" conceptualization of the initial economic development process was later incorporated into Walt W. Rostow's well-known account of the "take-off" into self-sustained growth, in which the "dislodging of a rock" is represented by the "take-off of an airplane." Essential to the big push notion are the economic concepts of external effects (that economic operations in one area of the economy can have direct, non-market effects on economic operations in other areas of the economy), and economies of scale (that if economic commodities are produced on a large scale, specialization and division of labor will enable their production at lower unit cost). The basic message of big push theory is that things cannot be done in a small way: a little shove—even a lot of little shoves at different points in time—will not dislodge that rock. What is needed is not a series of little shoves but rather one big, coordinated push.[16]

For example, if a developing country constructs one big shoe factory (to use Rosenstein-Rodan's illustration), and nothing else, that factory will likely quickly wither away into bankruptcy. On the other hand, if that developing country constructs a large number of factories producing a large number of commodities, many of which are complementary to one another, then they are all likely to prosper—and the economy as a whole is likely to prosper along with them. It is not, however, merely a matter of having a large number of factories producing marketable commodities. Social infrastructure capital also plays a critical role: roads, railways, harbors, airports, schools, hospitals, and so on. Even though these kinds of things do not produce an immediate financial return, they must be provided in abundance, because the commercial success of the production enterprises depends on them. The upshot is that slow, tentative, cautious, marginal, incremental development efforts are unlikely to achieve success. Things must be done in a big and bold manner—just as the Soviets had done them during their own great push toward industrialization and urbanization from the late 1920s through the 1940s.

To properly understand the origin and subsequent fate of the big push concept, it is helpful to recall that Rosenstein-Rodan's seminal article was published in a leading economics periodical (the *Economic Journal* of the U.K. Royal Economic Association) at a time (1943) when the "Grand Alliance" of Britain, the United States, and the Soviet Union was engaged in a desperate struggle with the fascist powers of Nazi Germany and Imperial Japan. The pre-war ideological opposition between the market capitalism of Britain and the U.S. and the planned socialism of the Soviet Union was greatly de-emphasized, hushed up, ignored. The ruthless tyrant Joseph Stalin was transformed into friendly "Uncle Joe." As for the Soviet Union's industrialization drive, not much faith had been placed in that prior to World War II. It was widely assumed that the whole exercise merely represented "socialist bungling" on a vast scale, and that whatever minor economic progress had been made was the result of savage repression of the population by their Communist Party masters. It was also widely assumed that Nazi Germany must not be allowed to expand to the East, because if unopposed it would easily topple the "socialist house of cards" represented by the Soviet Union and thereupon incorporate the vast human and natural resources of that land, thus laying a firm basis for world conquest.

As often happens, events did not proceed according to the expectations and desires of the diplomats and militarists, and when Nazi Germany invaded Soviet Russia in June, 1941, it was with the full weight of its military forces, since by that time there was no organized military opposition to Germany anywhere on the Western European continent. Despite suffering staggering losses in men, material, and territory, the Soviet Union was not toppled like a house of cards. Instead it mustered determined resistance to what at the time was the largest, best organized, most mechanized and technologically advanced army in the world. Crucial to that resistance were modern artillery, tanks, airplanes and small arms. As the months and years wore on, and the Soviet forces gradually gained the upper hand over the German forces, a new, deep respect emerged for the Soviet Union's "big push" from a backward, primarily agricultural economy to a modern, primarily industrialized economy. Obviously that push had accomplished enormous progress, otherwise the Soviet Union would indeed have gone down like a house of cards before the Nazi war machine.

Thus when Rosenstein-Rodan published his seminal article in 1943, the background was that of growing appreciation for the Soviet program of comprehensive, forced-pace industrialization. Unfortunately, the cordial relations between the Soviet Union and the West did not long survive the Second World War. Very soon it was back to "business as usual" as far as the ideological conflict between communistic socialism and Western capitalism was concerned. With respect to the Soviet industrialization campaign of the 1930s, the emphasis in Western analysis returned to the various deficiencies and inefficiencies of the effort, and the terrible costs imposed by it on the Soviet population. Third World nations tempted to emulate the Soviet example were cautioned against the terrific strain any such emulation would put on their populations, strain that would most likely eventuate in bloody revolution and/or degeneration into oppressive dictatorship. Aside from ideological shifts, certain aspects of the big push concept contributed to its decline within the field of development economics. For one thing, Rosenstein-Rodan and other proponents of the concept never developed a formal mathematical model of the concept, partly because the key elements of the concept, namely external effects and economies of scale (the latter also known as "increasing returns to scale") were normally assumed away in mathematical model-building efforts in the economic mainstream from the 1950s onwards. From a technical standpoint, it was far more convenient to extract results from models based on constant returns to scale or decreasing returns to scale rather than increasing returns to scale, and which eliminated external effects from consideration.

In addition, influential development economists, such as Albert O. Hirschman, explicitly rejected the "big push" approach to economic development in favor of an "unbalanced growth" approach based on "linkages" between the various sectors of the economy. In the Hirschman view, good development results could in fact be attained by means of slowly and gradually developing the economy one sector at a time.[17] It could be, of course, that Albert Hirschman was merely making a virtue of necessity. There is always the question, after all, of where the big resources needed for the big push are coming from. In the case of the Soviet Union, the resources had been mustered by means of reducing the living standards of the Soviet population to bare subsistence. Even though the communist leadership did its best to maintain morale and commitment by appealing to the messianic role presumably being played by the Soviet Union in demonstrating the virtues of socialist planning to the rest of the world, the social pressures generated by a population reduced to subsistence consumption were so great that Joseph Stalin found it necessary, in order to maintain his personal grip on power, to implement a campaign of terror in the 1930s (of which the notorious "Moscow purge trials" were just the tip of the iceberg) that cost the lives of millions of Soviet citizens. Any nation contemplating a Soviet-style big push had to contemplate the costs of such an effort—assuming the resources for it were to come from within.

Another possibility, of course, was that the necessary resources would come from without, that is, in the form of foreign investment and/or foreign aid from the wealthy industrialized nations. In the immediate post-World War II world, with its rapidly developing Cold War, Third World nations did in fact receive a certain amount of external assistance, which they did their best to increase by means of playing off the capitalist and communist superpowers against one another. But as a practical matter, the external resources were far from sufficient to sustain a big push on the heroic scale envisioned by Paul Rosenstein-Rodan. A major impediment to increased foreign aid was the fact that the superpowers were already devoting large proportions of their current output to military purposes. This basic situation persisted throughout the more than four decades of intense Cold War prior to the collapse and dissolution of the Soviet Union in 1991. Throughout this period, numerous analysts and commentators on the international situation bemoaned the fact that huge economic resources that might be better spent on economic development were instead being plowed into military expenditures. They proposed a reallocation of resources from military purposes to economic development purposes, on the argument that economic development would increase prosperity, enhance political stability, and thereby reduce the need for military expenditures. This argument made little headway, however, against the conventional viewpoint that large-scale military expenditures made significant increases in foreign aid allocations "unaffordable."

Nevertheless, the intuitive appeal of the Rosenstein-Rodan concept of a "big push," in conjunction with the dramatic success of the Marshall Plan from 1948 through 1952 in the recovery of Western Europe from war damage, kept alive the policy vision of a global Marshall Plan on a monumental scale. It was argued by its advocates that such a program would deal decisively with a seriously debilitating problem of contemporary human civilization. Three such advocates were Stringfellow Barr, Seymour Melman, and George J. Church. All three of these individuals were American citizens who directed their appeals to their fellow citizens. Since their appeals were published, the relative economic strength of the United States has diminished somewhat. It is now certainly true that, whatever may have been the case in the past, it would be both politically and economically impractical for the United States to take a *dominant* role in an international economic development assistance effort designed to terminate the world poverty problem once and for all. At the same time, however, it remains the case that unless the United States takes a *major* role in such an effort (as opposed to a "dominant" role), it is unlikely that the other wealthy nations will muster the necessary resolution to undertake it. It might be suggested that although U.S. support for a Global Marshall Plan is no longer (if it ever was) necessary *and sufficient* for its success, it is certainly *necessary* for its success—and that this will remain the case into the foreseeable future.

Stringfellow Barr was a prominent historian, author, and academic administrator who became an important figure during the brief but intense post-World War II "world government boom." As a shock reaction to the atomic bombings of the unfortunate Japanese cities of Hiroshima and Nagasaki in 1945, an unprecedented level of interest in world federalism emerged during the five years that separated the end of the war from the commencement of the Korean War. The boom quickly fizzled out when it became apparent that the impending Cold War between the communist East and the noncommunist West made any sort of meaningful world government a practical impossibility.

During the ephemeral world government boom and thereafter, world federalist enthusiasts have viewed a world government primarily as an instrument for the reduction of the risk of a nuclear war among the superpowers. However, they have also viewed such a government as an instrument through which to overcome the long-term threat to international harmony and permanent peace represented by the economic gap between the rich nations and the poor nations. One of the earliest expressions of this particular vision was contributed by Stringfellow Barr, a member of the "Committee to Frame a World Constitution" formed by Robert Hutchins and Giuseppe Borgese of the University of Chicago in the immediate aftermath of the atomic bombings of Hiroshima and Nagasaki. In 1950, following completion of the Committee's work and the publication of their "Preliminary Draft of a World Constitution," the University of Chicago Press published a 30-page pamphlet by Barr entitled "Let's Join the Human Race." Barr asserted that the highly interdependent goals of world government and worldwide economic equalization should be pursued simultaneously, and that neither one was likely to be a success in the absence of the other. The flavor of Barr's style and substance is conveyed by the following quotes from "Let's Join the Human Race" (pp. 20-21):

> None of these obstacles to a common government is decisive. There is a much more serious obstacle. It is an obstacle that the philosopher Plato was speaking of when he said that most cities were not really one city but two—the city of the rich and the city of the poor. In the last century a Conservative prime minister of Britain wrote a novel under the subtitle, "The Two Nations"—the rich and the poor. History suggests that wherever a community is too sharply divided between rich and poor, one of two things happens: either the "city of the poor" rises and overthrows the other "city" or this other city imposes order by force on the city of the poor. If our generation were to set up a common government for the world community, before it moved aggressively to revive the world's economy, one of these two fates would sorely threaten it. In contemporary terms, the world government would be under heavy pressure to go Communist or to go Fascist.
>
> The City of the Rich, based largely on the economy of the United States, sees this problem less clearly than does the City of the Poor—the hungry, half-naked, diseased, and mostly colored millions. If Americans propose to them a common government "to keep law and order" in the world-wide City of Man, to control "the bomb," and let us all enjoy life in peace, then those who are not enjoying life and who fear the bomb much less than they fear famine may well be unmoved. There is a lot of ease and abundance in America for a bomb to destroy, so we go to bed at night asking, "How can we sleep?" But they ask, "When do we eat?" Those questions measure a yawning gulf between the Two Cities—cities that really do need one government. It is true that man shall not live by bread alone, but should this particular statement by Jesus Christ be quoted between meals to those who have had no meal at all?
>
> Another way to state the problem of the Two Cities is to say that though law and order have to be *enforced* in human communities by means of government, no government enforces them for long that does not bother about justice. Today the City of the Poor might well wish to know whether the City of the Rich really cares, before setting up political housekeeping with it. Nothing would reassure it more quickly or surely than a frontal assault by the whole City on the unspeakable misery of most of its inhabitants. That is why President Truman's "Point Four" remarks, even though timid and vague, briefly stirred not only the consciences of Americans but the hopes of men throughout the planet. The discussion which followed those remarks has now bogged down, because

> the false assumptions on which it was based could not sustain its weight. So "Point Four" has become a gimmick in the cold war against Russia; and the problem back of the cold war, back of the Korean catastrophe, and even back of World War III, if that should break out before these words are in print—that problem has not been tackled.

The themes and ideas in this short tract were later amplified in Barr's 1952 book *Citizens of the World*, which boasted a preface by Justice William O. Douglas of the U.S. Supreme Court.[18] Although somewhat dated at this point in time by its obsessive concern over the opposition between communism and capitalism (it was written just as the Cold War was reaching full maturity), *Citizens of the World* is in effect a remarkably comprehensive, careful, and forward-looking statement of the case for what we now understand as a Global Marshall Plan. Unlike most world federalists of his day, Barr viewed the North-South economic problem as no less serious an impediment to world government and lasting peace than the East-West ideological problem.

The high tide of optimism regarding worldwide economic prosperity may have been reached in the early 1960s, prior to the assassination of President John F. Kennedy and the subsequent gradual but inexorable descent of the United States into the Vietnam quagmire. A characteristic document from those years is Seymour Melman's 1961 book *The Peace Race*.[19] Melman's basic description of the titular term echoes the argument advanced in Stringfellow Barr's *Citizens of the World*: that the participation of the United States in a giant world economic development effort would not merely be "affordable" but positively beneficial to the domestic economy (*The Peace Race*, pp. 67-68):

> The "peace race" is a world policy for the West including competition and cooperation with the Soviet system. Competition is centered on an American effort to industrialize the world with freedom, and thereby win a world-wide political victory. Cooperation includes life-serving activities of every sort, of which controlled disarmament is the most important.
>
> The achievement of rapid industrialization with freedom is frustrated by the need to accumulate industrial resources out of the meager means of impoverished peasants. For this method, the ruthless police measures of the Soviet and especially the Chinese economies are well-suited, indeed essential. But the United States can underwrite the capital cost of industrialization. It can make industrial capital into a virtually "free good."
>
> The United States is the only industrial center in the world that has large unused production and labor resources, especially in the crucial industrial goods-producing industries. The unused production-might of the

> United States, a business and economic liability, can be turned into a strategic political and economic asset. Full order books and full employment would become the condition of American economic life.
>
> A second essential requirement for industrialization with freedom is the use of political and economic methods that include the right of independent organization and the encouragement of multiple sources of decision-making in society. I am confident that within the framework of these critical conditions the many-sided problems of economic development can be tackled with high morale and spectacular success.
>
> The cost of the peace race will amount, at maximum, to about 10 per cent of America's gross national product. A production increase of this size is attainable now, even while carrying the arms burden. The United States has not been producing at full capacity for several years. For the United States, starting the peace race does not require that the arms race first be ended. This possibility is open only for the United States.
>
> Already strained, the Soviet economy is incapable of the same feat as that of the United States. The Soviet bloc has no reserves of production capacity. Drastic shortages in housing, food, and consumer goods are the price of Soviet armaments.
>
> The Soviets will be compelled to seek disarmament in order to compete in a peace race. This is a link between competition for industrialization, a powerful move in its own right, and cooperation for disarmament. Also, as the peace race builds political confidence within the United States on the basis of solid political achievements, there will be greater readiness and competence to rely on the peace race and to terminate the arms race.

Melman's proposal is that the United States, by unilateral action or perhaps in concert with its wealthiest allied nations, commence a "peace race" with the Soviet Union by making a very large commitment to foreign aid, as much as 10 percent of GNP. In addition to dramatically accelerating economic progress in the Third World, and thereby undercutting the attractiveness of communism, this would put direct pressure on the Soviets to make proportional contributions. But the only way the Soviets will be able to do so will be by means of reducing their military expenditures. This will lay a strong foundation for mutual progress on arms reduction, thereby successively freeing up still greater resources for economic development.

It is only fair to point out that not only is Melman's "peace race" concept very much dated because of the post-1990 decline of the Cold War, but also his contention that a tremendous increase in U.S. foreign aid would be costless was strongly influenced by the severe economic recession of the late 1950s. At the present time in most of the wealthy nations, there is nothing approaching a critical unemployment problem; therefore expanding foreign aid cannot be justified as an anti-recession measure. Despite these caveats, Melman's basic vision continues to be valid: that the wealthy nations have it within their power, without undertaking inordinate economic sacrifices, to raise the poor nations to a standard of life closely comparable to the standard of life currently enjoyed by the wealthy nations.

In the June 12, 1978, issue of *Time*, George J. Church published a two-page "*Time* Essay" entitled "The Case for a Global Marshall Plan." Although the term "Global Marshall Plan" was not unknown prior to Church's contribution, the appearance of the essay in a prominent news magazine endowed the term (and the concept behind it) with a degree of recognition and respectability that it had not previously enjoyed. Some representative quotes from Church's contribution are as follows:

> More than a third of the people in the world suffer from serious malnutrition. In 36 countries, income averages less than $265 per person per year; in another 34, less than $520. These figures from the World Bank point up the desperate poverty in many of the 100 nations that are euphemistically classified as less developed countries (LDCs). People in the industrialized countries with pressing economic problems of their own might well say, "So what?" Poverty has long been a fact of life, and Americans especially feel that they have done more than their share in giving foreign aid since World War II. It is not, however, a question of altruism. The advanced countries have an urgent self-interest in improving a situation [global economic inequality] that in a few years may well overshadow any other international issue. The self-interest is partly political: poverty in the LDCs provides fertile soil for demagogues. . . These strains have bred North-South tensions that easily match in bitterness the East-West ideological clashes. At conference after conference, LDCs have demanded a "new international economic order" involving vaguely defined transfers of wealth from North to South. Northern statesmen, with much justice, have regarded this rhetoric as a kind of impractical Robin Hoodism. But with no discernible justice, the industrial countries have kept a tight lid on their assistance to LDCs. The Northern attitude is myopically stingy. . . Says West German Economics Minister Count Otto Lambsdorff: "I do not believe that a kind of Marshall Plan for the Third World—which today would have to be shouldered jointly by the U.S., Europe and Japan—is a feasible solution." Yet a new version of the Marshall Plan that rebuilt Europe after World War II may well be the most workable solution. Only such a plan could overcome the widespread feeling among voters that much aid to LDCs is wasted because it consists of piecemeal efforts by the givers to finance uncoordinated projects. . . Any

> Marshall Plan for the developing nations would admittedly be imperfect. But consider the alternatives: for the LDCs, continued poverty; for the industrial nations, endless political threats and damage to their own economies. Rich and poor countries do not have to like each other to realize they have a common interest they cannot escape.

Although *Time Magazine* is certainly an influential venue, Church's essay, published almost 40 years ago, obviously did not inspire a groundswell of political support at that time leading to the inauguration of a real-world Global Marshall Plan. It may, however, have helped to maintain appropriations to USAID at a somewhat higher level than might otherwise have been the case.

Perhaps the best known of the more recent invocations of the term "Global Marshall Plan" was in Al Gore's book *Earth in the Balance: Ecology and the Human Spirit*, written while he was serving as U.S. Senator and published in June 1992, shortly before he was elected vice-president of the United States.[20] Although no dramatic developments are attributable to the publication of this book, as a bestseller written by a highly placed government official, it inspired considerable enthusiasm in some circles. The book has become something of a "bible" for the Global Marshall Plan Initiative, a political pressure group mostly active in Western Europe.[21]

As its sub-title indicates, Gore's book is chiefly an impassioned plea for policies favoring environmental sustainability. Given the pressures put on the natural environment by rapid development in terms of economic production and average living standards (per capita income), there is an inevitable short-term tradeoff between environmental quality and economic growth. While the rich countries of today are able to impose relatively stringent environmental regulations, a high level of environmental quality is not so affordable to relatively poor developing countries. Were the LDCs of today to implement the environmental policies of the rich countries, their economic progress might come grinding to a halt—at a minimum, it would probably be seriously retarded. To achieve dramatic progress toward halting and then reversing global environmental deterioration, it may first be necessary, as a precondition, to implement a Global Marshall Plan to achieve a high level of material prosperity throughout the developing world, and thereby a high level of economic equality over all the nations of the world.

The tone of *Earth in the Balance*, and much of the literature produced by adherents of the Global Marshall Plan Initiative, is suggestive of the Millennium Development Goals (MDGs), produced by the Millennium Summit sponsored by the United Nations in the millennial year

2000. The MDGs might be described as a "wish list" of highly commendable objectives, such as the eradication of extreme poverty and hunger, and the achievement of universal primary education throughout the world. Although all U.N. member nations endorsed the MDGs in principle, national allocations to various aspects of the program have been limited and progress has been spotty. Of course, numerous critics have dismissed the MDGs as mere wishful thinking, unsupported by any serious analysis of their feasibility, nor by any comprehensive, practical plan toward their realization.

If a Global Marshall Plan of the nature and on the scale envisioned in this research were to be implemented in the real world, there might then exist a non-negligible possibility that the Millennium Development Goals would actually be achieved within a reasonable period of time. This would certainly not occur within 15 years, which was the proposed time frame when the MDGs were proposed in 2000. A time frame of 50 years would be more realistic for a real-world GMP. But any long journey starts out with a first step. This book reports significant economic evidence that such a program might actually succeed. It therefore constitutes an argument that the first step should be taken.

3

A Global Marshall Plan Model

Although the basic idea of a Global Marshall Plan has been in circulation for a very long time, almost from the time of the original Marshall Plan (European Recovery Program) of 1948-1951, professional economists have done virtually no work at all toward serious technical examination and evaluation of its potential performance. This is not merely unfortunate, it is virtually shameful. Considering the seriousness of the problem of global economic inequality, and considering the dramatic progress that might be made against the problem through a determined, comprehensive Global Marshall Plan, at least a few economists should be working diligently to shed light on the possibility.

The reason why this is not the case, one can only presume, is that the vast majority of contemporary economists are very much oriented toward the here and now: they much prefer studying "the world as it is" (positive economics) in preference to "the world as it should be" (normative economics). Apparently the latter is simply too subjective and unscientific for a discipline that greatly prides itself on being relentlessly objective and scientific. It is not that economists avoid studying any proposal at all for progressive policy innovations toward the improvement of human society. But only those proposals that seem serious candidates for adoption in the relatively near future are likely to attract their attention. A tremendous expansion of existing foreign aid programs into a Global Marshall Plan is not presently on the list of proposals that fall into this category.

The fundamental reason why a Global Marshall Plan is not on the contemporary policy agenda is the strongly entrenched preconception, at all levels of society from academic economists to the man in the street, that such an undertaking would be costly and futile. It would (it is supposed) involve a terrible waste of economic resources. The citizens of the wealthy donor nations would be taxed heavily to provide funds for the program. These funds would be mostly squandered through a combination of incompetence, greed, and dishonesty among those directly involved with the functioning of the program. As a consequence, any economic benefit to the impoverished masses of the developing nations would be negligible to nonexistent.

This is the dominant preconception today—the question remains whether or not it is a correct, valid, legitimate preconception. Up to now, this remaining question has not been seriously addressed by the economics profession. It is my intention to rectify this situation. The research reported in this book was undertaken with the objective of applying economic methodology to the study of a full-scale Global Marshall Plan, that is, to a multilateral effort mounted by all or most of the nations of the world with the sole and explicit purpose of making major inroads, within the relatively proximate future, against the problem of global economic inequality. The present chapter sets forth the theoretical specification of the model, describes its numerical implementation, and discusses its validation. The following chapter will describe its application to the potential impact of a Global Marshall Plan on the world economy, with special reference to the inequality situation.[1]

The GMP model (so designated because it pertains to the potential performance of a Global Marshall Plan—GMP) is a model of the world economy with nations as economic units and years as time periods. The model represents an effort to achieve a reasonable compromise between the diverse objectives of realistic economic content, tight focus on the main question of interest, analytical simplicity, and computational convenience. Key elements of the model are the production function, the consumption function, the transfer allocation function determining each nation's foreign aid contribution, and the share function determining each nation's foreign aid receipts. Owing to the model's tight focus on foreign aid, the single model link between the component national economies consists of transfers of generalized capital investment resources through the GMP. The model does not encompass various other links between national economies such as foreign trade, private foreign investment, and private voluntary transfers.[2]

Variables are subscripted with an *i* for "nation *i*" and a *t* for "time period *t*." There are 146 nations in the dataset, comprising all nations that had populations over one million people in 1980. The dataset consists of World Bank data on the populations and per capita incomes of these nations from 1980 through 2010. Data from the 31-year period 1980 through 2010 are used to validate the model: that is, to show that with reasonable parametric specifications, model simulations over this interval produce a reasonably close fit between model results and the observed empirical data. The GMP model *policy simulations*, as opposed to the validation simulation, cover the 51-year period from 2010 through 2060. These will be discussed in the following chapter.

Probably the single most critical assumption incorporated in the model is that the same Cobb-Douglas production function holds in all nations. The production function, shown in equation (3.1) below, gives output Y as a function of inputs generalized capital K and population P (used as a numerical proxy for productive labor). It is an abstraction from reality, of course, to utilize population for productive labor, because the ratio of productive labor to total population is not the same over all nations. However, usage of labor force participation rates to infer productive labor from total population would be problematical, even if such rates were reliably available for all nations, because in the poorer agrarian nations a considerable amount of productive labor is actually provided within the household by children or other dependents who are not considered to be labor force participants.

Statistical data are utilized for Y and P in the numerical implementation of the model, but K, *generalized* capital, represents a hypothetical construct for which existing statistical proxies such as "plant and equipment," even if they were reliably available for all nations, would not be appropriate. "Generalized capital" is the value of all reproducible inputs *other than* physical labor power. In addition to the usual "plant and equipment," it would definitely include the value of educational and training inputs into the labor force (human capital components) as well as the value of publicly provided productive resources such as roads, bridges, dams, and schools (social capital components).

Generalized capital plays a pivotal role in the GMP model. It is presumed: (1) that the extreme differentials in per capita output between nations in the contemporary world may be all or mostly attributed to extreme differentials in current endowments of generalized capital between nations; and (2) that generalized capital is transferable between nations, in the sense that a given investment in generalized capital may be installed in any nation and it will have the same impact on production. Needless to emphasize, these are both highly controversial assumptions. It has long been proposed by politically conservative economists that the bulk of the productivity differentials in the world today may be attributed to imbedded cultural and institutional factors that are virtually impervious to human control.

If this proposition were correct, then in order for the model under consideration here to be realistic, it would be necessary that the total factor productivity coefficient A be very different over nations, instead of being equal for all nations. Of course, if the observed productivity differentials in the world today are the result of A differentials rather than K differentials, then a program such as the GMP examined herein, that would alter the future allocation of world investment in K as between nations, would have a very small impact on the distribution of production over nations. Quite simply, the program would be ineffective. This possibility is modeled by means of a parameter designated ξ, which represents the proportion of the initial per capita income differentials that may be attributed to differentials in total factor productivity coefficients, as opposed to differentials in generalized capital stocks. It is shown in Chapter 4 below that if the ξ parameter becomes too high, the GMP will not be effective. That this unfortunate outcome is merely *possible*, however, is perhaps not a sufficient justification for abandoning hope and never even trying a GMP.

Once total output in each nation has been produced according to the Cobb-Douglas production function, it is then allocated between four uses: military output M; consumption C; transfer fund contribution T; and domestic investment I. In a GMP-less world, no nation makes a contribution into the GMP. In a GMP world, the richer nations would make contributions into a transfer fund, from which the poorer nations would draw shares S. These shares would be applied to investment in generalized capital K. The rules embodied in the GMP model for determining contributions and shares are very much of an ad hoc nature. They are meant to be appealing from a common sense point of view, but they have no explicit justification in terms of economic efficiency or social welfare theory. The rules are specified so that transfer fund contributions are larger for richer nations, while transfer fund shares are larger for the poorer and more populous nations.

THEORETICAL SPECIFICATION

The production function of country i at time t is specified to be a Cobb-Douglas form in generalized capital K and population P:

$$Y_{i,t} = A_{i,t} K_{i,t}^{\alpha} P_{i,t}^{\beta} \tag{3.1}$$

where Y = output, K = generalized capital, P = population, A = total factor productivity (a parameter), and where the power parameters α and β are such that $0 < \alpha, \beta < 1$ and $\alpha + \beta = \nu$. The parameter α is the output elasticity of generalized capital, and the parameter β is the output elasticity of population/labor. These are required to be positive numbers less than one by the conventional economic assumption of positive but diminishing marginal product of a factor of production. The parameter v, whose value depends on α and β, is the degree of homogeneity of the production function. If $v < 1$, we have the case of diminishing returns to scale: a proportionate increase in K and P increases output Y by less than the proportionate amount. If $v = 1$, we have the case of constant returns to scale: a proportionate increase in K and P increases output Y by the same proportionate amount. Finally, if $v > 1$, we have the case of increasing returns to scale: a proportionate increase in K and P increases output Y by more than the proportionate amount.

The parameters α and β in equation (3.1) may be expressed in terms of $\alpha*$ and v. Let $\alpha* = \alpha/v$ and $\beta* = \beta/v$. Then $\alpha* + \beta* = 1$ and $\beta* = 1 - \alpha*$. Therefore, given numerical values for $\alpha*$ and v, we calculate first $\alpha = \alpha* v$, then $\beta* = 1 - \alpha*$, and finally $\beta = \beta* v$. We will refer to $\alpha*$ as "adjusted generalized capital elasticity of output" because it is obtained by dividing generalized capital elasticity of output (α) by the degree of homogeneity ($v = \alpha + \beta$).

The parameter A in equation (3.1) above represents total factor productivity. The concept of the Global Marshall Plan is to allocate new K resources, generated mostly in the wealthier nations, across all nations in such a way that the poorer and more populous nations receive proportionately larger shares of these new resources. The effectiveness of the GMP in equalizing living standards across the world would depend on the extent to which the currently observed differentials in living standards are a function of unequal stocks of generalized capital K rather than of differentials in the total factor productivity coefficients A. The parameter ξ is introduced in the following: this parameter measures the extent to which per capita income differentials are a function of differences in total factor productivity coefficients rather than of differences in generalized capital endowments.

The present discussion pertains exclusively to the initial period $t = 0$, therefore the time period subscript is omitted. Let $y_1 = Y_1/P_1$ be per capita income in the richest nation. Then total output in the richest nation is $Y_1 = y_1 P_1$. Now let k_1 be a model parameter representing the ratio of generalized capital in the richest nation K_1 to total output Y_1 in the richest nation: $k_1 = K_1/Y_1$. By this definition, $K_1 = k_1 Y_1$. The Cobb-Douglas production function for the richest nation is:

$$Y_1 = A_1 K_1^{\alpha} P_1^{\beta} \tag{3.2}$$

and therefore A_1 is solved for as follows:

$$A_1 = \frac{Y_1}{K_1^{\alpha} P_1^{\beta}} \tag{3.3}$$

Now consider some nation i poorer than nation 1. Its Cobb-Douglas production function for output Y_i in the initial period is:

$$Y_i = A_i K_i^{\alpha} P_i^{\beta} \tag{3.4}$$

In terms of per capita income y_i (frequently denoted herein as PCY):

$$y_i = \frac{Y_i}{P_i} = \frac{A_i K_i^{\alpha} P_i^{\beta}}{P_i} = A_i K_i^{\alpha} P_i^{\beta-1} \tag{3.5}$$

There are two extreme cases with respect to the observed difference between per capita income in nation 1 and per capita income in nation i: (1) the entire observed differential between y_1 and y_i is owing to differences in total factor productivity coefficients A ($k_i = k_1$ and $A_i < A_1$); (2) the entire observed differential between y_1 and y_i is owing to differences in generalized capital stocks K ($A_i = A_1$ and $K_i < K_1$).

In the first case, the k_i ratio in nation i is the same as the k_1 ratio in the richest nation, so that generalized capital in nation i is:

$$K_i^o = k_1 Y_i \tag{3.6}$$

Substitute equation (3.6) above into equation (3.5) for y_i and solve for A_i. This gives us the A_i which is consistent with the first hypothesis that all y differentials are the result of total factor productivity differentials:

$$A_i^o = \frac{y_i}{(K_i^o)^{\alpha} P_i^{\beta-1}} = \frac{y_i}{(k_1 Y_i)^{\alpha} P_i^{\beta-1}} \tag{3.7}$$

In the second case, the A_i parameter in nation i is the same as the A_1 parameter in the richest nation:

$$A_i' = A_1 \tag{3.8}$$

Now let the actual A_i be a weighted average of the two extreme case A's:

$$A_i = \xi A_i^o + (1-\xi) A_i' \tag{3.9}$$

where ξ is a parameter in the range from 0 to 1 inclusive. The actual K_i is then calculated from the weighted average A_i:

$$K_i = \left(\frac{Y_i}{A_i P_i^{\beta}} \right)^{1/\alpha} = \left(\frac{Y_i}{(\xi A_i^o + (1-\xi) A_i') P_i^{\beta}} \right)^{1/\alpha} \tag{3.10}$$

If $\xi = 0$, then all the A_i are equal to A_1 and all differentials in per capita income are owing to differentials in generalized capital K_i. If $\xi = 1$, then every nation has the same amount of K_i in proportion to output Y_i as does nation 1, and all differentials in per capita income are owing to differentials in the total factor productivity coefficients A_i. If ξ is between 0 and 1, then the differentials in per capita income are partially owing to differentials in generalized capital stock and partially owing to differentials in total factor productivity coefficients.

Once output Y in a certain nation has been produced, it is allocated over four uses: (1) military expenditure M; (2) consumption C; (3) gross transfer T; and (4) domestic investment I. Of these, the determination of military expenditure is the simplest. Military expenditure in each period for each nation is taken to be a certain proportion of output:

$$M_{i,t} = m_{i,t} Y_{i,t} \tag{3.11}$$

The situation with respect to consumption C is more complicated. We start by postulating a linear "potential per capita consumption function" that relates the potential per capita consumption c' of the nation's population to the nation's per capita disposable income y^d after the military expenditure obligation has been met:

$$c'_{i,t} = a + b y^d_{i,t} = a + b \frac{Y_{i,t} - M_{i,t}}{P_{i,t}} \tag{3.12}$$

where a and b are respectively the intercept and slope parameters of the linear function ($0 < b < 1$). Since by definition potential per capita consumption $c' = C'/P$ (where C' = total amount of potential consumption), the linear function for the total amount of potential consumption may be written as:

$$C'_{i,t} = \left(a + b \frac{Y_{i,t} - M_{i,t}}{P_{i,t}} \right) P_{i,t} = aP_{i,t} + b(1 - m_{i,t}) Y_{i,t} \tag{3.13}$$

where the second RHS term shows the result of substituting the military expenditure equation (3.11) into (3.12). In cases of poorer nations with low per capita income, it is possible that C' computed from equation

(3.13) exceeds the value of $Y - M$. In these cases, it is presumed that military expenditure takes precedence over consumption (this is why M may be referred to as the "military obligation"). Thus actual consumption C is the minimum of potential consumption and disposable income:

$$C_{i,t} = \min(C'_{i,t}, Y_{i,t} - M_{i,t}) \tag{3.14}$$

Now define the residual R as output less military expenditure and consumption:

$$R_{i,t} = Y_{i,t} - M_{i,t} - C_{i,t} \tag{3.15}$$

Assuming that $C = C'$ and the residual is therefore positive, part of the residual is allocated into investment I in the nation's own generalized capital stock, and the remainder goes to a transfer contribution T into the global transfer fund to be allocated to increasing the generalized capital stocks of the poorer nations according to the Global Marshall Plan. The question is: How much of a richer nation's residual R goes into I and how much goes into T?

The proposed "transfer allocation function" relates the *proportion* of a particular nation's residual that goes into the global transfer fund, denoted by λ, to the *ratio*, denoted by r, of per capita income in that particular nation (y) to per capita income in the richest nation ($y^{\max}$). The function contains two parameters: (1) $r^{\min}$ is the lowest ratio at which a nation would make a contribution into the transfer fund; (2) $\lambda^{\max}$ is the highest proportion that would be contributed into the global transfer fund by the richest nation. In the benchmark policy simulation, $r^{\min}$ is set equal to 0.20, and $\lambda^{\max}$ is set equal to 0.25. Setting $r^{\min}$ equal to 0.20 indicates that any nation sufficiently poor that its ratio of per capita income to per capita income in the richest nation is less than 0.20 (one-fifth), would make *no* contribution into the global transfer fund ($\lambda = 0$). Setting $\lambda^{\max}$ equal to .25 indicates that the maximum proportion of the residual contributed into the global transfer fund, this contribution being made by the richest nation (in which $r = 1$), would be 0.25 (one-fifth). The transfer allocation function is presumed to be linear in the range from $r = r^{\min}$ to $r = 1$. The function may be represented as follows:

$$\lambda_{i,t} = 0 \text{ if } r_{i,t} < r^{\min} \tag{3.16}$$

$$\lambda_{i,t} = \lambda^{\max} \frac{r_{i,t} - r^{\min}}{1 - r^{\min}} \text{ if } r_{i,t} \geq r^{\min} \tag{3.17}$$

where

$$r_{i,t} = y_{i,t} / y_t^{\max} \tag{3.18}$$

$$y_t^{\max} = \max(y_{i,t}, i = 1 \text{ to } n) \tag{3.19}$$

Note from equation (3.17) that if $r_{i,t} = r^{\min}$ then $\lambda_{i,t} = 0$. If $r_{i,t} = 1$, then $\lambda_{i,t} = \lambda^{\max}$. In the range from $r_{i,t} = r^{\min}$ to $r_{i,t} = 1$, $\lambda_{i,t}$ is a linear function of $r_{i,t}$ with slope $\lambda^{\max}$.

Once the transfer allocation function has determined the proportion λ of a particular nation's residual that is contributed into the global transfer fund, the total amount of the nation's transfer fund contribution is given by:

$$T_{i,t} = \lambda_{i,t} R_{i,t} \tag{3.20}$$

The total amount of the transfer fund *TT* is then the sum over all *n* nations of the individual nations' transfer contributions:

$$TT_t = \sum_{i=1}^{n} T_{i,t} \tag{3.21}$$

With respect to the determination of the share of each nation in the total transfer fund *TT*, we desire a formula that would give proportionately more to nation *i* on the basis of both its poverty level and its population size, since both poverty level and population are indicators of the nation's "need" for new generalized capital resources. Define the "difference" *d* as the difference between the maximum per capita consumption over all nations and the per capita consumption in nation *i*:

$$d_{i,t} = c_t^{\max} - c_{i,t} \tag{3.22}$$

where

$$c_t^{\max} = \max(c_{i,t}, i = 1 \text{ to } n) \tag{3.23}$$

The larger the difference *d*, the larger the poverty of nation *i*. The "population-weighted difference" is the product of the difference factor *d* and the nation's population *P*. It is proposed that the proportional share *s* of a given nation in the total transfer function be the ratio of the nation's population-weighted difference to the total population-weighted difference over all nations:

$$s_{i,t} = \frac{d_{i,t}P_{i,t}}{\sum_{i=1}^{n} d_{i,t}P_{i,t}} \quad (3.24)$$

The absolute amount S of nation i's share s in the total global transfer fund TT would then be:

$$S_{i,t} = s_{i,t}TT_t \quad (3.25)$$

From the nature of equation (3.24), every nation in the world except for the richest nation would have a positive proportionate share s in the global transfer fund and hence a positive absolute share amount S. At the same time, all nations with ratios r greater than $r^{\min}$ would have positive transfer contribution ratios λ and hence positive absolute transfer contribution amounts T. The net transfer contribution T^n of a nation would be its absolute transfer contribution amount T less its absolute share amount S:

$$T^n_{i,t} = T_{i,t} - S_{i,t} \quad (3.26)$$

Define the net transfer ratio t^n in nation i as the ratio of net transfer contribution to total output:

$$t^n_{i,t} = \frac{T^n_{i,t}}{Y_{i,t}} = \frac{T_{i,t} - S_{i,t}}{Y_{i,t}} \quad (3.27)$$

This measure is akin to the "foreign aid contribution ratio" used to assess the relative generosity of wealthier nations in providing economic development assistance to poorer nations.

The development of the global economy from period t to period $t + 1$ is shown in the following set of equations:

$$\tau_{t+1} = (1+\varphi)\tau_t \quad (3.28)$$

$$A_{i,t+1} = (1+\tau_{t+1})A_{i,t} \quad (3.29)$$

$$g_{i,t+1} = (1+\gamma)g_{i,t} \quad (3.30)$$

$$P_{i,t+1} = (1+g_{i,t+1})P_{i,t} \quad (3.31)$$

$$I_{i,t} = R_{i,t} - T_{i,t} \tag{3.32}$$

$$K_{i,t+1} = (1-\delta)K_{i,t} + I_{i,t} + \chi S_{i,t} \tag{3.33}$$

Equations (3.28) and (3.29) relate to the development of total factor productivity over time. The parameter τ governs the rate of change of the total factor productivity coefficient A, while the rate of change of τ is governed by the parameter ϕ. If the rate of change of technological progress is increasing over time, then $\phi > 0$; if the rate of change of technological progress is decreasing over time, then $\phi < 0$; and if the rate of technological progress is constant over time, then $\phi = 0$.

Equations (3.30) and (3.31) relate to population increase over time. The parameter g governs the rate of change of population P, while the rate of change of g is governed by the parameter γ. If the rate of population increase is increasing over time, then $\gamma > 0$; if the rate of population increase is decreasing over time, then $\gamma < 0$; and if the rate of population increase is constant over time, then $\gamma = 0$.

Finally, equations (3.32) and (3.33) relate to the development of generalized capital K over time. As shown in equation (3.32), domestic investment in generalized capital is given by I, which is equal to the residual R less the transfer fund contribution T. There are two parameters in equation (3.33) which represent loss factors. The δ parameter represents standard depreciation in generalized capital, while the χ parameter represents that part of the nation's share in the total transfer fund that is actually transformed into effective generalized capital. This parameter may be something less than 1, owing to the possibility of significant administrative expenses, and/or to the diversion of significant resources to private uses through graft and corruption.

NUMERICAL IMPLEMENTATION

The dataset used for GMP model validation purposes was taken from the World Bank's World Development Indicators databank. This dataset consists of annual values from 1980 through 2010 (31 years inclusive) for total population P and for four comparable per capita income (PCY) measures for the 146 nations that were listed in the data source as having populations of one million or more in 1980.

Table 3.1 presents information on the four comparable per capita income measures included in World Development Indicators. The upper part A of the table shows descriptive statistics for the four measures for the year 2010, while the lower part B shows key GMP model results for both the validation interval 1980-2010 and the policy simulation interval

Table 3.1
Descriptive Statistics and Key GMP-Model Results for
Four World Bank Measures of Per Capita Income (PCY)

A. Descriptive Statistics (2010)	PCY1	PCY2	PCY3	PCY4
Maximum	86,850	65,374	58,130	52,080
Minimum	190	141	350	312
Range	86,660	62,233	57,780	51,768
Mean	11,584	9,233	13,057	11,489
Coefficient of Variation	23762	20309	15289	13496
B. Key GMP-Model Results	PCY1	PCY2	PCY3	PCY4
Mean R-Squared (1980-2010)	0.8994	0.9584	0.9086	0.9436
WMRatio (2060) without GMP	0.1542	0.1232	0.2789	0.2581
WMRatio (2060) with GMP	0.6347	0.6511	0.6551	0.6350
MnRatio (2060) without GMP	0.0016	0.0016	0.0045	0.0049
MnRatio (2060) with GMP	0.5462	0.5602	0.5770	0.5504

Notes:
PCY1: GNI per capita Atlas method (current US $)
PCY2: GNI per capita (constant 2005 US $)
PCY3: GNI per capita, Purchasing Power Parity (current international $)
PCY4: GNI per capita, Purchasing Power Parity (constant 2005 international $)

2010-2060. These latter statistics will be explained in the following, but for the moment the only thing that needs to be noted about them is that they are not very different numerically. It was found from experiment that qualitatively the results from the simulations are the same regardless of which particular World Bank measure of per capita income is used. Therefore to streamline the exposition, only results using PCY4 (GNI per capita, Purchasing Power Parity, constant 2005 international $) will be reported in this book. This measure of PCY is arguably the most sophisticated, because it takes into account inflationary influences, as well as utilizing the Purchasing Power Parity approach, which most economists believe represents a better measure of relative living standards among nations. Hereinafter, unless specified otherwise, per capita income (PCY) refers to PCY4. The appendix to this chapter shows the 146 nations in the dataset: on the left they are rank-ordered on the basis of 2010 PCY, and on the right they are ranked-ordered on the basis of 2010 total population.

Source data on total population is complete for the 146 nations in the dataset. Source coverage for the four comparable per capita income measures is less complete. Depending on the specific measure, certain nations have missing data for one or more years between 1980 and 2010. And in the case of a few nations, there is no data on per capita income for any of these years. To deal with missing data, the following methods were utilized.

In the case of nations which have per capita income for some but not all years, a three step procedure was utilized. First, the first year in which data on per capita income is available for a specific nation was determined. Second, the ratio between per capita income in that nation and per capita income in the United States for that year was determined. Third, this ratio was applied to the known per capita income figure in the United States to estimate the per capita income figure for the specific nation in each year for which data is not available.

For nations that have no per capita income data at all for any of the years 1980 through 2010, they were given per capita income of "similar" nations. In the case of PCY4, there were seven nations in this category: Korea Dem Rep was given the same per capita income figures as Vietnam; Kosovo was given the same per capita income figures as Bosnia-Herzegovina; Myanmar was given the same per capita income figures as Thailand; Somalia was given the same per capita income figures as Zambia; South Sudan was given the same per capita income figures as Zambia; Zimbabwe was given the same per capita income figures as Zambia; and Cuba was given the same per capita income figures as Dominican Rep.

With 146 nations in the GMP model dataset, obviously it would be impractical to present results for each individual nation. Although there will be some reference in the following to results for specific nations (e.g., the 30 richest donor nations), for the most part results will be described for seven "income groups" of nations defined on per capita income, specifically PCY4 (GNI per capita, Purchasing Power Parity, constant 2005 international $). The 146 nations in the dataset were sorted in the order of decreasing PCY4: the first 20 were assigned to income group 1; the next 20 to income group 2; the next 20 to income group 3, and so on. All the groups contain 20 nations, except for group 7 which contains 26 in order to cover all 146 nations. The means of various statistics reported herein for the seven groups are not simple means but rather populated-weighted means. For example, the mean PCY of income group 1 is shown in Table 3.2 as $37,080. This is not the simple mean of the PCYs for the 20 nations in group 1; rather each national PCY in the group is weighted by the proportion of the total population of the group represented by the population of that nation. Table 3.2 shows basic statistics for the seven groups of nations for 2010. At the bottom of this table is a listing of the various nations included within each group.

Table 3.2
Seven Income Groups of Nations: Basic Statistics, 2010

Group	Nations	Population	PCY Range	Mean PCY
1	20	798,960,319	55,080-30,123	37,080
2	20	342,931,651	26,932-13,844	22,428
3	20	838,797,104	13,690-8,984	11,509
4	20	1,740,228,966	8,586-5,653	6,865
5	20	1,769,300,501	5,298-2,747	3,310
6	20	820,266,916	2,747-1,333	1,991
7	26	512,219,325	1,311-312	908
Total	146	6,822,704,782		

Group 1 Nations: Singapore, Kuwait, Norway, Hong Kong SAR China, United States, Switzerland, United Arab Emirates, Netherlands, Austria, Sweden, Canada, Germany, Belgium, Australia, Denmark, United Kingdom, Japan, Finland, Ireland, France.
Group 2 Nations: Italy, Korea Rep, Spain, Israel, Slovenia, Trinidad and Tobago, New Zealand, Greece, Czech Republic, Portugal, Saudi Arabia, Oman, Slovak Republic, Argentina, Poland, Hungary, Estonia, Croatia, Libya, Lithuania.
Group 3 Nations: Russian Federation, Chile, Malaysia, Panama, Latvia, Uruguay, Turkey, Belarus, Lebanon, Iran Islamic Rep, Mexico, Bulgaria, Romania, Venezuela RB, Costa Rica, Algeria, Brazil, Kazakhstan, South Africa, Macedonia FYR.
Group 4 Nations: Azerbaijan, Colombia, Tunisia, Cuba, Dominican Republic, Puerto Rico, Peru, Albania, Myanmar, Thailand, Ecuador, Bosnia and Herzegovina, Kosovo, China, Jamaica, Turkmenistan, Ukraine, Namibia, El Salvador, Egypt Arab Rep.
Group 5 Nations: Armenia, Jordan, Paraguay, Sri Lanka, Angola, Syrian Arab Republic, Cote d'Ivoire, Guatemala, Morocco, Bolivia, Indonesia, Georgia, Philippines, Honduras, Mongolia, Nicaragua, Moldova, India, Uzbekistan, Korea Dem Rep.
Group 6 Nations: Vietnam, Congo Rep, Iraq, Pakistan, Yemen Rep, Madagascar, Lao PDR, Mauritania, Cameroon, Lesotho, Kyrgyz Republic, Cambodia, Sudan, Tajikistan, Papua New Guinea, Senegal, Bangladesh, Nigeria, Kenya, Mali.
Group 7 Nations: Benin, Tanzania, Nepal, Burkina Faso, Somalia, South Sudan, Zambia, Zimbabwe, Ghana, Chad, Rwanda, Uganda, Haiti, Sierra Leone, Ethiopia, Guinea, Afghanistan, Mozambique, Togo, Malawi, Central African Republic, Niger, Burundi, Eritrea, Liberia, Congo Dem Rep.

Turning to the question of benchmark parameter values, we first take note of the fact that the theoretical content of contemporary economics is far more voluminous than the empirical content. A tremendous amount of raw data is collected, recorded, and published, but virtually all of this data is produced by the complex real world rather than by the controlled experiments from which are derived the great majority of precise and reliable empirical results in the physical sciences. Normally in economics, the numerical parameters of theoretical relationships must be econometrically estimated from non-experimental data. Owing to a variety of problems, ranging from unrepresentative and inaccurate data to equation misspecification and under-identification, these estimates are often unreliable. Even with respect to the most fundamental economic concepts (the aggregate consumption function, the aggregate production function, the supply of labor function, and so on), very little consensus exists even as to the appropriate mathematical forms of these functions, let alone the numerical values of those parameters that occur in any specific mathematical form.

The problem is compounded in the case of the equations of the GMP model developed herein. These equations represent hypothetical cross-national relationships, and only a very small percentage of econometric studies undertake estimation of cross-national relationships. The vast majority of such studies are based on data from a single nation. Moreover, our interest here is in an interactive system (the GMP model) rather than in any specific equation in the system. It is often the case that individual equations that seem to display a good fit to the data (high R-Squareds, significant *t*-values, etc.) do not work well when incorporated into larger systems. Finally, the purpose of the GMP model is to examine the potential impact of an unprecedented policy innovation: a Global Marshall Plan. Obviously the parameters of the transfer function of this program cannot be estimated from any currently existing data. In fact, it could be plausibly speculated that a policy innovation so monumental in scope as the Global Marshall Plan would have major ramifications throughout the entire world economy. Therefore the relationships and parameters that hold today, in the absence of such a program, might be substantially different from those that could hold in the future, under the operation of the program.

The upshot of all this is that it would be futile to aspire to a high level of numerical precision and accuracy in specifying the parameters of the GMP model. Benchmark parameter values will be utilized in this study that satisfy the following criteria: (1) they are consistent with basic *a priori* economic theory; (2) they lie within the wide boundaries of plausibility established by an impressionistic appreciation of related empirical literature; (3) they produce a reasonably satisfactory fit between the empirical data and the model results over the validation period extending from 1980 through 2010. Of course, the uncertainty that exists with respect to model parameter values means that an important part of the research is "sensitivity analysis": the determination of how model simulations are affected by changes in numerical parameter values. The basic without-GMP and with-GMP simulations for the benchmark parameter values suggest that an actual Global Marshall Plan might be highly successful, greatly accelerating the economic growth of the poor nations and substantially reducing inequality, yet at the same time maintaining high rates of growth in the rich nations. A natural suspicion would be that the results are "too good to be true" and that they are the consequence of "overly optimistic" benchmark parameter values. This suspicion will be carefully examined and evaluated in the sensitivity analyses reported in Chapter 4 below.

We commence with the production function, equation (3.1) above. This Cobb-Douglas form contains two parameters that are both time-invariant and constant across nations: α is the elasticity of output with respect to generalized capital K, and β is the elasticity of output with respect to population P. According to the basic economic presumption of diminishing returns to a factor of production, these parameters must be positive numbers less than 1. There have been numerous statistical studies of this Cobb-Douglas form, mostly across time in a single nation or across industries or regions within a single nation, and using physical capital for K and labor force for P. These efforts normally produce an α estimate in the range from .1 through .3, and a β estimate in the range from .6 to .9. The sum of the two parameters, $v = \alpha + \beta$, is the degree of homogeneity of the function. Most studies suggest that the degree of homogeneity of a Cobb-Douglas production function is approximately unity. The benchmark values for these parameters were set at $\alpha = .2$, $\beta = .8$, and therefore $v = \alpha + \beta = 1$. This implies $\alpha^* = \alpha/v = \alpha/(\alpha + \beta) = .2$. In the sensitivity analyses reported below in Chapter 4, variations in these production function parameters are reported in terms of α^* and v rather than in terms of α, β, and v. This is economical since α, β, and v are related by the equation $v = \alpha + \beta$.

The total factor productivity parameter A definitely varies over time and potentially varies over nations. Its initial value for each nation is determined by two parameters: k_1, the initial-period ratio between generalized capital K and output Y in the richest nation (nation 1), and ξ, the parameter that determines the extent to which differentials in per capita income over nations are (1) the result of differentials in generalized capital K over nations versus (2) the result of differentials in the initial value of the total factor productivity coefficient A over nations. This parameter will be referred to, somewhat inelegantly, as the "K differential vs. A differential coefficient." Capital-output ratios based on physical capital tend to be in the range from 5 to 10, but physical capital is only one component of generalized capital, in addition to which it was found by experiment that unrealistic results emerge from simulations in which k_1 is in the range from 5 to 10. The benchmark value of this parameter was therefore set to 25. The benchmark value of the ξ parameter was set to 0, which corresponds to the case in which all differentials in per capita output between nations are attributable to differentials in generalized capital K between nations.

The rate of disembodied technological progress (i.e., the rate of change of the total factor productivity coefficient A) is τ, which in the GMP model is actually a variable rather than a parameter because it is allowed to change over time. The parameter representing the rate of change of disembodied technological progress is ϕ. Since disembodied technological progress τ is itself the rate of change of the total factor productivity coefficient A, this means that ϕ can also be regarded as the second rate of change of total factor productivity. The two GMP model parameters requiring numerical specification are τ_0, the rate of change of disembodied technological progress in the initial period, and ϕ, the constant second rate of change of disembodied technological progress after the initial period. Most of the numerous estimates of the long-term rate of disembodied technological progress fall in the range from 1 to 3 percent per annum. Therefore the benchmark value of τ_0 is set at .012 (1.2 percent per annum). It is a highly speculative matter whether the *rate of change* of disembodied technological progress in the recent past has been positive or negative, and equally so whether the situation in this regard in the recent past can be expected to persist into the future. Therefore the benchmark value of ϕ is set to zero (0), implying no change in the rate of change of disembodied technological progress during the period of concern.

The GMP model consumption function embodied in equations (3.12)-(3.14) above involves the parameters a and b, representing respectively the intercept and slope of a linear relationship between the dependent variable potential per capita consumption and the independent variable per capita disposable income. Both of these are taken as pure parameters: invariant over both time and nations. The b parameter is equivalent to the famous Keynesian Marginal Propensity to Consume (MPC), which is universally presumed to be a positive number less than 1. The benchmark value of this parameter is set to .75. The a parameter represents "autonomous consumption," that hypothetical level of consumption that would transpire if disposable income were zero. Of course, in practice if disposable income were zero, consumption would also be zero. It is probably more useful, therefore, to think of a simply as the intercept associated with a linear approximation to the true consumption function, which almost certainly is non-linear. The benchmark value of a is set to 2500. To put this number into perspective, the average per capita income in U.S. dollars over the 146 nations in the World Bank dataset as of 1980 was $11489.

In equations (3.12)-(3.14) representing the model consumption function, there is also implicit, through equation (3.11), the parameter $m_{i,t}$: the proportion of total output necessarily allocated to military uses. In general, this parameter varies over both nations and time. In the numerical application of the model, however, this parameter varies over nations but not over time. The World Development Indicators databank contains the variable "Military expenditure (% of GNP)." The mean value of this variable from 2000 to 2010 was utilized to estimate $m_{i,t}$ for each nation, and this value was used for all years in all computations for both the validation interval (1980-2010) and the policy simulation interval (2010-2060). Since our principal interest is in the policy simulation interval, it would certainly be useful to have good figures for military expenditure proportions throughout these years. But as the future course of international relations is highly unpredictable, so also are the perceived needs of the various nations for military expenditures. It is to be hoped that international relations will improve, tensions will ease, and most nations will gradually reduce their military spending. If that happens, it would probably improve the prospects that a real-world Global Marshall Plan would be undertaken and pursued energetically. To the extent that some resources previously devoted to military purposes could be shifted directly into GMP transfers, this would help to answer the inevitable question that will be put forward by critics in the wealthy donor nations: "But where is the money coming from?" From the formal structure of the model, it is apparent that the money is not coming out of current consumption in the wealthy nations; rather it is coming out of investment funds that would have been invested domestically, but instead are invested in developing countries. But that might be too subtle for the critics. On the other hand, if one dollar that went previously into defense now goes into the GMP, that is easier to understand. Be that as it may, we cannot predicate that there will be a major decline in defense spending among the wealthy donor nations, and thus we cannot make an assumption that the $m_{i,t}$ parameter will decline between 2010 and 2060.

With respect to population growth, the rate of population growth definitely varies over nations, and potentially varies over time as well. Any variation in the rate of population growth for each nation is governed by the value of the parameter γ, which is both time and nation invariant. The population growth rate for nation i at time t, $g_{i,t}$, is determined by the initial population growth rate for that nation, $g_{i,1}$, and the population growth change parameter γ. The initial rate of population growth for each nation is estimated by the observed rate of geometric population growth between 1980 and 2010. From the geometric growth equation:

$$P_T = P_0(1+g)^T \tag{3.34}$$

where P_T is the terminal year population, P_0 is the initial year population, T is the number of inclusive years between 0 and T, and g is the constant rate of geometric growth, g is computed as:

$$g = \left(P_T / P_0\right)^{1/T} - 1 \tag{3.35}$$

For purposes of the validation simulation, the observed population figures for the nations are utilized. For the policy simulations, the populations of the nations after 2010 must be estimated. The geometric growth rate of population between 1980 and 2010, as computed by (3.35), provides the initial value of this parameter. Population for each nation from 2010 to 2060 is calculated from the population growth equations (3.30)-(3.31). The benchmark γ is set equal to zero, implying no change in the growth rates of population across nations between 2010 and 2060. Just as reductions in military spending would improve the success prospects of a Global Marshall Plan, so too would reductions in population growth. In fact, population growth rates have been declining somewhat for most nations over the recent past. Nevertheless, it would be unduly optimistic to build this trend into the policy simulations by specifying the benchmark γ value to be a negative number.

Two parameters occur in equation (3.33), which represents growth in the generalized capital stock K of a nation: δ is a standard depreciation factor, and χ is the proportion of a nation's share S in the global transfer function that is effectively converted into generalized capital (the "conversion effectiveness coefficient"). Unfortunately, there is no empirical basis for either of these parameters. Physical depreciation is rarely taken into account in studies pertaining to aggregate capital accumulation (i.e., capital accumulation at the national level). In most macro-econometric models, equations such as (3.33) are considered definitions (identities) not to be estimated. Obviously, physical capital does depreciate, but modeling of this factor is apparently more successful at the individual firm level than at the national level. The benchmark value for δ is therefore 0, indicating that physical depreciation is not taken into account in the benchmark case.

As for the conversion effectiveness coefficient, χ, there is obviously no empirical basis for this since no such thing as a Global Marshall Plan has ever been attempted in the real world. In the absence of such a program, no empirical basis exists for estimating the value of this parameter.

Table 3.3
GMP Model Benchmark Parameter Values

Symbol	Explanation	Value
α^*	adjusted elasticity of output with respect to generalized capital	0.2
v	degree of homogeneity of Cobb-Douglas production function	1.0
k_1	initial-period ratio of generalized capital to output in richest nation	25
ξ	*K* differential vs. *A* differential coefficient (source of per capita income differentials)	0
τ_0	initial-period rate of change of disembodied technological progress (*A* coefficient)	0.012
ϕ	second rate of change of disembodied technological progress (*A* coefficient)	0
a	intercept of the linear consumption function in disposable income	2500
b	slope of the linear consumption function in disposable income	0.75
m_i	military obligation coefficient (ratio of military expenditure to total product)	varies
$g_{i,0}$	initial-period rate of change of population of nation i	varies
γ	second rate of change of population	0
δ	physical depreciation coefficient	0
χ	conversion effectiveness coefficient	1

The benchmark value for χ is 1, indicating full conversion of share amount into generalized capital. Clearly this is a very optimistic assumption, as is the assumption that physical depreciation does not apply to the stock of generalized capital ($\delta = 0$). The effect of less optimistic assumptions ($\delta > 0$ and $\chi < 1$) will be investigated in sensitivity analyses, as reported in Chapter 4 below.

The benchmark numerical specifications of the various parameter values are summarized in Table 3.3. These numerical values are consistent with *a priori* economic theory as well as with empirical indications forthcoming from relevant statistical literature. As shown in the following section of the present chapter, they also produce a benchmark validation simulation that demonstrates that the GMP model is capable of producing a reasonable approximation to real world per capita income growth during the 1980-2010 interval.

VALIDATION OF THE MODEL

Before applying an economic simulation model to estimate the potential consequences of a economic policy innovation, it is customary to "validate" the model by determining that it tracks "reasonably well" the observed variable values during a period in which there was no policy innovation. The better the fit to the empirical data during the validation period, the more likely it is that the model constitutes a "reasonable approximation to reality" that will more accurately predict the effect of the innovation.

In the case of the present project, the validation period covers the 31 years covered by the World Bank dataset: 1980 to 2010. A validation simulation computes the variable values of the GMP model between 1980 and 2010 with the second of the two GMP transfer function parameters set equal to zero. Recall that the two transfer function parameters, as shown in equations (3.16) and (3.17) above, are: (1) $r^{\min}$ is the lowest ratio between a given nation's per capita income and the richest nation's per capita income at which the given nation would make a contribution into the global transfer fund; and (2) $\lambda^{\max}$ is the highest proportion of a given nation's residual (the difference between output and the sum of military expenditure and consumption) that would be contributed into the global transfer fund by the richest nation. If $\lambda^{\max} = 0$, this effectively short-circuits the Global Marshall Plan: *none* of any given nation's residual, regardless of the value of the nation's ratio, is contributed into the transfer fund. Results from the validation simulation of the GMP model, using the benchmark parameter values shown in Table 3.3 above, are presented in Tables 3.4 and 3.5 and the accompanying Figures 3.1 and 3.2.

Table 3.4 shows a comparison of weighted mean PCY growth as estimated by the model with empirical weighted mean PCY growth, for income groups 1 and 7. Group 1 represents high income nations, while group 7 represents low income nations. Figure 3.1 shows a comparison of weighted mean PCY growth as predicted by the model versus as observed empirically, for all seven groups. The upper panel of this figure shows results for the richest 4 groups, while the lower panel shows results for the poorest 3 groups. Note the difference in the scaling of the vertical axis: the upper panel goes from a minimum of 0 to a maximum of 40,000, while the lower panel goes from a minimum of 500 to a maximum of 3,500. If figures for all seven groups were put into a single graph with the scaling of the upper panel, the plots for groups 5, 6, and 7 would all be too close to the horizontal axis to be distinguishable.

Table 3.4
Tabular Comparison: Weighted Mean PCY Growth for Income Groups 1 and 7, 1980-2010 at 2-Year Intervals, Model versus Empirical

	Income Group 1			Income Group 7		
year	Model	Empir.	% diff	Model	Empir.	% diff
1980	21778	21778	0.00	711	711	0.00
1982	22443	21996	2.03	723	709	1.84
1984	23142	23563	−1.79	733	701	4.63
1986	23864	24777	−3.69	743	683	8.85
1988	24610	26596	−7.47	753	716	5.16
1990	25370	27770	−8.64	762	703	8.40
1992	26157	28139	−7.04	767	654	17.36
1994	26976	29067	−7.19	773	639	20.88
1996	27826	30393	−8.44	780	675	15.50
1998	28714	32064	−10.45	790	686	15.13
2000	29632	34107	−13.12	800	707	13.16
2002	30578	34414	−11.15	809	731	10.73
2004	31566	35954	−12.20	819	764	7.18
2006	32586	37746	−13.67	828	803	3.10
2008	33632	37857	−11.16	838	857	−2.23
2010	34718	37080	−6.37	848	908	−6.59

From an examination of the percentage differences between model and empirical PCY in Table 3.4, it is seen that the model slightly underestimates the PCY for the richest group of nations for most of the 1980-2010 period, while it slightly overestimates PCY for the poorest group of nations through the period. However, the absolute percent differences are not too high. The highest single percent error in absolute terms is 20.88 percent for group 7 in 1994.

Figure 3.1 illustrates visually the tracking performance of the GMP model for all seven groups of nations. It is apparent that the model results fit the empirical data best for the highest and lowest of the income groups, and less well for the middle-income groups 4 and 5. The GMP model underestimates of PCY growth are most pronounced for these middle-income groups. It should be noted, however, that the degree of underestimation for group 5 is exaggerated by the relatively small range of the vertical axis of the lower panel. Over the majority of the seven groups, the model tracks real-world GNP growth reasonably well, certainly well enough to justify a degree of confidence that the GMP model represents a reasonable approximation to reality.

Figure 3.1
Graphical Comparison: Weighted Mean PCY Growth for Seven Income Groups, 1980-2010, Model versus Empirical

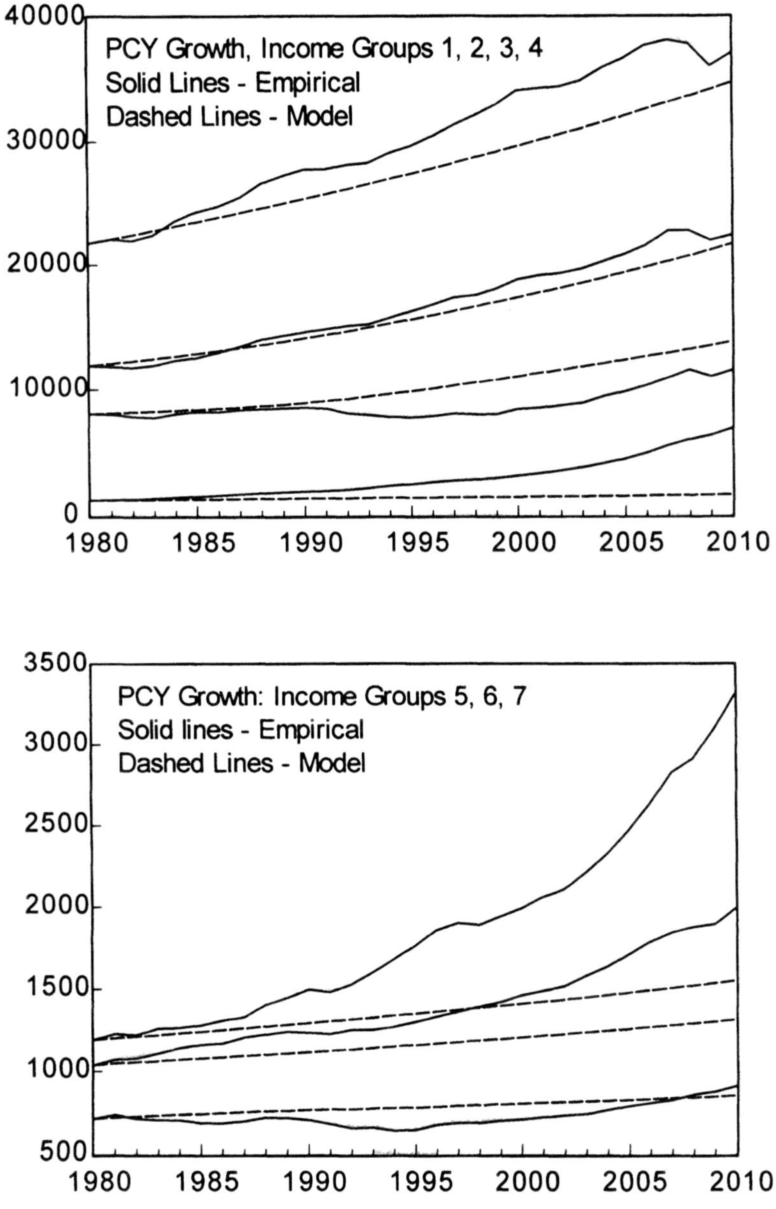

In addition to looking at relative model versus empirical PCY growth for groups of nations over the 1980-2010 validation interval, another approach to evaluating goodness of fit is to look at aggregate measures of inequality over all nations in the dataset. We will utilize two such measures: Weighted Mean Ratio (WMRatio); and Minimum Ratio (MinRatio). The "ratio" r was utilized above in the specification of the transfer allocation function in equations (3.16) and (3.17): it is defined as the ratio of the per capita income of a specific nation to the per capita income of the richest nation in the dataset for a specific time period. Per capita income is alternatively represented herein by PCY or y. The latter, of course, is more convenient for purposes of writing formulas for various statistics. The formulas for WMRatio and MinRatio for period t are as follows:

$$\text{WMRatio} = \sum_{i=1}^{n} \frac{P_{i,t}}{\Sigma P_{i,t}} r_{i,t} = \sum_{i=1}^{n} \frac{P_{i,t}}{\Sigma P_{i,t}} \frac{y_{i,t}}{y_t^{\max}} \qquad (3.36)$$

$$\text{MinRatio} = \frac{y_t^{\min}}{y_t^{\max}} \qquad (3.37)$$

where n is the number of nations (146), $P_{i,t}$ is population of nation i at time t, $\Sigma P_{i,t}$ is total population over all nations at time t, $y_{i,t}$ is per capita income (PCY) of nation i at time t, $y_t^{\max}$ is maximum per capita income over all nations at time t, and $y_t^{\min}$ is minimum per capita income over all nations at time t. Both of these measures can be described as "inverse" or "negative" measures of inequality: the lower they are, the higher the degree of inequality, while the higher they are, the lower the degree of inequality.

Table 3.5 shows a comparison of WMRatio and MinRatio as estimated by the model with empirical WMRatio and MinRatio over the validation interval. Figure 3.2 plots these figures: the upper panel for WMRatio, and the lower panel for MinRatio. From these exhibits, it is apparent that the model does a reasonable job of tracking inequality trends over the validation interval. With respect to WMRatio, the model indicates a slight decrease in inequality throughout the entire interval: the WMRatio figures are drifting upwards. The empirical WMRatio figures show a modest trend towards slightly greater inequality for most of the period, a trend that is dramatically reversed over the last five years of the interval, so that at its end, the model and empirical figures are quite close together. The situation is approximately the same with respect to MinRatio: a slight widening between the model and empirical figures for

Table 3.5
Tabular Comparison: Two Summary Measures of Inequality over All Nations, 1980-2010 at Two-Year Intervals, Model versus Empirical

	WMRatio			MinRatio		
year	Model	Empir.	% diff	Model	Empir.	% diff
1980	0.1284	0.1284	0.00	0.0042	0.0042	0.00
1982	0.1273	0.1303	2.31	0.0042	0.0042	1.03
1984	0.1221	0.1314	7.59	0.0042	0.0042	1.73
1986	0.1208	0.1328	9.94	0.0041	0.0043	4.00
1988	0.1187	0.1346	13.37	0.0041	0.0044	6.56
1990	0.1197	0.1366	14.11	0.0041	0.0045	9.75
1992	0.1193	0.1389	16.40	0.0041	0.0047	12.72
1994	0.1168	0.1413	21.01	0.0042	0.0048	14.84
1996	0.1158	0.1438	24.20	0.0041	0.0048	15.34
1998	0.1120	0.1467	31.03	0.0041	0.0047	13.98
2000	0.1103	0.1494	35.42	0.0035	0.0047	34.24
2002	0.1175	0.1513	28.75	0.0036	0.0047	28.69
2004	0.1191	0.1552	30.32	0.0030	0.0048	59.42
2006	0.1458	0.1645	12.89	0.0045	0.0050	11.69
2008	0.1826	0.1760	-3.56	0.0054	0.0052	-3.98
2010	0.1882	0.1797	-4.51	0.0060	0.0052	-12.85

most of the validation interval, with the gap closing at the end of the interval.

The effect of the severe global recession during the 2000-2010 decade is clearly manifested in these figures. The effect is particularly pronounced for MinRatio because of the sharp drop in this figure for the year 2003. But for both WMRatio and MinRatio, the recovery toward the end of the 2000-2010 decade brings the empirical figures and the model estimates into fairly close alignment. The fact that trends as predicted by the model were steady, while trends as they occurred in the real world were considerably more variable, is a reflection of the fact that the GMP model is intended for long-term policy evaluation and not for short-term forecasting. The model does not try to take into account the various shock factors that cause short-term fluctuations in the real world. The global recession of the 2000s was a traumatic event for the hundreds of millions that were directly affected by it, and it certainly strengthens the case for some kind of global anticyclical policy of a sort not presently possible. But in long-term historical perspective the recession will probably be perceived as a mere "blip." What is important for present purposes is the indication from Table 3.5 and Figure 3.2 that the GMP model tracks long-term inequality reasonably well.

Figure 3.2
Graphical Comparison: Two Summary Measures of Inequality over All Nations, 1980-2010, Model versus Empirical

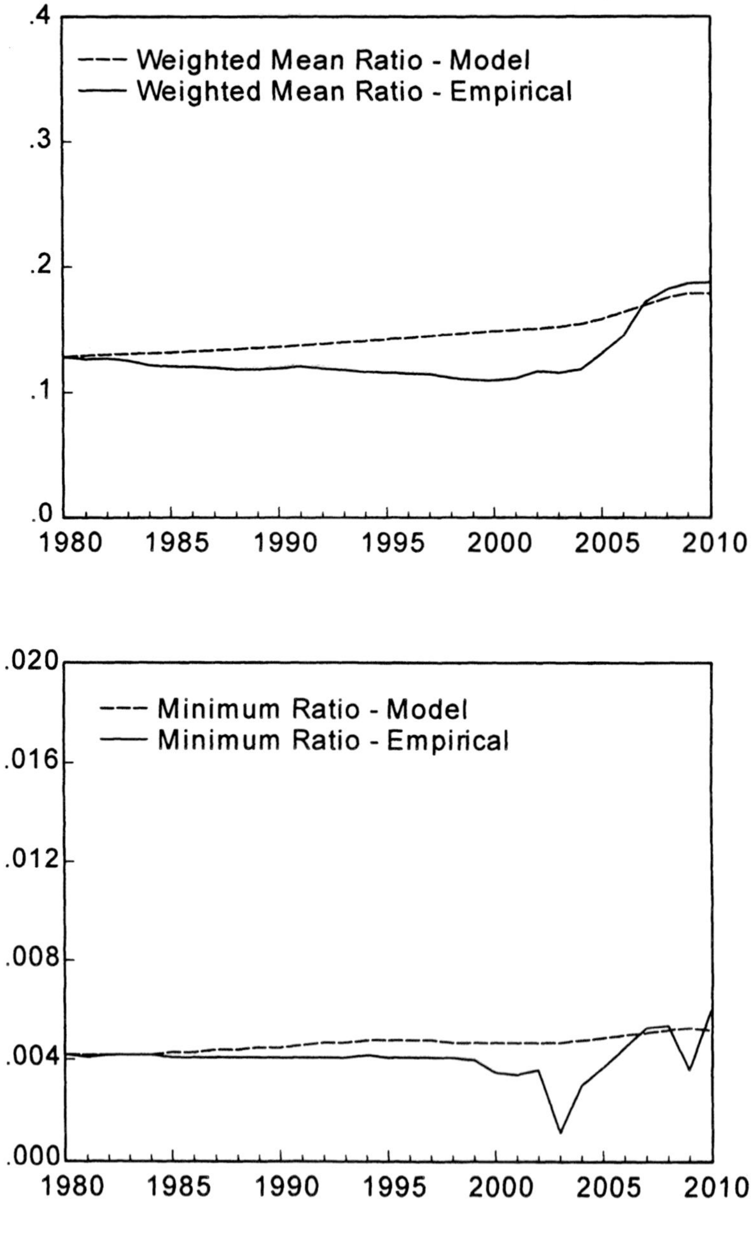

A standard statistical measure of goodness of fit is the R-Squared (RSQ). In our application, the empirical variable is observed per capita income (y = PCY) over the 146 nations and 31 years of the World Bank dataset, and the model variable is computed per capita income ($\hat{y}$) from the GMP model over the same nations and years. For purposes of the model computations, the initial year (1980) is 0 and the final year (2010) is 30. The R-Squared over the 31 years for the each nation i is given by:

$$\text{RSQ} = \frac{\sum_{t=0}^{30} (\hat{y}_{i,t} - \bar{y}_i)^2}{\sum_{t=0}^{30} (y_{i,t} - \bar{y}_i)^2} \tag{3.38}$$

where $\bar{y}_i$ is the mean per capita income for nation i over the 31 years in the dataset.

The R-Squared statistic is a customary measure of overall goodness of fit of an estimated regression equation. From its computational nature, it must lie in the range from 0 (indicating no correlation at all between the actual value of the dependent variable and its estimated value from the regression equation) to 1 (indicating a perfect correlation between actual and estimated values of the dependent variable—a plot of the actual values against the estimated values follows a 45-degree straight line). One of the advantageous properties of R-Squared is that it is a pure number that is unaffected by the units of measure utilized for the dependent variable. The R-Squared is qualitatively described as "the proportion of variation in the dependent variable that is explained by variation in the set of independent variables included in the regression equation." An important caveat is that the term "explained" is being used here in the sense of "statistically associated with," and that a statistical association does not necessarily manifest a causative relationship.

Obviously with 146 nations in the dataset, it would be impractical to look directly at the RSQ statistics for each nation. However, a summary statistic may be computed from the nation-level statistics: the Weighted Mean R-Squared (WMRSQ). In computing the weighted means over nations (as in the case of the WMRatio statistic introduced above), the weights are each nation's 2010 population as a proportion of total 2010 population over the 146 nations. The formula for this summary statistic is as follows:

$$\text{WMRSQ} = \sum_{i=1}^{146} \frac{P_{i,30}}{P_{30}} \frac{\sum_{t=0}^{30} (\hat{y}_{i,t} - \overline{y}_i)^2}{\sum_{t=0}^{30} (y_{i,t} - \overline{y}_i)^2} \tag{3.39}$$

where P_{30} is total population in period 30 (2010).

An additional summary statistic was computed for the validation run: the R-Squared over the 146 nations for the final year empirical and model per capita income. This is a cross-sectional rather than a time series statistic; it looks at the model data fit to the empirical data in the last period of the validation interval. Designated RSQ30 for the 30th period cross-sectional R-Squared, its formula is as follows:

$$\text{RSQ30} = \frac{\sum_{i=1}^{146} (\hat{y}_{i,30} - \overline{y}_{30})^2}{\sum_{i=1}^{146} (y_{i,30} - \overline{y}_{30})^2} \tag{3.40}$$

where $\overline{y}_{31}$ is the mean per capita income in period 30 (2010) over the 146 nations.

During the validation phase, the GMP model was simulated for many different combinations of parameter values. The purpose was to find a set of numerical parameter values that is consistent with *a priori* economic theory and that produces a reasonably satisfactory fit between the observed data and the model results on per capita income over the 146 nations in the dataset between 1980 and 2010. The numerical parameter values shown above in Table 3.3, utilized in a no-GMP validation simulation (i.e., $\lambda^{\max} = 0$), produce the following numerical values of the above two summary statistics:

WMRSQ = .8351
RSQ30 = .8744

These values indicate that the explanatory power of the GMP model for PCY growth over the validation interval of 1980 to 2010 is well over 80 percent for both summary statistics. According to conventional numerical standards within the economics profession, these values show that the GMP model provides a "good fit" to the observed data on per capita income. This strengthens the likelihood that the model represents a reasonable approximation to reality.

Chapter 3 Appendix
Nations in the World Bank Dataset

146 Nations Rank-Ordered by 2010 Per Capita Income			146 Nations Rank-Ordered by 2010 Population		
Country	Population	PCY	Country	Population	PCY
Singapore	5,076,700	52,080	China	1,337,705,000	6,791
Kuwait	2,991,580	51,612	India	1,205,624,648	3,088
Norway	4,889,252	47,342	United States	309,326,225	42,541
Hong Kong	7,024,200	43,751	Indonesia	240,676,485	3,764
United States	309,326,225	42,541	Brazil	195,210,154	9,891
Switzerland	7,824,909	41,401	Pakistan	173,149,306	2,490
United Arab Em.	8,441,537	36,509	Nigeria	159,707,780	1,522
Netherlands	16,615,394	36,339	Bangladesh	151,125,475	1,595
Austria	8,389,771	35,232	Russian Fed	142,389,000	13,690
Sweden	9,378,126	34,894	Japan	127,450,459	31,846
Canada	34,126,547	34,599	Mexico	117,886,404	11,853
Germany	81,776,930	34,240	Philippines	93,444,322	3,562
Belgium	10,895,586	33,517	Ethiopia	87,095,281	884
Australia	22,065,300	33,227	Vietnam	86,932,500	2,747
Denmark	5,547,683	33,147	Germany	81,776,930	34,240
United Kingdom	62,271,177	33,086	Egypt	78,075,705	5,653
Japan	127,450,459	31,846	Iran	74,462,314	12,027
Finland	5,363,352	31,763	Turkey	72,137,546	12,549
Ireland	4,474,356	30,987	Thailand	66,402,316	7,633
France	65,031,235	30,123	France	65,031,235	30,123
Italy	60,483,385	26,932	United King.	62,271,177	33,086
Korea Rep	49,410,000	26,806	Congo DR	62,191,161	312
Spain	46,070,971	26,558	Italy	60,483,385	26,932
Israel	7,623,600	25,486	Myanmar	51,931,231	7,633
Slovenia	2,048,583	24,654	South Africa	49,991,300	9,318
Trin. & Tobago	1,328,095	23,812	Korea Rep	49,410,000	26,806
New Zealand	4,367,800	23,762	Colombia	46,444,798	8,078
Greece	11,307,502	23,328	Spain	46,070,971	26,558
Czech Republic	10,519,792	21,898	Ukraine	45,870,700	5,935
Portugal	10,637,346	21,025	Tanzania	44,973,330	1,271
Saudi Arabia	27,258,387	20,744	Kenya	40,909,194	1,464
Oman	2,802,768	19,318	Argentina	40,374,224	16,745

146 Nations Rank-Ordered by 2010 Per Capita Income			146 Nations Rank-Ordered by 2010 Population		
Country	Population	PCY	Country	Population	PCY
Slovak Republic	5,430,099	19,019	Poland	38,183,683	16,658
Argentina	40,374,224	16,745	Algeria	37,062,820	9,966
Poland	38,183,683	16,658	Sudan	35,652,002	1,743
Hungary	10,000,023	16,158	Canada	34,126,547	34,599
Estonia	1,340,161	15,799	Uganda	33,987,213	1,039
Croatia	4,417,800	15,313	Morocco	31,642,360	4,166
Libya	6,040,612	14,154	Iraq	30,962,380	2,653
Lithuania	3,286,820	13,844	Peru	29,262,830	7,850
Russian Fed.	142,389,000	13,690	Venezuela RB	29,043,283	10,705
Chile	17,150,760	13,360	Uzbekistan	28,562,400	2,751
Malaysia	28,275,835	13,294	Afghanistan	28,397,812	816
Panama	3,678,128	13,195	Malaysia	28,275,835	13,294
Latvia	2,239,008	13,065	Saudi Arabia	27,258,387	20,744
Uruguay	3,371,982	12,584	Nepal	26,846,016	1,214
Turkey	72,137,546	12,549	Korea DR	24,500,520	2,747
Belarus	9,490,000	12,198	Ghana	24,262,901	1,190
Lebanon	4,341,092	12,119	Mozambique	23,967,265	798
Iran	74,462,314	12,027	Yemen Rep	22,763,008	2,353
Mexico	117,886,404	11,853	Australia	22,065,300	33,227
Bulgaria	7,534,289	11,119	Syria	21,532,647	4,363
Romania	21,438,001	10,813	Romania	21,438,001	10,813
Venezuela RB	29,043,283	10,705	Madagascar	21,079,532	2,111
Costa Rica	4,669,685	10,165	Sri Lanka	20,653,000	4,542
Algeria	37,062,820	9,966	Cameroon	20,624,343	1,923
Brazil	195,210,154	9,891	Angola	19,549,124	4,501
Kazakhstan	16,323,287	9,439	Cote d'Ivoire	18,976,588	4,273
South Africa	49,991,300	9,318	Chile	17,150,760	13,360
Macedonia FYR	2,102,216	8,984	Netherlands	16,615,394	36,339
Azerbaijan	9,054,332	8,586	Kazakhstan	16,323,287	9,439
Colombia	46,444,798	8,078	Niger	15,893,746	591
Tunisia	10,549,100	8,075	Burkina Faso	15,540,284	1,204
Cuba	11,281,768	8,043	Malawi	15,013,694	755
Dominican Rep	10,016,797	8,043	Ecuador	15,001,072	7,556
Puerto Rico	3,721,208	8,043	Cambodia	14,364,931	1,840
Peru	29,262,830	7,850	Guatemala	14,341,576	4,182

146 Nations Rank-Ordered by 2010 Per Capita Income			146 Nations Rank-Ordered by 2010 Population		
Country	Population	PCY	Country	Population	PCY
Albania	3,150,143	7,693	Mali	13,985,961	1,333
Myanmar	51,931,231	7,633	Zambia	13,216,985	1,200
Thailand	66,402,316	7,633	Zimbabwe	13,076,978	1,200
Ecuador	15,001,072	7,556	Senegal	12,950,564	1,651
Bosnia and Herz.	3,845,929	7,448	Chad	11,720,781	1,132
Kosovo	1,775,680	7,448	Greece	11,307,502	23,328
China	1,337,705,000	6,791	Cuba	11,281,768	8,043
Jamaica	2,701,200	6,558	Belgium	10,895,586	33,517
Turkmenistan	5,041,995	6,177	Guinea	10,876,033	818
Ukraine	45,870,700	5,935	Rwanda	10,836,732	1,047
Namibia	2,178,967	5,894	Portugal	10,637,346	21,025
El Salvador	6,218,195	5,806	Tunisia	10,549,100	8,075
Egypt Arab Rep	78,075,705	5,653	Czech Rep	10,519,792	21,898
Armenia	2,963,496	5,298	Bolivia	10,156,601	4,050
Jordan	6,046,000	5,252	Dominican R.	10,016,797	8,043
Paraguay	6,459,721	4,966	Hungary	10,000,023	16,158
Sri Lanka	20,653,000	4,542	South Sudan	9,940,929	1,200
Angola	19,549,124	4,501	Haiti	9,896,400	998
Syrian Arab Rep	21,532,647	4,363	Somalia	9,636,173	1,200
Cote d'Ivoire	18,976,588	4,273	Benin	9,509,798	1,311
Guatemala	14,341,576	4,182	Belarus	9,490,000	12,198
Morocco	31,642,360	4,166	Sweden	9,378,126	34,894
Bolivia	10,156,601	4,050	Burundi	9,232,753	477
Indonesia	240,676,485	3,764	Azerbaijan	9,054,332	8,586
Georgia	4,452,800	3,592	U. Arab Emir.	8,441,537	36,509
Philippines	93,444,322	3,562	Austria	8,389,771	35,232
Honduras	7,621,204	3,372	Switzerland	7,824,909	41,401
Mongolia	2,712,738	3,296	Tajikistan	7,627,326	1,730
Nicaragua	5,822,209	3,163	Israel	7,623,600	25,486
Moldova	3,562,062	3,097	Honduras	7,621,204	3,372
India	1,205,624,648	3,088	Bulgaria	7,534,289	11,119
Uzbekistan	28,562,400	2,751	Hong Kong	7,024,200	43,751
Korea DR	24,500,520	2,747	Papua NG	6,858,945	1,700
Vietnam	86,932,500	2,747	Paraguay	6,459,721	4,966
Congo Rep	4,111,715	2,711	Lao PDR	6,395,713	2,096

146 Nations Rank-Ordered by 2010 Per Capita Income			146 Nations Rank-Ordered by 2010 Population		
Country	Population	PCY	Country	Population	PCY
Iraq	30,962,380	2,653	Togo	6,306,014	766
Pakistan	173,149,306	2,490	El Salvador	6,218,195	5,806
Yemen Rep	22,763,008	2,353	Jordan	6,046,000	5,252
Madagascar	21,079,532	2,111	Libya	6,040,612	14,154
Lao PDR	6,395,713	2,096	Nicaragua	5,822,209	3,163
Mauritania	3,609,420	2,061	Sierra Leone	5,751,976	977
Cameroon	20,624,343	1,923	Eritrea	5,741,159	444
Lesotho	2,008,921	1,913	Denmark	5,547,683	33,147
Kyrgyz Rep	5,447,900	1,898	Kyrgyz Rep	5,447,900	1,898
Cambodia	14,364,931	1,840	Slovak Rep	5,430,099	19,019
Sudan	35,652,002	1,743	Finland	5,363,352	31,763
Tajikistan	7,627,326	1,730	Singapore	5,076,700	52,080
Papua New Guin.	6,858,945	1,700	Turkmenistan	5,041,995	6,177
Senegal	12,950,564	1,651	Norway	4,889,252	47,342
Bangladesh	151,125,475	1,595	Costa Rica	4,669,685	10,165
Nigeria	159,707,780	1,522	Ireland	4,474,356	30,987
Kenya	40,909,194	1,464	Georgia	4,452,800	3,592
Mali	13,985,961	1,333	Croatia	4,417,800	15,313
Benin	9,509,798	1,311	New Zealand	4,367,800	23,762
Tanzania	44,973,330	1,271	Cen. Afr. Rep	4,349,921	715
Nepal	26,846,016	1,214	Lebanon	4,341,092	12,119
Burkina Faso	15,540,284	1,204	Congo Rep	4,111,715	2,711
Somalia	9,636,173	1,200	Liberia	3,957,990	400
South Sudan	9,940,929	1,200	Bosnia-Herz.	3,845,929	7,448
Zambia	13,216,985	1,200	Puerto Rico	3,721,208	8,043
Zimbabwe	13,076,978	1,200	Panama	3,678,128	13,195
Ghana	24,262,901	1,190	Mauritania	3,609,420	2,061
Chad	11,720,781	1,132	Moldova	3,562,062	3,097
Rwanda	10,836,732	1,047	Uruguay	3,371,982	12,584
Uganda	33,987,213	1,039	Lithuania	3,286,820	13,844
Haiti	9,896,400	998	Albania	3,150,143	7,693
Sierra Leone	5,751,976	977	Kuwait	2,991,580	51,612
Ethiopia	87,095,281	884	Armenia	2,963,496	5,298
Guinea	10,876,033	818	Oman	2,802,768	19,318
Afghanistan	28,397,812	816	Mongolia	2,712,738	3,296

146 Nations Rank-Ordered by 2010 Per Capita Income				146 Nations Rank-Ordered by 2010 Population		
Country	Population	PCY		Country	Population	PCY
Mozambique	23,967,265	798		Jamaica	2,701,200	6,558
Togo	6,306,014	766		Latvia	2,239,008	13,065
Malawi	15,013,694	755		Namibia	2,178,967	5,894
Cen. African Rep	4,349,921	715		Macedonia	2,102,216	8,984
Niger	15,893,746	591		Slovenia	2,048,583	24,654
Burundi	9,232,753	477		Lesotho	2,008,921	1,913
Eritrea	5,741,159	444		Kosovo	1,775,680	7,448
Liberia	3,957,990	400		Estonia	1,340,161	15,799
Congo Dem Rep	62,191,161	312		Trin-Tobago	1,328,095	23,812

4

APPLICATION OF THE GMP MODEL

What might be the effect of a very large-scale economic development assistance program that would shift massive amounts of new generalized capital resources from the rich nations to the poor nations over the next several decades? Such a program would involve a tremendous expansion of the foreign development assistance programs of today. It would in fact constitute a Global Marshall Plan, a gigantic scaling up of the original Marshall Plan that greatly accelerated Europe's economic recovery from the devastation of World War II. The GMP model that was set forth, numerically implemented, and validated in the previous chapter will now be applied to the question of interest.

The GMP model policy simulation results to be presented in this chapter suggest that the effect might well be dramatic. Such a program might well produce a remarkable acceleration in the economic growth of the developing nations, while imposing only slight costs on the rich donor nations in terms of a slightly slower rate of economic growth. The world poverty problem might well be greatly alleviated within a 50-year period. This does not mean that the problem of inequality would be completely eliminated. But the gap between the richest and poorest nations would be significantly reduced, and sufficient progress would have been made in the poorest nations that they could no longer be deemed "poor" in absolute terms.

It must be emphasized strongly that this potential equalization of living standards across nations would be according to the principle of "common progress," and would not constitute "redistribution" as that term is normally understood. The normal understanding of "redistribution," as carried out through public policy intervention within nations, does indeed entail a direct shift of consumption expenditures from wealthier households who foot the tax bill, to poorer households who receive various social benefits. It is widely presumed at the present time that the only economically feasible means of significantly raising the living standards of the poor nations would be through a redistribution program that mimics the redistribution programs within nations. There would be large-scale direct transfers of final consumption goods—transfers that would necessarily seriously diminish living standards within the rich nations. Without doubt, a major program of this sort would not be politically feasible. The populations of the rich nations, while they can and do approve of small-scale public and private transfers to other nations of the sort seen today, will not support the economic development of the poor nations if the cost of the development program will be such as to seriously reduce their own living standards. That would put too great a strain on the sense of moral responsibility and humanitarian compassion among people living in the rich nations.

But the GMP model policy simulations reported here suggest that an unacceptable amount of strain would *not* be placed on rich peoples' capacity for moral responsibility and humanitarian compassion. The objectives of the GMP could likely be achieved with only a very slight, virtually unnoticeable, retardation in the *rate of growth* of living standards in the rich nations. The essential point is that the living standards of the rich nations would continue to rise throughout the operation of the Global Marshall Plan. There would be a substantial degree of convergence in living standards, but the point of convergence would be considerably higher than the present-day living standards even in the richest nations. Thus progress would be *common*, shared by all, even the richest nations. This outcome would be entirely different from that of a crude program of simple redistribution, as redistribution is normally thought of: living standards over all nations equalized at a low level, implying serious reductions in the living standards of the richest nations to gain slight increases in the living standards of the poorest nations.

Lest this fundamental conclusion be overstated, it must be conceded at the outset that optimistic simulation results are *not* obtained over *all* reasonable ranges of parameter values. Some of the simulation results confirm what is intuitively evident: that the Global Marshall Plan *might* be a dismal failure. Later in this chapter, we will investigate the sensitivity of the GMP model simulation results to parametric variation, and will determine those parameters most likely to undermine the desired outcome. It will be seen that within the context of the model, there are various ways in which the intentions of the program might be thwarted. The theoretical structure of the model clearly admits the possibility of failure.

Therefore, it is unnecessary for those whose "instincts" inform them that a Global Marshall Plan on the envisioned scale would necessarily be a colossal disaster, to criticize and reject the GMP model under investigation herein. It is merely necessary to criticize and reject one or more of the benchmark numerical parameter values shown in Table 3.3 above.

But if the theoretical structure of the GMP model (as opposed to its benchmark parameter values) is indeed accepted as a reasonable approximation to reality, the question of the potential effect of a massive worldwide economic development program could be moved farther away from the realm of *a priori* theoretical speculation and closer to the realm of empirical investigation. The question would devolve to "What are the actual numerical values of these particular parameters?" This is a much more narrowly focused question than "What are the economic relationships that bear on the success or failure of economic development assistance programs, and how important are these relationships likely to be in the real world?" The former question is more likely than the latter to yield an answer sufficiently compelling to form a secure basis for a policy decision on whether or not to actually initiate a massive worldwide economic development assistance program.

The fact that the GMP model utilized in this research clearly admits the possibility of failure of a real-world GMP constitutes testimony to its theoretical legitimacy: it augments our subjective judgment that the model represents a reasonable approximation to reality. If we could choose *any* numerical parameter values we pleased, and the simulation results would continue to show a high level of equalization over the entire world coupled with continued economic progress in the richest nations, then our common sense would tell us that these results were too good to be true, that they were not be trusted, and that there must be something fundamentally wrong with the model itself. Paradoxically enough, the fact that under some parameter values the GMP model indicates that the program would be a failure, lends more weight and credibility to the indication forthcoming from the benchmark simulation: that a real-world GMP might well drastically ameliorate the problem of world poverty and inequality within a relatively brief period of historical time, without imposing unacceptable costs on the rich nations. The benchmark GMP model simulation described in this chapter provides hard evidence that humanity has in fact within its grasp the solution to the greatest single hazard (now that the Cold War has dissipated) to continuing human progress in the contemporary world.

BENCHMARK POLICY SIMULATION

The GMP model policy simulations reported herein cover a 51-year period commencing in 2010 and concluding in 2060. Since the beginning year of 2010 has already passed into history, these simulations represent "what-if" experiments: they estimate what would have happened had a real-world Global Marshall Plan been started in 2010—or not started in 2010. The benchmark simulations utilize the parameter values shown in Table 3.3 above. There are two such simulations: the without-GMP simulation and the with-GMP simulation. Since a GMP was not in fact started in 2010, the without-GMP simulation is more in the nature of a simple forecast, as opposed to an estimation of the effects of a policy innovation.

In the without-GMP simulation, the parameters of the transfer allocation function are set so that no nation pays any part of its national income into the transfer fund. The transfer allocation function utilized in the GMP model relates the *proportion*, denoted by λ, of a particular nation's residual (total output less military expenditures and consumption expenditures) that goes into the global transfer fund, to the *ratio*, denoted by r, of per capita income in that particular nation (c) to per capita income in the richest nation (y^{max}). This function contains two parameters: (1) r^{min} is the lowest ratio at which a nation would make a contribution into the transfer fund; (2) λ^{max} is the highest proportion that would be contributed into the global transfer fund by the richest nation. The transfer allocation function is presumed to be linear (i.e., a straight line) in the range from $r = r^{min}$ to $r = 1$. To "disable" a potential GMP, i.e., to run a without-GMP simulation, it is merely necessary to set λ^{max} equal to 0 (zero). In this case, it does not matter what the nation's ratio is, because whatever the ratio is, the nation pays no proportion of its residual (and hence no proportion of its GNI) into the transfer fund.

In the benchmark with-GMP policy simulation reported here, the r^{min} parameter value is set to 0.25, and the λ^{max} parameter value is set to 0.20. Setting r^{min} equal to 0.25 indicates that any nation sufficiently poor that its ratio of per capita income to per capita income in the richest nation is less than 0.25 (25 percent), would make *no* contribution into the global transfer fund ($\lambda = 0$). Setting λ^{max} equal to 0.20 indicates that the maximum proportion of the residual contributed into the global transfer fund, this maximum contribution being made by the richest nation (in which $r = 1$), would be 0.20 (20 percent). Note that paying 20 percent of a nation's residual into the transfer fund does not denote paying 20 percent of that nation's GNI into the transfer fund, because the residual is a relatively small proportion of GNI. For example, according to the base-

Table 4.1
Tabular Comparison: Weighted Mean PCY Growth for Income Groups 1 and 7, Projected 2010-2060 at 2-Year Intervals, with and without GMP

	Income Group 1			Income Group 7		
year	with	w/o	% diff	with	w/o	% diff
2010	37080	37080	0.00	908	908	0.00
2012	38044	38064	-0.05	7958	919	765.62
2014	39031	39074	-0.11	9314	931	900.63
2016	40043	40110	-0.17	10323	942	995.36
2018	41080	41172	-0.22	11588	954	1114.46
2020	42141	42260	-0.28	13604	966	1308.33
2022	43225	43374	-0.34	15882	978	1523.98
2024	44334	44514	-0.41	18107	990	1728.74
2026	45466	45680	-0.47	20210	1002	1916.17
2028	46621	46871	-0.53	22202	1015	2087.84
2030	47799	48086	-0.60	24107	1027	2246.63
2032	48997	49325	-0.66	25949	1040	2395.16
2034	50216	50587	-0.73	27747	1053	2535.55
2036	51454	51870	-0.80	29515	1066	2669.46
2038	52710	53173	-0.87	31266	1079	2798.14
2040	53982	54495	-0.94	33010	1092	2922.65
2042	55269	55834	-1.01	34754	1105	3043.80
2044	56568	57187	-1.08	36505	1119	3162.26
2046	57882	58553	-1.15	38269	1133	3278.60
2048	59210	59929	-1.20	40050	1147	3393.25
2050	60546	61313	-1.25	41854	1160	3506.62
2052	61889	62701	-1.29	43685	1175	3619.01
2054	63237	64091	-1.33	45544	1189	3730.71
2056	64588	65480	-1.36	47436	1203	3841.96
2058	65940	66866	-1.39	49365	1218	3952.98
2060	67292	68246	-1.40	51331	1233	4063.96

line with-GMP simulation, in 2010 the United States would have paid 2.686 percent of its national income into the transfer fund.

Table 4.1 shows estimated PCY growth from 2010 to 2060 with and without the GMP for two income groups of nations: the richest group 1 and the poorest group 7. The PCY figures refer to population-weighted mean PCY over the nations in the two groups. For each group, the percentage difference between PCY with and without GMP is shown for each year. This table clearly illustrates the central result of this research: that a real-world GMP might have a tremendous accelerating effect on economic living standards in the poor recipient nations, while only a very modest decelerating effect on economic living standards in the rich donor nations. For the richest group 1 of nations, weighted mean PCY is estimated to increase from $37,080 in 2010 to $67,292 in 2060 if there is a GMP in operation, relative to an increase from $37,080 in 2010 to $68,246 in 2060 if there is no GMP in operation. The difference between with-without PCY in 2060 is −1.40 percent. Meanwhile, for the poorest group 7 of nations, weighted mean PCY is estimated to increase from $908 in 2010 to $51,331 in 2060 if there is a GMP in operation, relative to an increase from $908 in 2010 to $1,233 in 2060 if there is no GMP in operation. The difference between with-without PCY in 2060 for the poorest group of nations is approximately 4,064 percent.

To say that the results presented in Table 4.1 are remarkable would be a gross understatement. The losses in terms of slightly lower growth for the minority of very rich nations are minuscule relative to the tremendous gains of the poorest nations. This, of course, raises the question of plausibility. Are not these results simply too good to be true? Would not the actual situation under a hypothetical future Global Marshall Plan have little or nothing in common with the benchmark GMP model simulations presented here? Obviously, the only way to answer these kinds of questions definitively would be to initiate a real-world Global Marshall Plan and observe the outcome. Short of that, discussion of these questions must necessarily remain highly speculative. Nevertheless, the questions have to be addressed. The probability that a real-world GMP will actually be initiated (on a provisional and experimental basis to determine its likelihood of success) will be enhanced to the extent that a case may be made—albeit a speculative case—that these benchmark GMP model results are *not*, despite understandable initial impressions to the contrary, wholly implausible.

A first step toward the development of this case is simply to point out that the results shown in Table 4.1 are a consequence of one of the oldest and most universally accepted economic principles of all: the law of diminishing returns to a factor of production. The factor of production in this case is generalized capital, comprising not only the value of physical plant and machinery, but also the value of human capital resources (knowledge and skills achieved via education and training) and the value of social capital resources (roads, bridges, dams, schools, and so on). According to the law of diminishing returns, as the absolute amount of a particular input to the productive process increases, the marginal product of that input decreases. That is to say, fixed increases in the amount of the input utilized will generate steadily decreasing amounts of additional output as the total amount of the input utilized increases. In graphical terms, the relationship between input and output is concave upward-sloping ("bowed over").

The rich nations are utilizing large amounts of generalized capital, therefore the marginal product of generalized capital in these nations is low. The poor nations are utilizing small amounts of generalized capital, therefore the marginal product of generalized capital in these nations is high. Consequently, if a certain increment of generalized capital that would have been installed in a rich nation, is instead installed in a poor nation, the reduction in potential output of the rich nation will be small, while the increase in actual output of the poor nation will be large. This proposition, in itself, is hardly a matter for debate. But according to the benchmark GMP model simulations with and without a Global Marshall Plan in operation, the numerical implications of this proposition, in the context of the world problem, are far more dramatic than have ever been imagined by most economists.

Without doubt most economists today would be inclined to resist the numerical indications of the benchmark simulations since they pose such a direct challenge to the wisdom of current policy in this area, which confines economic development assistance to inconsequential amounts. But the important thing to recognize and appreciate is that there is nothing in these simulation results contrary to received economic theory. In fact, the *qualitative* proposition that poor nations gain more from economic development transfers than these transfers cost the rich nations, is fully consistent with the virtually axiomatic law of diminishing returns to a factor of production, and would in fact be accepted by a large majority of economists. It is simply the *quantitative significance* of this qualitative proposition with which economists would tend to have difficulty. But the difficulty stems from the conflict with established policy, not from a conflict with economic principles.

To reiterate, the Cobb-Douglas production function utilized in the GMP model is represented as follows:

$$Y_{i,t} = A_{i,t} K_{i,t}^{\alpha} P_{i,t}^{\beta} \tag{4.1}$$

where Y = output, K = generalized capital, P = population (a proxy for labor), and α and β are parameters. The Marginal Product of generalized capital in this function may be written as follows:

$$\text{MP}_{\text{K}} = \frac{\partial Y_{i,t}}{\partial K_{i,t}} = \frac{\alpha A_{i,t} P_{i,t}^{\beta}}{K_{i,t}^{1-\alpha}} \tag{4.2}$$

The MP_K equation shows that Marginal Product is positively affected by the *A* coefficient (total factor productivity) and by the population level *P*, but negatively affected by the level of generalized capital *K*. The benchmark GMP model simulations assume that the entire difference between the per capita income of any one nation and that of any other nation is the result of a difference in generalized capital stocks, and that none of the difference is attributable to a difference in the total factor productivity coefficients between the two nations That is to say, the *A* coefficient is the same for all nations. This presumption leads to very large differences in initial generalized capital stocks *K* and very large differentials in MP_K between various nations. For a few illustrative nations, computation of the above formula using 2010 data results in the following:

United States MP_K =	0.0072
Japan MP_K =	0.0229
Russian Fed. MP_K =	0.6691
Brazil MP_K =	2.4557
China MP_K =	11.0509
Nigeria MP_K =	4380.0060

The huge difference in Marginal Product of generalized capital in Nigeria relative to the United States is a result of the tremendous difference in generalized capital *K*. Thus if a certain increment in generalized capital is installed in Nigeria rather than in the United States, the "clout" of that certain increment, in terms of increased output, is much greater. Thus it is the principle of diminishing returns to a factor of production, in conjunction with the very large disparities currently existing in generalized capital stocks across nations, that accounts for the remarkable difference between the without-GMP simulation result and the with-GMP simulation result. This does not make the results any less remarkable, but it does make them more understandable—we can see a logical economic reason why these results might indeed be valid, despite initial impressions to the contrary.

Figure 4.1 provides a visual representation of some of the information in Table 4.1, but it improves on Table 4.1 by including all seven groups of nations instead of only the richest and poorest groups. The upper panel shows a plot of estimated PCY for the seven groups if there is no Global Marshall Plan in operation; the lower panel shows a plot of estimated PCY if there is a Global Marshall Plan in operation. The upper panel indicates continuation of the existing trend toward a widening gap between the richest and poorest nations, while the lower panel shows a remarkable degree of equalization over the 2010-2060 interval.

Figure 4.1
Graphical Comparison: Weighted Mean PCY Growth for Seven Income Groups, Projected 2010-2060, with and without GMP

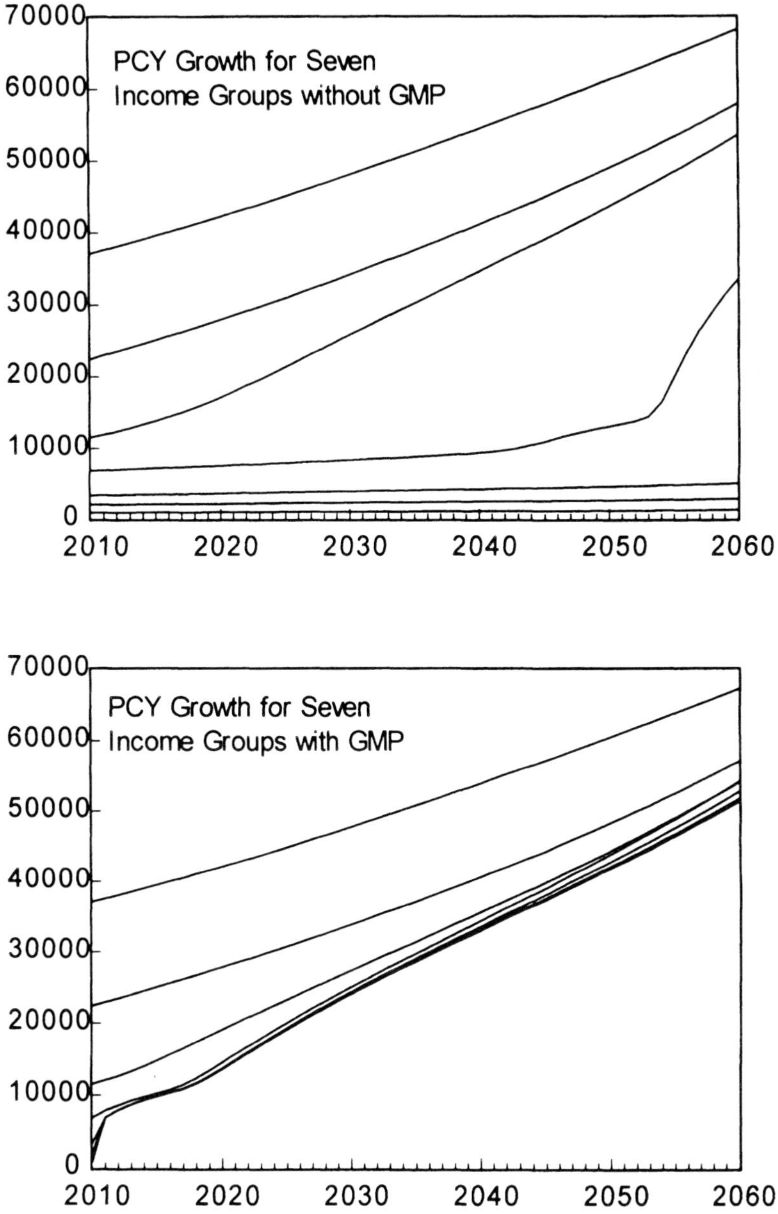

From the upper panel of Figure 4.1, it appears that without a Global Marshall Plan, we may expect "more of the same." The economic gap will continue to widen: the rich nations will get richer, while the low-income nations continue the same slow-growth pattern they have exhibited for the last several decades. This simulation result does not suggest that the problem of world inequality is going to "solve itself" anytime soon. There is, however, one notable exception to the pattern of widening economic disparity: as a whole the nations in middle-income group 4 experience a dramatic growth "takeoff" toward the end of the 2010-2060 interval. This exception will be discussed below.

But aside from the apparent anomaly of group 4, there is no evidence of any sort of economic convergence of the relatively poor nations on the relatively rich nations. On the other hand, if a Global Marshall Plan were set into motion, there could, according to the with-GMP simulation illustrated by the lower panel of Figure 4,1, occur a truly remarkable amount of progress toward overcoming the economic gap within a 51-year time span. The contrast between the without-GMP simulation and the with-GMP simulation can only be described as profound. True, we do not see absolute convergence in the sense that the poorest nations, at the end of the 51-year period, would have living standards as high as those in the richest nations at that time. However, these results do suggest that the living standards of what are the poorest nations of today would have improved sufficiently, by the end of the period, to be comparable to those of the richest nations today. They also suggest that all nations, from the relatively rich to the relatively poor, would be growing at comparable rates.

Of course, the GMP model does not encompass all factors affecting economic growth. Clearly it does not encompass various short-term factors affecting growth. If we were to undertake a real-world GMP, the actual growth patterns of various nations would be highly variable: growth would not be according to smooth curves shown in Figure 4.1. In addition to that, there are several long-term factors that influence the long-term rates of economic growth of the various nations. It is unlikely, for example, that Japan will continue the high-growth pattern it has exhibited over the last 50 years through the next 50 years. As for the poor nations of today, under a GMP some would no doubt be benefited more than others. As a result, there could well be some substantial alterations in the relative economic positions of nations. The possibility exists, even, that some of the poor nations of today may end up overtaking the richest nations of today. For example, China might overtake the United States in terms of per capita income within a 50-year period. If that were to happen, however, China would at some point change from a recipient nation to a donor nation within the GMP. Recall that a nation's receipts from the foreign aid transfer fund depend on its relative economic prosperity. The more prosperous a nation becomes, the less it would receive in foreign aid. As a nation becomes steadily richer, at some point it would shift from being a recipient nation to being a donor nation. China is the single most important example of this possibility, but the possibility would also apply to many mid-income nations of today.

The strongest indication from the with-GMP simulation is not what it projects for individual nations, but rather what it suggests about the entire family of nations. What it suggests is a leveling of the "global economic playing field," as it were: that is to say, the development of a global economy in which there are not two qualitatively different types of nations: those that have been very rich for a long period of time and those that have been quite poor for a long period of time. Instead, we would see a world in which all nations were characterized by living standards that are high by our present standards, but in which the finer degrees of prosperity would fluctuate over time. The relative economic status of the nations would vary, so that at one point in time nation A would be richer (in terms of PCY) than nation B, while at a later time their relative positions would be reversed. But the differentials in PCY would not be so large and so persistent for these differentials to be a source of hostility and conflict among nations. For example, in 2010 Norway had a PCY of $47,342 while the United Kingdom had a PCY of $33,086. This is a substantial differential, but it is not enough to cause the people of the United Kingdom (most of them at any rate) to feel relatively poor, and to experience unhealthy impulses toward envious resentment against the people of Norway.

Let us return now to the anomaly mentioned above: according to the upper panel of Figure 4.1, the nations in group 4, as a whole, will in fact experience a dramatic acceleration in their economic growth rates toward the end of the 2010-2060 period even if there is no Global Marshall Plan in operation. Apparently most of the nations in group 4 would at this point experience what economic historian Walt W. Rostow described as the "takeoff into sustained growth" in his classic treatise *The Stages of Economic Growth: A Non-Communist Manifesto* (1960). It seems quite surprising that a non-stochastic model (i.e., a model that incorporates no "random shock variables"), such as the GMP model studied herein, should contain within itself the capability of producing such a major transition for some nations in such a short period of time.

To investigate this indication, a long-term simulation of 250 periods was done using the GMP model without a GMP. It was determined that eventually every nation, even the poorest, eventually encounters this takeoff point. The key is the residual $R_{i,t}$ for each nation, defined as total output less military expenditure and consumption (see equations (3.11) through (3.15) in Chapter 3 above). Consumption, in turn, is the minimum of (1) potential consumption from a linear consumption function, and (2) consumption as the difference between national output and military expenditure. If it is the case that potential consumption from the linear consumption function is larger than the difference between national output and military expenditure, then consumption gives way to military expenditure, and actual consumption becomes the difference between national output and military expenditure. In this case the residual is zero:

$$R_{i,t} = Y_{i,t} - C_{i,t} - M_{i,t} = Y_{i,t} - (Y_{i,t} - M_{i,t}) - M_{i,t} = 0 \tag{4.3}$$

This situation is the norm among the poor nations. But it is also the case that given the model assumptions, sooner or later, even for the poorest nations, potential consumption will exceed the difference between national output and military expenditure, and the residual will become positive. At that point, a large proportion of the residual (less the contribution to the GMP transfer fund—assuming a GMP is in operation) starts going into domestic investment in generalized capital. Given the high Marginal Product of the small stock of generalized capital in any given poor nation, economic growth takes off. Through a long-term computation (250 periods) of the GMP model, it was ascertained, for example, that the critical takeoff point occurs around 2083 for Egypt, around 2125 for Indonesia, and around 2245 for Bangladesh.

The basic thrust of this book, of course, is that the GMP model policy simulations described herein constitute significant evidence in support of the potential effectiveness of a Global Marshall Plan and that such a program ought to be initiated in the real world on an experimental basis for a reasonable period of time sufficiently long to establish whether or not the program, if continued, would be a success. At the present time, most economists are very skeptical that a very large-scale economic development assistance program would be anything more than a gigantic waste of resources. Those sharing the majority viewpoint on this issue at the present time might be inclined to argue that the result displayed in Figure 4.1 for the group 4 nations suggests that a Global Marshall Plan is unnecessary. This is because sooner or later *all* the poor nations of today can be expected to achieve the same sort of "economic critical mass" that propelled the group 4 nations into rapid growth. In other words, this simulation result suggests that the problem of world poverty will indeed eventually "solve itself" if we merely remain patient and continue waiting for a sufficiently long period of time.

The problem with this interpretation of the evidence is that it is based on the presumption that the GMP model set forth and numerically simulated in this research is in fact sufficiently valid for the results to be taken seriously as guides to real-world potentialities. But if this presumption is made, then we should surely be prepared to take seriously the fundamental finding of the research. The fundamental finding of the research is that, very possibly, the problem of world poverty could be effectively resolved within a fairly brief period of historical time, and without seriously reducing the rate of economic progress achieved by the rich nations. What the research results tell us is that it is probably not necessary to remain patient and wait for a long period of time for the world poverty problem to "solve itself." The without-GMP results shown in Figure 4.1 suggest that only the mid-income 20 nations in group 4 will attain rapid growth within the next 50 years. But the with-GMP results suggest that all of the nations in the poorer income groups will achieve a high level of prosperity if a GMP is undertaken—without this causing a substantial diminution in the growth of the richer nations.

The substantial impact of a Global Marshall Plan on aggregate measures of inequality is shown in Table 4.2 and the accompanying Figure 4.2, which pertain to WMRatio and MinRatio. The "ratio" for a given nation is the ratio of that nation's per capita income to the maximum per capita income over all nations in the World Bank dataset. The Weighted Mean Ratio (WMRatio), formally defined above in equation (3.36), is the population-weighted mean ratio over all nations in the dataset. The lower this statistic, the greater the degree of inequality. The Minimum Ratio (MinRatio), formally defined above in equation (3.37), is the minimum ratio over all the nations in the dataset. It is also a negative measure of inequality: the lower is this statistic the greater the degree of inequality. Table 4.2 gives these inequality measures at two year intervals, while the accompanying figure is based on annual data.

As can be seen, if there is no GMP over the 2010-2060 period, these inequality measures are forecasted to hold fairly steady, while if there is a GMP, both measures are forecasted to improve dramatically. With respect to WMRatio, the numerical data show a very slight rate of improvement (which is virtually imperceptible in the plot) up to approximately the early 2050s, at which point the rate of improvement increases and is clearly discernible in the plot. The increasing rate of improvement in the latter part of the 2010-2060 period is caused by the previously discussed takeoff among the group 4 nations, which is shown in the upper panel of Figure 4.1 above. The WMRatio statistic applies to the entire group of nations, so that when one group experiences takeoff, this affects WMRatio. MinRatio, on the other hand, pertains to the poorest nation in

Table 4.2
Tabular Comparison: Two Summary Measures of Inequality over All Nations, Projected 2010-2060 at Two-Year Intervals, with GMP and without GMP

	WMRatio			MinRatio		
year	with	without	% diff	with	without	% diff
2010	0.1882	0.1882	0.00	0.0060	0.0060	0.00
2012	0.2448	0.1896	29.09	0.1498	0.0060	2408.10
2014	0.2634	0.1913	37.70	0.1727	0.0060	2799.51
2016	0.2782	0.1930	44.13	0.1884	0.0059	3071.84
2018	0.2980	0.1951	52.78	0.2021	0.0059	3313.18
2020	0.3261	0.1975	65.15	0.2133	0.0059	3513.00
2022	0.3559	0.2000	77.95	0.2238	0.0059	3702.74
2024	0.3841	0.2026	89.57	0.2368	0.0059	3937.14
2026	0.4099	0.2051	99.79	0.2579	0.0058	4313.15
2028	0.4336	0.2076	108.85	0.2841	0.0058	4778.50
2030	0.4556	0.2099	117.08	0.3117	0.0058	5272.02
2032	0.4762	0.2120	124.68	0.3387	0.0058	5759.24
2034	0.4957	0.2139	131.74	0.3643	0.0058	6227.37
2036	0.5109	0.2142	138.50	0.3859	0.0057	6677.83
2038	0.5246	0.2143	144.74	0.4054	0.0056	7103.65
2040	0.5374	0.2144	150.61	0.4233	0.0056	7511.39
2042	0.5495	0.2147	155.87	0.4399	0.0055	7903.99
2044	0.5609	0.2160	159.71	0.4553	0.0054	8284.07
2046	0.5717	0.2178	162.52	0.4697	0.0054	8653.87
2048	0.5820	0.2191	165.63	0.4832	0.0053	9015.30
2050	0.5919	0.2200	169.06	0.4959	0.0052	9369.96
2052	0.6013	0.2206	172.58	0.5079	0.0052	9719.22
2054	0.6102	0.2257	170.40	0.5193	0.0051	10064.23
2056	0.6189	0.2406	157.20	0.5302	0.0050	10406.00
2058	0.6271	0.2512	149.66	0.5405	0.0050	10745.37
2060	0.6350	0.2581	146.00	0.5504	0.0049	11083.11

the entire dataset. In the absence of a Global Marshall Plan, the value of MinRatio remains virtually constant over the 2010-2060 period. From both the numbers in Table 4.2, and the plots in Figure 4.2, the tremendous potential impact of a Global Marshall Plan is dramatically evident. With a GMP in operation, WMRatio is estimated to rise from 0.1882 in 2010 to 0.6350 in 2060, while MinRatio is estimated to rise from 0.0060 in 2010 to 0.5504 in 2060. For both of these measures, their value under a situation of perfect international equality, in which every nation had the same per capita income, would be 1. Certainly perfect international equality is not the objective to a Global Marshall Plan. But a *reasonable* degree of equality is desirable—and potentially attainable.

Figure 4.2
Graphical Comparison: Two Summary Measures of Inequality over All Nations, Projected 2010-2060, with and without GMP

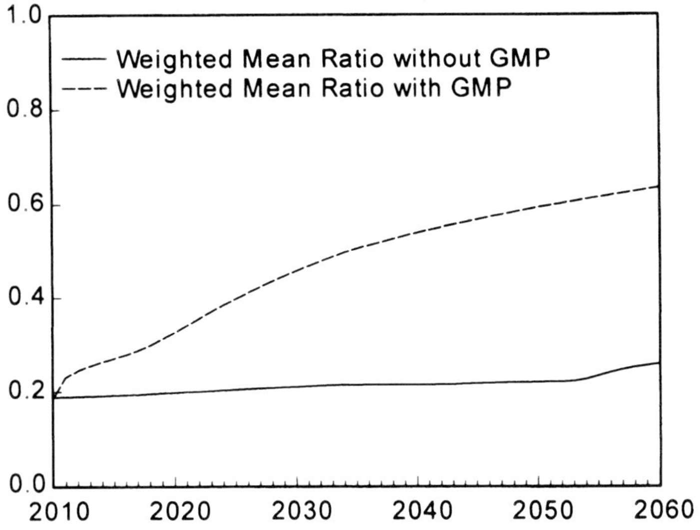

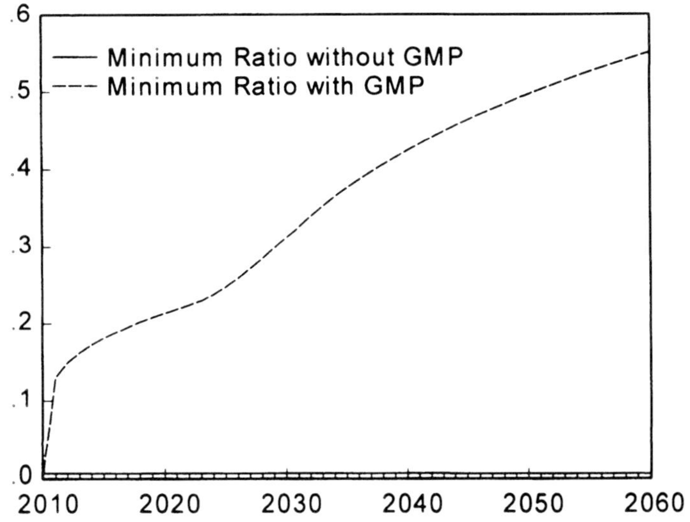

BURDEN OF THE GMP

The central indication of the benchmark simulation described in the foregoing section is that very rapid acceleration in the living standards of the poor nations is possible without excessive diminution of the rate of rise of living standards in the rich nations. From an economic point of view, the burden of the GMP is the reduced rate of increase of per capita income in the rich nations if there is a GMP in operation, relative to the situation if there were not a GMP in operation. A comparison of the upper and lower panels of Figure 4.1 suggests that the growth rates of the rich nations are little affected by whether or not a GMP is undertaken.

This point is sufficiently important to be worth reiteration. Figure 4.1 shows the Weighted Mean Ratios for seven groups of nations with and without a GMP in operation. Figure 4.3 below shows the with-without situation for two specific nations: the United States is an exemplar of the rich donor nations, while Nigeria is an exemplar of the poor recipient nations. The solid lines in this figure represent the situation without a GMP; the dashed lines represent the situation with a GMP. With a GMP, there is a very modest—hardly perceptible—downward shift for the United States, while the upward shift for Nigeria is extraordinary.

Figure 4.3
Graphical Comparison: Projected PCY Growth 2010-2060
for the United States and Nigeria, with and without GMP

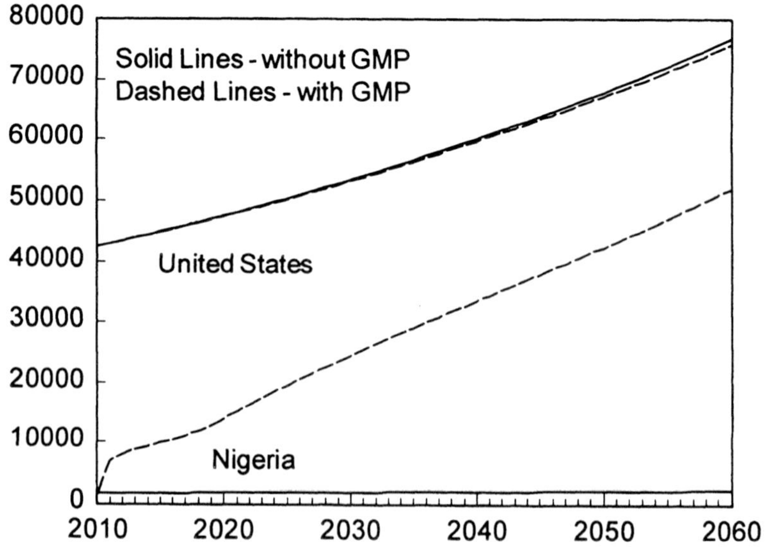

Table 4.3.
Burden of the GMP: Forgone PCY Growth from 2010 to 2060 for the 30 Richest Nations in 2010

Nation	PCY in 2010	Projected PCY in 2060 without GMP	Projected PCY in 2060 with GMP	% diff.
Singapore	52080	78967	78056	−1.153
Kuwait	51612	77558	76646	−1.176
Norway	47342	86460	85462	−1.154
Hong Kong	43751	78265	77178	−1.390
United States	42541	76917	75840	−1.400
Switzerland	41401	77722	76588	−1.458
United Arab Emirates	36509	48826	48723	−0.211
Netherlands	36339	72596	71374	−1.683
Austria	35232	72399	71148	−1.728
Sweden	34894	71677	70430	−1.740
Canada	34599	67930	66694	−1.819
Germany	34240	72327	71062	−1.749
Belgium	33517	70569	69297	−1.803
Australia	33227	65360	64128	−1.885
Denmark	33147	70487	69211	−1.811
United Kingdom	33086	69949	68686	−1.805
Japan	31846	69063	67767	−1.877
Finland	31763	68492	67203	−1.882
Ireland	30987	65530	64249	−1.956
France	30123	66061	64779	−1.940
Italy	26932	64752	63437	−2.031
Korea Rep	26806	62112	60843	−2.043
Spain	26558	62813	61517	−2.063
Israel	25486	55890	54973	−1.641
Slovenia	24654	63067	61752	−2.084
Trinidad and Tobago	23812	61227	59935	−2.112
New Zealand	23762	59606	58352	−2.103
Greece	23328	60950	59682	−2.082
Czech Republic	21898	61915	60610	−2.109
Portugal	21025	60669	59391	−2.106

Table 4.3 presents numerical information on the burden of the GMP in terms of reduced per capita income growth for the richest 30 nations in the dataset as of 2010. These would be among the leading donor nations to a real-world Global Marshall Plan. The nations are listed in the table in descending order of 2010 PCY. The percentage difference in projected 2060 PCY between the with-GMP and without-GMP situation for the United States is −1.400 percent. In general it is observed that the general

magnitude of reduced growth among these nations is in the order of –1.5 to –2.0 percent. By most people's standards, these are not large amounts.

From an economic point of view, the most fundamental way of assessing the cost of a Global Marshall Plan to the rich nations is to determine the reduction in economic growth they would experience as a consequence of allocating some of their economic residual away from domestic investment in generalized capital and toward the global transfer fund. An alternative way to look at the cost of the program is in terms of the proportion of a nation's total current output that would go to the global transfer fund. The actual amount of the transfer fund contribution would be a *net* amount: the difference between a certain nation's gross transfer fund contribution and that same nation's share. Every nation in the world except the richest nation would be allocated a share of the global transfer fund. For the rich donor nations, this would be an accounting figure and not an actual payment. If this share amount is less than the gross transfer fund contribution, then the nation would pay the difference into the fund. This would be the case for the rich donor nations. If the share amount is greater than the gross transfer fund contribution, then the nation would receive the difference as a disbursement from the fund. This would be the case for the poor recipient nations. So the upshot of this accounting method is that the rich donor nations would make actual payments into the fund, while the poor recipient nations would receive payments from the fund.

Table 4.4 shows the projected burden of the GMP for the richest 30 nations in terms of the percentage of national income that would be paid into the fund, at ten-year intervals from 2010 to 2060. The figures range from a maximum of about 4 percent of national income to under 1 percent of national income. For the United States, the percentages start at 2.686 percent in 2010 and drift up to somewhat over 3 percent starting in 2030. Although the United States is the fifth nation on the list in terms of per capita income, owing to the very large absolute size of U.S. national income, it would be the single largest contributor into the Global Marshall Plan, just as it has been the largest single disburser of foreign aid over the last several decades. Aside from the United States, other major contributors on the top-30 list are the nations of Western Europe, and Japan, as well as several others from around the world (Canada, Australia, Singapore, Hong Kong, etc.). Some nations are on the top-30 list that might not have been expected. For example, the Republic of Korea (South Korea) was long considered to be a developing nation, but as of 2010 it was sufficiently prosperous to join the list of top donors. Owing to their substantial oil export revenues, the United Arab Emirates and Kuwait are also on this list.

Table 4.4
Burden of the GMP: Contributions of the 30 Richest Nations in 2010, Percentage of National Income, 2010-2060 at Ten-Year Intervals

Nation	GMP Contributions as Percentage of National Income					
	2010	2020	2030	2040	2050	2060
Singapore	3.825	3.895	3.961	3.873	3.629	3.323
Kuwait	3.726	3.780	3.826	3.715	3.446	3.113
Norway	3.366	3.668	3.975	4.171	4.255	4.330
Hong Kong	2.954	3.189	3.392	3.465	3.424	3.366
United States	2.686	2.917	3.106	3.169	3.125	3.065
Switzerland	2.658	2.929	3.159	3.269	3.282	3.289
United Arab Emirates	1.938	1.638	1.151	0.405	0.409	1.120
Netherlands	2.010	2.287	2.482	2.562	2.568	2.584
Austria	1.890	2.186	2.395	2.493	2.527	2.577
Sweden	1.831	2.119	2.315	2.399	2.420	2.456
Canada	1.803	2.031	2.145	2.128	2.036	1.949
Germany	1.754	2.066	2.285	2.401	2.462	2.546
Belgium	1.670	1.966	2.156	2.238	2.265	2.314
Australia	1.616	1.820	1.891	1.823	1.685	1.553
Denmark	1.618	1.918	2.112	2.198	2.234	2.293
United Kingdom	1.585	1.874	2.053	2.124	2.142	2.183
Japan	1.470	1.771	1.951	2.024	2.053	2.109
Finland	1.451	1.742	1.909	1.967	1.979	2.016
Ireland	1.372	1.627	1.736	1.722	1.658	1.614
France	1.225	1.501	1.629	1.646	1.623	1.629
Italy	0.851	1.168	1.308	1.351	1.380	1.451
Korea Rep	0.823	1.092	1.166	1.125	1.063	1.034
Spain	0.819	1.112	1.212	1.203	1.176	1.184
Israel	0.579	0.737	0.644	0.404	0.141	0.065
Slovenia	0.584	0.921	1.052	1.089	1.127	1.210
Trinidad and Tobago	0.497	0.825	0.927	0.926	0.922	0.959
New Zealand	0.482	0.778	0.835	0.778	0.714	0.685
Greece	0.404	0.724	0.812	0.804	0.800	0.840
Czech Republic	0.252	0.631	0.770	0.826	0.900	1.027
Portugal	0.146	0.522	0.641	0.674	0.725	0.825

Each nation's contribution into the GMP transfer fund, as a percentage of its national income, is affected by the nation's military obligation. These obligations vary widely across nations. Some poor nations spend quite a lot on their military establishments, while some rich nations spend relatively little. Recall that the empirical figures utilized for the military obligations of the nations were estimated from military spending during the 2000-2010 decade, and in the benchmark with-GMP simulation, these are assumed to remain constant over the 2010-2060 interval.

Obviously this is a strong assumption, and without doubt there would be substantial fluctuations in military spending over the next 50 years according to the vagaries of international relations. This is one of several reasons why actual PCY growth of the participating nations would not follow smooth curves. But within an overall situation of considerable variability among the nations, there is good reason to expect that the general trend would be upward.

Another factor that would affect each donor nation's share of national income contributed to the GMP transfer fund is the specific measure of per capita income utilized. As described above in the numerical implementation of the GMP model, the World Bank database includes four different comparable measures of per capita income (see Table 3.1). To streamline the exposition, only results using the fourth measure (GNI per capita, Purchasing Power Parity, constant 2005 international $) are reported here. Although the overall implications remain the same whichever PCY measure is utilized, there are some significant differences in detail. For example, the estimated percentages of U.S. national income that would go into the GMP for the four different PCY measures are as follows: PCY1: 1.384 percent; PCY2: 1.861 percent; PCY3: 2.746 percent; PCY4: 2.686 percent. Looking at these figures, it is easy to envision that in the negotiations leading up to the formalization and implementation of a real-world Global Marshall Plan, representatives from the United States might be inclined to argue that PCY1 is actually a more accurate measure of actual PCY than any of the others. One possible solution to such an imponderable issue as this would be to utilize the average contribution percentage over the four PCY measures.

While it is to be expected that in working out the details of a real-world Global Marshall Plan, there might be a considerable amount of haggling, jockeying, and horse-trading among representatives of the donor nations to work out an acceptable compromise, at the same time it is to be hoped that with the prospect of such a gigantic and noble enterprise before them, all the participating nations will be inspired by a sense of determination and shared purpose that will keep the haggling, jockeying, and horse trading from becoming too rancorous and disruptive. It is a significant fact that the percentages shown in Table 4.4 tend to be at or below the customary percentages heretofore devoted to military purposes by most nations. Indeed, one of the selling points for a real-world Global Marshall Plan is that rising prosperity around the world would reduce international tensions and allow many if not most nations to reduce their military expenditures significantly.

To summarize, the important indication from Table 4.4 is not the precise numerical information on contributions of specific rich nations, but rather the fact that the net transfer percentages are not excessively high. For the richest nations the percentages are *high*, to be sure, but they are not *excessively* high. During the Cold War era, and even afterwards, many of the rich nations allocated more than these percentages to military spending. If the benchmark GMP model simulation were to tell us that the rich nations would have to allocate 10, 20, or 30 percent of their national incomes in order for a Global Marshall Plan to be successful, then we could more legitimately conclude that the concept was wholly impractical. But the actual percentages are more in the order of 2, 3, or 4 percent. These numbers may be within the realm of political feasibility.

SENSITIVITY ANALYSIS

Previous sections of this chapter have examined the benchmark GMP model simulations: the benchmark simulation without a Global Marshall Plan in operation, and the benchmark simulation with such a program in operation. The without-GMP simulation indicates continuation of the present situation: increasing inequality owing to the fact that the average living standards (as measured by per capita income) of the rich nations are growing faster than those of the poor nations. The with-GMP simulation suggests that a very large-scale economic development assistance program might generate a tremendous amount of economic equalization across all nations of the world without imposing a serious cost on the rich nations. The cost to the rich nations would be in the form of a slightly lower rate of growth in living standards. This by no means indicates a decline in average living standards within the rich donor nations. Presuming that the benchmark simulation results represent a reasonable approximation to potential reality, the desirability of a real-world Global Marshall Plan would be manifest to most people .

The conventional viewpoint in the world today, however, particularly within the richer nations, is that a very large-scale economic development assistance program along the lines of the envisioned GMP would be a colossal and very expensive failure. Such a program would impact heavily on economic growth in the rich nations, reducing it very substantially. At the same time, improvement in the poor nations would be at best modest and at worst negligible. The natural reaction to the benchmark GMP model results described above stemming from this conventional viewpoint is that these results are simply too good to be true. Either the GMP model itself is in error (does not represent an adequate approximation to real-world variables and relationships), or the benchmark parameter values are in error (do not represent adequate approximations to the real-world numerical parameter values). At this point the model itself will not be defended other than to say that it is based on very conventional and widely accepted economic principles, such as, for example, the law of diminishing Marginal Product of a factor of production. The numerical values of the model's parameter values are another story—it cannot be reasonably maintained that these values are "very conventional and widely accepted." Whatever actual numbers are utilized for the parameters of an economic policy model are normally subject to a considerable uncertainty and error. This is certainly the case with respect to the GMP model.

Therefore, in assessing the policy implications of any particular economic policy model, such as the GMP model, considerable weight is normally placed on sensitivity analysis: on the investigation of how changes in the parametric input into the model simulation affect the numerical output. The question addressed is how robust are particular qualitative policy indications against changes in parameter values? Do these qualitative policy indications change dramatically if parameter values are changed slightly? If so, we deem the initial policy indications to be non-robust. On the other hand, do these qualitative policy indications remain basically intact despite substantial variation in the numerical values of the parameters? If so, we deem the initial policy indications to be robust.

The final section of the present chapter examines the sensitivity of the simulation results to variations in numerical parameter values. On the whole, the results to be described here suggest that the basic qualitative indication of the benchmark GMP model simulations (with and without a GMP in operation) is indeed highly robust against parametric variation. Most model parameters may be varied over significant ranges, and the model simulations continue to show that a great deal of economic equalization is possible at minimal cost to the rich nations.

There are, however, two critical exceptions to this rule. Indeed, it is frankly acknowledged that with sufficiently adverse numerical values for these two parameters, the GMP model simulation results are fully consistent with pessimistic expectations regarding the prospects of a very large-scale economic development assistance project along the lines of a Global Marshall Plan. The two critical parameters are: the K differential vs. A differential coefficient (ξ); and the conversion effectiveness coefficient (χ). It is tangibly demonstrated that with adverse numerical values for either one of these two parameters, the effectiveness of the Global Marshall Plan would be greatly weakened. In fact, with sufficiently unfavorable parameter values, the program would be basically futile. That is to say, it would have no meaningful impact at all on the world inequality situation. Nevertheless, two important countervailing points are brought to light by the analysis: (1) the improving effect of the GMP on the world inequality problem continues to be very substantial unless the numerical values of these parameters depart from benchmark values by improbably large amounts; (2) even if the parameter values of these two parameters are such that the GMP is virtually useless as far as raising living standards in the poor countries is concerned, the program does *not* have a significantly adverse effect on the rate of rise of living standards in the rich nations.

Since the effects of adverse values of ξ and χ are virtually identical, to streamline the exposition we will look only at ξ. Furthermore, since these results are by far the most significant of all the results obtained from the sensitivity analysis, they will be discussed thoroughly at the outset, with brief consideration of the other, more optimistic results, postponed to the end of this section.

The first of the two parameters which have a profound impact on the potential success or failure of an actual Global Marshall Plan is symbolized by ξ. This is the parameter that determines the extent to which observed differentials in initial-period per capita income y among the 146 nations of the World Bank dataset may be attributed to differentials in generalized capital stock endowments K, as opposed to differentials in total factor productivity coefficients A. The benchmark value of the "K differential vs. A differential coefficient" (as it is inelegantly referred to) is 0 (zero), which indicates that *all* differentials in per capita income are the result of differentials in generalized capital stocks (the total factor productivity coefficients A are the same over all nations). At the opposite end of the spectrum would be $\xi = 1$, according to which *all* differentials in per capita income are the result of differentials in total factor productivity coefficients (the ratios of generalized capital K to total output Y are the same over all nations). If the value of $\xi = .5$, this would indicate that one-half of the differentials in per capita income y could be attributed to differentials in generalized capital K, and the other one-half of the differentials could be attributed to differentials in the total factor productivity coefficients A.

Table 4.5 shows the impact of variation in the ξ parameter on the two summary measures of inequality WMRatio and MinRatio in 2060 (the final year of the policy simulation interval), and also on the projected PCY in 2060 of two specific nations: the United States is an exemplar of the rich donor nations, while Nigeria is an exemplar of the poor recipient nations. The first column of Table 4.5 contains values for the ξ parameter from a minimum of 0 to a maximum 1. For a ξ value of 0, the 2060 value of WMRatio is 0.6350, indicating a very large decrease in global inequality, while if the ξ value is 1, the 2060 value of WMRatio is

0.1512, indicating no decrease at all in inequality. For MinRatio, the respective results are as follows: 0.5504 if ξ equals 0, and 0.0062 if ξ equals 1. Thus the results for MinRatio correspond exactly to the results for WMRatio. With $\xi = 0$ there is a tremendous amount of equalization; with $\xi = 1$ there is virtually no equalization despite the operation of the Global Marshall Plan. It is not an exaggeration to say that the success or failure of a real-world GMP depends critically on this one parameter.

Table 4.5
Sensitivity Analysis: Effect of Critical Parameter ξ Variation on Economic Equalization

ξ	WMRatio (2060)	MinRatio (2060)	U.S. PCY (2060)	Nigeria PCY (2060)
0.00	0.6350	0.5504	75840	51987
0.05	0.6008	0.5078	75871	48538
0.10	0.5668	0.4654	75902	45101
0.15	0.5331	0.4232	75934	41680
0.20	0.4998	0.3812	75965	38268
0.25	0.4668	0.3392	75997	34871
0.30	0.4342	0.2973	76028	31484
0.35	0.4018	0.2558	76060	28102
0.40	0.3698	0.2159	76092	24721
0.45	0.3382	0.1807	76124	21348
0.50	0.3072	0.1548	76157	18015
0.55	0.2774	0.1382	76189	14829
0.60	0.2507	0.1224	76221	12088
0.65	0.2292	0.1069	76254	10259
0.70	0.2126	0.0921	76287	9034
0.75	0.1987	0.0775	76320	7822
0.80	0.1861	0.0629	76353	6619
0.85	0.1749	0.0485	76386	5424
0.90	0.1651	0.0342	76420	4245
0.95	0.1569	0.0200	76453	3122
1.00	0.1512	0.0062	76487	2303

With respect to the effect of ξ variation on a representative recipient nation, we see that for a ξ value of 0, the projected 2060 Nigerian PCY is \$51,897, while if the ξ value is 1, the projected 2060 Nigerian PCY is \$2,303. With respect to the effect of ξ variation on a representative donor nation, we see that for a ξ value of 0, the projected 2060 United States PCY is \$75,840, while if the ξ value is 1, the projected 2060 United States PCY is \$76,487. Figure 4.4 shows the effect of three ξ values (0, 0.5, and 1) on projected PCY growth from 2010 to 2060 with a GMP for the United States (upper panel) and Nigeria (lower panel).

Figure 4.4
Effect of Variation in Critical Parameter ξ on Projected PCY Growth with GMP, 2010-2060, United States and Nigeria

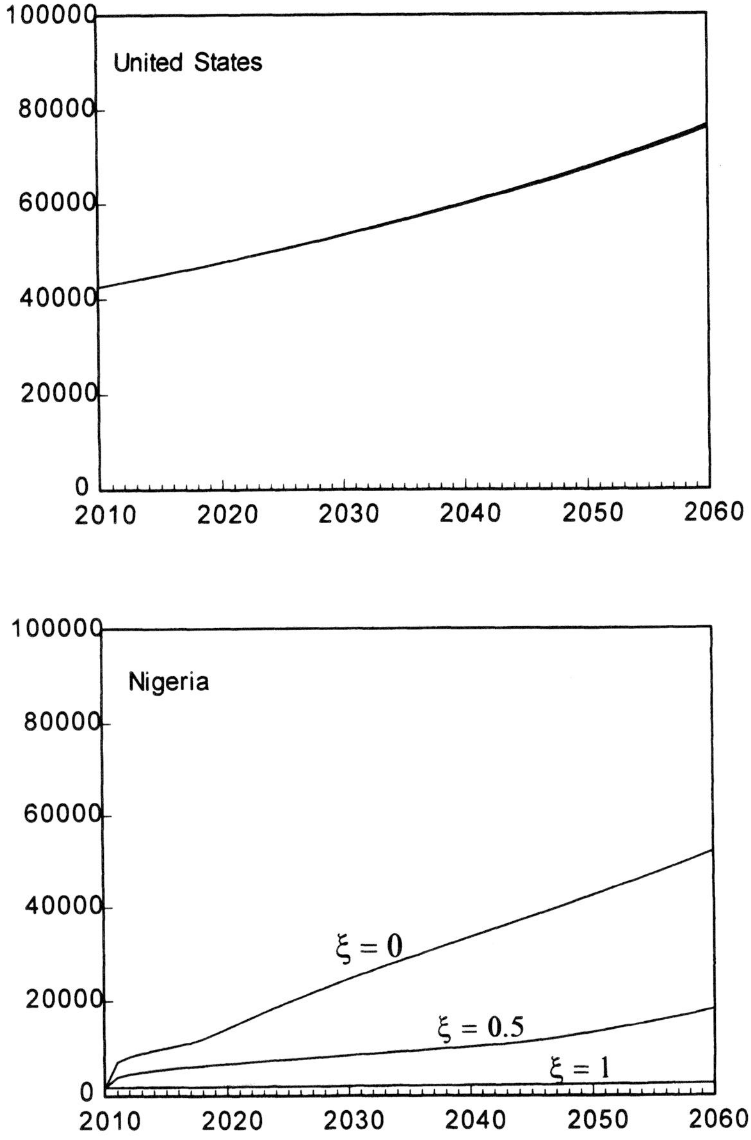

As can be seen from the United States plot in the upper panel of Figure 4.4, variation in the value of ξ has extremely little effect on PCY growth in the United States: the plots for $\xi = 0$, 0.5, and 1 are virtually indistinguishable. Meanwhile, for Nigeria there is a profound effect on projected PCY growth for ξ variation over these three values. For $\xi = 0$, projected PCY growth is very strong, while for $\xi = 1$, projected PCY growth is virtually nonexistent. What this information suggests is that higher values of ξ relative to the benchmark value would have a major depressing effect on PCY growth in the poor recipient nations, but virtually no effect on PCY growth in the rich donor nations. In the "worst case scenario," meaning that the value of ξ is 1 and that current differentials in per capita income are entirely the result of differentials in total factor productivity, and that no part of the differentials can be attributed to differentials in generalized capital, then the effect of the Global Marshall Plan on global economic inequality would be nil—but this unfortunate outcome would not significantly diminish the economic status of the rich nations.

Another important point is brought to light by these results: that even if the value of ξ is very much above its optimistic benchmark value of 0, the Global Marshall Plan would still have a major alleviating effect on the global economic inequality situation. For example, we note from Table 4.5 that if $\xi = 0.5$, the projected WMRatio for 2060 would be 0.3072. which is very much above its 2010 value of 0.1882. Similarly, from Figure 4.4 we note that PCY growth in Nigeria is still quite substantial even if $\xi = 0.5$. In short, higher values of ξ relative to its benchmark value would be very unfortunate from the point of view of the developing nations that would be the beneficiaries of the Global Marshall Plan, but this would have a virtually imperceptible effect on the economic prospects for the rich nations that would be supporting the program. In other words, the cost of a real-world GMP to the rich nations would remain quite minor whatever the value of ξ.

A final point is worthy of mention. If the actual value of the critical parameter ξ is indeed well below the optimistic benchmark value of 0, this would mean that a real-world Global Marshall Plan would manifest its ineffectiveness very quickly. The basic thrust of this research is that the benchmark results support the proposition that a real-world GMP should be initiated *on a tentative and experimental basis*. The research as a whole, which shows that success or failure might be determined by a single parameter, herein denoted ξ, definitely does *not* support the proposition that a real-world GMP should be continued onward for year after year and decade after decade even if the program is continuing to be manifestly unsuccessful in making progress toward its objectives. If a real-world GMP is not making much headway, GMP model simulations show why this could be the case: the ξ value is too high. Exactly the same outcome could occur if the conversion effectiveness coefficient χ is too low (is significantly below its optimistic benchmark value of 1). The GMP model thus encompasses not one but two factors that could cause failure. Since it is self-evident from common sense that pessimistic prognostications about a real-world GMP might be valid, it is in a sense reassuring that the GMP model does in fact encompass this possibility. If simulation results indicated that success would be achieved whatever the numerical values of the model parameters, then we could justifiably conclude that the model cannot possibly be an adequate approximation to reality.

But the GMP model as theoretically specified does indeed admit of the possibility that a real-world GMP might be a complete failure. One possibility is that the ξ parameter is much higher than its optimistic benchmark value of 0. The ξ parameter is not a "typical" parameter (such as α in the production function or a in the consumption function) that comes into play continuously throughout the simulation period. Rather it comes into play only in determining the initial values of generalized capital stocks K and the total factor productivity coefficients A. We turn now to sensitivity results for various model parameters that are continuously operative throughout the simulation interval. Not counting the ξ parameter, Table 3.1 contains 12 parameters for which numerical variation is possible. Obviously it would be impractical to report anything more than a few illustrative results.

To keep things manageable, the reported results are confined to those presented in Table 4.6, which shows the projected Weighted Mean Ratio (WMRatio) with a Global Marshall Plan in operation in year 50 of the simulation period (2060) for a variety of numerical parameter values. To reiterate, WMRatio is the weighted mean of the ratio of each nation's per capita income to the richest nation's per capita income, where the weights are each nation's proportion of the total population of the 146 nations included in the World Bank dataset utilized in this research. The lower this measure, the more unequal is the international distribution of income. Conversely, the higher this measure, the more equal is the international distribution of income. The computed value of this measure using actual data for 2010 is 0.1882. According to the benchmark simulation without a GMP, this measure is estimated to rise somewhat to 0.2581 in 2060. According to the benchmark simulation with a GMP, this measure to estimated to rise dramatically to 0.6350 in 2060.

Table 4.6 consists of four sections, each of which shows the effect on WMRatio in period 50 of symmetric variation in two parameters around

Table 4.6
Sensitivity Analysis: Effect of Selected Parametric Variation on Economic Equalization

	Weighted Mean Ratio (WMRatio) in Period $t = 50$ (2060)				
	$\alpha^* = 0.10$	$\alpha^* = 0.15$	$\alpha^* = 0.20$	$\alpha^* = 0.25$	$\alpha^* = 0.30$
$v = 0.80$	0.2999	0.2754	0.2483	0.2191	0.1919
$v = 0.90$	0.5265	0.4888	0.4211	0.3379	0.2519
$v = 1.00$	0.7857	0.7197	0.6350	0.5253	0.3929
$v = 1.10$	0.8268	0.8269	0.8236	0.7813	0.6378
$v = 1.20$	0.6895	0.6829	0.6751	0.6670	0.6578
	$k_1 = 15$	$k_1 = 20$	$k_1 = 25$	$k_1 = 30$	$k_1 = 35$
$\tau_0 = 0.004$	0.6538	0.6113	0.5778	0.5505	0.5274
$\tau_0 = 0.008$	0.6805	0.6399	0.6081	0.5820	0.5602
$\tau_0 = 0.012$	0.7051	0.6658	0.6350	0.6097	0.5885
$\tau_0 = 0.016$	0.7280	0.6899	0.6598	0.6351	0.6142
$\tau_0 = 0.020$	0.7494	0.7126	0.6832	0.6589	0.6383
	$a = 2000$	$a = 2250$	$a = 2500$	$a = 2750$	$a = 3000$
$b = 0.65$	0.7121	0.7081	0.7037	0.6989	0.6936
$b = 0.70$	0.6868	0.6812	0.6751	0.6681	0.6602
$b = 0.75$	0.6535	0.6450	0.6350	0.6236	0.6106
$b = 0.80$	0.6041	0.5886	0.5705	0.5495	0.5251
$b = 0.85$	0.5138	0.4794	0.4365	0.3842	0.3356
	$\phi = -0.02$	$\phi = -0.01$	$\phi = 0$	$\phi = 0.01$	$\phi = 0.02$
$\gamma = -0.02$	0.6284	0.6378	0.6496	0.6646	0.6839
$\gamma = -0.01$	0.6224	0.6320	0.6440	0.6593	0.6790
$\gamma = 0$	0.6128	0.6227	0.6350	0.6507	0.6708
$\gamma = 0.010$	0.5967	0.6068	0.6196	0.6356	0.6565
$\gamma = 0.020$	0.5687	0.5793	0.5926	0.6095	0.6313

their respective benchmark values, holding all other parameters at their benchmark values. For example, the first section of the table pertains to α^* and v, respectively the adjusted elasticity of output with respect to generalized capital, and the degree of homogeneity of the Cobb-Douglas production function. The respective benchmark values of these two parameters are $\alpha^* = 0.20$ and $v = 1.00$. The parameter α^* is varied through 0.10, 0.15, 0.20, 0.25, 0.30; the parameter v is varied through 0.80, 0.90, 1.00, 1.10, and 1.20. The middle cell of the 5x5 matrix of results corresponds to the benchmark case in which the terminal WMRatio = 0.6350. It is observed that the level of equality attained by the GMP is negatively related to α^* and positively related to v. The worst-case scenario in this section of the table is for $\alpha^* = 0.30$ and $v = 0.80$, in which case WMRatio = 0.1919. This is actually the worst-case scenario in the entire table.

The second section of Table 4.6 pertains to k_1 and τ_0, respectively the initial-period ratio of generalized capital to output in the richest nation, and the initial-period rate of change of disembodied technological progress. The respective benchmark values of these two parameters are $k_1 = 25$ and $\tau_0 = 0.012$. The k_1 parameter is varied through 15, 20, 25, 30 and 35; the τ_0 parameter is varied through 0.004, 0.008, 0.012, 0.016, and 0.020. The results indicate that terminal-period equality is negatively related to k_1 and positively related to τ_0. The worst-case scenario in the case of these two parameters is $k_1 = 35$ and $\tau_0 = 0.004$, in which case the projected 2060 WMRatio = 0.5274.

The third section of Table 4.6 pertains to a and b, respectively the intercept of the linear consumption function in disposable income, and the slope of this consumption function. The respective benchmark values of these two parameters are $a = 2500$ and $b = 0.75$. The a parameter is varied through 2000, 2250, 2500, 2750, and 3000; the b parameter is varied through 0.65, 0.70, 0.75, 0.80, and 0.85. The results indicate that terminal-period equality is negatively related to both a and b. The worst-case scenario for these two parameters is $a = 3000$ and $b = 0.85$, in which case the projected 2060 WMRatio = 0.3356.

The fourth section of Table 4.6 pertains to ϕ and γ, respectively the second rate of change of disembodied technological progress, and the second rate of change of population. The respective benchmark values of these two parameters are $\phi = 0$ and $\gamma = 0$. The ϕ parameter is varied through –0.02, –0.01, 0, 0.01, and 0.02; similarly the γ parameter is varied through –0.02, –0.01, 0, 0.01, and 0.02. The results indicate that terminal-period equality is positively related to ϕ and negatively related to γ. The worst-case scenario for these two parameters is that $\phi = -0.02$ and $\gamma = 0.02$, in which case the projected 2060 WMRatio = 0.5687.

These results are all economically plausible. For example, in the third section of the table, higher values of the a and b parameters in the consumption function mean that the amount of the residual in the wealthy nations would be smaller, thus contributions into the transfer fund would be smaller. For another example, in the fourth section of the table, the ϕ parameter governs the rate of change of technological progress while the γ parameter governs the rate of change of population growth. It is plausible that if the rate of technological progress speeds up, this will improve the prospects for equalization, while if the rate of population growth speeds up, this will reduce these prospects.

It is made plain by Table 4.6 that if the parameter values of the GMP model are sufficiently adverse, then simulations of a GMP will be pessimistic. For example, if we set every one of the eight parameters covered by Table 4.6 at their worst-case scenario values, the terminal-period WMRatio would be 0.1912. Even in this worst case, however, a GMP would entail modest improvement over the measured WMRatio in 2010 of 0.1882. In any event, it is only preconception that would insist that adverse parameter values are more probable than favorable parameter values, and that pessimistic projections are more probable than optimistic projections. Among the four sections of Table 4.6, there are a total of 100 WMRatio values. Of these 100, the great majority would represent a substantial improvement over the 2010 WMRatio of 0.1882. It is also worth recalling that the benchmark parameter values were specified to generate a good fit between model PCY growth and empirical PCY growth over the 1980-2010 validation interval. As we get farther away from the benchmark values, the validation interval fit becomes weaker.

A speculative objection to the good results obtained from the benchmark simulations is that they may be highly dependent on the benchmark parameter values. According to this objection, slight variations in these parameter values could and probably would lead to much impaired simulation results. Evidence presented in this section casts doubt on this particular objection. Most GMP model parameters may be varied substantially around their benchmark values without significantly altering the main qualitative results of the research. It must be conceded, however, that there are some parameters that, if they are given values greatly different from their benchmark values, will cause the potential impact of a Global Marshall Plan on global inequality to become minor or even negligible. The primary example of this is ξ, the parameter that determines the extent to which the initial empirical differences in per capita income are the result of differences in total factor productivity over nations, as opposed to differences in generalized capital stocks. But an important countervailing point emerges from the sensitivity experiments: whether or not a GMP has a major impact on the global inequality problem, such a program would impose minor costs on the rich nations. One looks in vain through the sensitivity results for indications that parameter values exist for which the cost of a Global Marshall Plan to the rich nations would be substantial.

5

SUMMARY AND CONCLUSION

Among the many objections that could be lodged against the present proposal for a Global Marshall Plan (GMP), one of the more important is that "there is not one shred of worthwhile evidence" that such a program would achieve significant success. The research reported here responds to this objection: it definitely provides at least a "shred" of worthwhile evidence that a GMP in fact would be successful.

But another possible response to this objection, aside from the findings reported here, is that "there is not one shred of worthwhile evidence" that a GMP would *not* achieve significant success. The GMP envisioned here would involve transfers of investment resources from the rich nations to the poor nations a great many times larger than the current transfers, a quantum jump larger. Thus far in human history, a foreign development assistance program on this scale has not been attempted. Thus, in a strict sense, no "worthwhile evidence" of any sort exists—evidence supportive either of the program's success or its failure.

If a GMP on the scale envisioned here is undertaken and pursued for one or two decades, and little or no progress is made toward reducing the economic gap between the rich nations and the poor nations, then that would constitute worthwhile evidence that the program was doomed to failure. By the same token, if a GMP is undertaken and pursued for one or two decades, and significant progress *is* made toward reducing the economic gap between the rich nations and the poor nations, then that would constitute worthwhile evidence that the program was destined for success. "Worthwhile evidence," in this very strict sense, can only be achieved by means of actual experiment. For example, prior to December 17, 1903, when the Wright brothers flew their tiny craft near Kitty Hawk,

North Carolina, there was no worthwhile evidence (in the very strict sense) that mankind would ever be able to build a mechanically propelled machine capable of flying through the air (as opposed to floating through the air as had already been accomplished with balloons) under the burden of a human passenger.

Of course, if we loosen up to an extent on how we define "worthwhile evidence," then it can certainly be said that worthwhile evidence exists concerning the potential performance of a real-world GMP—just as worthwhile evidence existed prior to December 17, 1903, regarding the possibility of powered flight. For many years prior to the Wright brothers' historic flight at Kitty Hawk, those informed of progress being made in gasoline engines and gliders were reasonably confident that the two could be combined to achieve a successful airplane. Meanwhile, among those uninformed of this progress, presuming they were also deficient in both imagination and optimism, the standard attitude was "If God had intended humans to fly, He would have given us wings." The same kind of mentality that pronounced this verdict on the possibility of powered flight at the beginning of the twentieth century would now, in the twenty-first century, react to a proposal for a Global Marshall Plan with an analogous verdict: "If God had intended all human beings to attain high living standards, He would have made the world economy such that all human beings attain high living standards." It is to be hoped that the latter verdict will eventually be proved just as inane and inaccurate as the former.

But admittedly, in one very important sense the achievement of worldwide economic equality in the twenty-first century will be far more difficult than was the achievement of powered flight in the twentieth century. This is because the cost of experimentation, in trying to find a solution to the problem of worldwide economic inequality, is far greater than it was in trying to develop a workable aircraft. The total economic resources utilized by the Wright brothers in their modest workshop were a tiny fraction of U.S. GNI at the time. Even if one added together *all* the economic resources utilized by *all* those experimenting with powered aircraft in that era, those resources would still have been a tiny fraction of U.S. GNI. This certainly cannot be said of a real-world experiment with a Global Marshall Plan.

On the other hand, while the resources necessary to conduct a definitive experiment with a real-world GMP would be tremendous in an absolute sense, the research reported here suggests they would be fully manageable in a relative sense, and they would moreover be virtually unnoticeable in terms of forgone growth by the rich nations. In other words, there would be extremely little forgone growth: growth in living standards with a GMP in operation would be only very slightly below growth in living standards without a GMP in operation. Of course if this were *not* the case, and it turned out that the more optimistic indications from the present research were invalid, a real-world GMP would very quickly be cut back drastically and quite likely phased out altogether.

With respect to evidence on potential success or failure, at this point in time there is nothing that could be described as "compelling" one way or the other. Pessimists can cite the large quantities of foreign aid dispensed in the past—despite which the economic gap continues to grow. Optimists can cite the fact that although the rich nations are growing more quickly than the poor nations, most poor nations are in fact growing at a respectable, non-negligible rate, and it seems intuitively plausible that at least some of this growth is attributable to the foreign aid contributions of the rich nations. Pessimists can point to the fact that there is no obvious relationship in the raw data between foreign aid and growth, and in addition several sophisticated econometric studies have been unable to find a statistically significant effect of aid on growth. Optimists can point out the difficulty of verifying causative relationships using the non-experimental data generated by the real world, and in addition can cite the fact that some sophisticated econometric studies have indeed indicated a statistically significant positive effect of foreign aid on economic growth.

This book has described and discussed some relevant economic research conducted by the present author on the potential success or failure of a hypothetical Global Marshall Plan. To my knowledge, this research is unique in terms of the question being addressed: whether or not a sufficiently large international economic development effort, involving all nations large and small, rich and poor, and which could accurately be described by the term "Global Marshall Plan," would be likely to achieve a high level of economic equality throughout the world within a relatively abbreviated period of historical time. To my mind, this is an extremely important question that deserves far more attention than it has received to date from the economics profession.

No doubt the main reason for this inattention is that at the present time almost all economists assume that the answer to this particular question is self-evidently in the negative. Economists are often chided, criticized, and even ridiculed for the dubious assumptions they habitually make. Although not presently recognized as such, this happens to be a particularly glaring example of this unfortunate tendency. To abstain from research on an important economic issue because the outcome of any such research is *assumed*, is hardly consistent with that spirit of high-minded scientific inquiry that economists self-righteously proclaim as their guiding motivation and inspiration. But as the saying goes: "It is never too late to change." I earnestly hope that my own research on this issue will inspire other economists to become seriously interested in it, and to develop models explicitly designed to provide tentative answers to what is probably the most important economic policy question of the contemporary age.

In the meantime, my own research provides a starting point. That starting point is decidedly optimistic. The research clearly indicates a non-negligible possibility that a real-world GMP could be a spectacular success, with a high degree of convergence being achieved in the living standards of all nations—without this causing a serious decline in the rate of increase of living standards in the rich nations. In other words, the research shows the possibility that a high level of worldwide economic equality can be achieved on the basis of the "common progress" principle. The poor nations of today can be brought to a high level of prosperity without this causing any diminishment in the high level of prosperity currently being enjoyed by the rich nations. In other words, progress would be common to all nations.

Of course it must be strongly emphasized that the research discussed herein does not constitute "proof," in either the scientific sense or the legal sense, that a real-world GMP would in fact be a success. "Proof" of *any* proposition, whether positive or negative, about the outcome of an untried policy measure is beyond the power of social science, even at its most methodologically sophisticated. Contemporary social science makes much use of mathematics, and mathematical manipulations, if they are performed correctly according to established mathematical principles, are impervious to error. This does not imply the infallibility of analysis based on mathematical models. If the assumptions which provide the starting point of the analysis are invalid, then the conclusions will be invalid despite flawless mathematical manipulations.

Similarly, there is no guarantee of the infallibility of conclusions based on arithmetical calculations performed by a computer. Use of computers is certainly a strong guarantee against serious arithmetical errors. But according to the well-known maxim enunciated at the dawn of the computer age—"garbage in, garbage out." Aside from questions concerning the conceptual foundations ("assumptions") of the research, there is the fact that the research indicates not only that a real-world GMP could be a spectacular success—but also that it could be a spectacular failure. The outcome of success or failure depends on the numerical values of certain model parameters. Even if we were prepared to assume that the model was a reasonable approximation of reality, we have no way of knowing the exact numerical values of its parameters. Indications of success are achieved with what I consider to be a sensible, reasonable set of numerical parameter values.

But I have also shown that with numerical parameter values that I consider to be much less plausible—but which others might deem more plausible—there are indications of failure. Specifically, if the critical ξ parameter is sufficiently close to the numerical value of 1, then according to the model simulations the GMP program would be a complete failure. In a way, this outcome reinforces the plausibility of the GMP model as a conceptual construct. If the conceptual construct indicated that a real-world GMP would necessarily be a success, regardless of the numerical values of the model's parameters, then we could be legitimately skeptical of the conceptual construct. There is such a thing, in social scientific work as well as in the ordinary business of life, of results that are "too good to be true." That is, they are too good to be believable. But this is not the case with respect to the research reported here. Paradoxically, the fact that the model results admit the possibility of failure lends more credence, rather than less, to the model's primary indication of the significant possibility of success.

How "strong" are these results in a practical sense? How much do they support the proposition that humanity should attempt a Global Marshall Plan? Given the qualification that the GMP would be initiated *on a provisional and experimental basis*, and that the continuation of the program in the long term would depend on a demonstrably high level of success in the early going (the first 10 to 15 years), then I personally would say that these results lend a very great deal of support to undertaking a real-world GMP. But admittedly this is a subjective judgment based on many years of nurturing a high level of optimism concerning the future prospects of global human civilization. To some, this level of optimism about the future cannot be justified by any sort of calm, rational, and objective evaluation of the past history and current status of human civilization. But while I cannot deny that throughout its history the human race has imposed upon itself terrible trials and tribulations, nevertheless, if we compare humanity's average condition during the Stone Age to its average condition today, the improvement is clear to most.

In principle, our conclusions about important policy questions should not be based on preconceived notions and unquestioned assumptions, but rather on deliberative analysis based on the facts as we know them. I would urge that among the facts that ought to be taken into proper consideration regarding the success probability of a real-world GMP, are the research results described, discussed, and evaluated in this book. I would ask that the evidence presented here be considered with an open mind, and reflected upon seriously.

EVALUATING THE RESEARCH

The research reported herein has utilized the economic methodology of computer simulation of a numerically implemented model to develop formal evidence on the potential performance of a very large-scale economic development assistance effort termed the Global Marshall Plan (GMP). The GMP model (so named for its purpose) utilizes nations as economic units and years as time periods.

For each nation, there is a production function, a consumption function, a transfer allocation function, a share determination function, and a set of transition equations from one period to the next. The production function is a standard Cobb-Douglas form in generalized capital and labor (proxied by population). The consumption function is a standard linear form in disposable income (income left after the "military obligation" has been met). The amount of national income left after deducting military expenditures and consumption expenditures is termed the nation's "residual." The transfer allocation function is such that richer nations pay larger proportions of their residuals into the total transfer fund. The remaining proportion of each nation's residual goes into domestic investment in generalized capital. The share determination function is such that poorer and more populous nations get larger shares of the total transfer fund. The shares of the poorer nations represent foreign aid receipts devoted to the accumulation of generalized capital. Generalized capital differs from ordinary capital: it includes, in addition to ordinary plant and machinery, the categories of education and training expenditures, and social infrastructure capital.

The empirical basis of the GMP model consists of the World Bank dataset, which contains per capita income y and population P from 1980 through 2010 for the 146 nations that had populations of 1,000,000 or more in 1980. This dataset is used to validate the GMP model. The benchmark numerical parameter values of the model are consistent with a priori economic theory, they lie within the boundaries of plausibility established by relevant empirical literature, and they produce GMP model results in per capita income over the 1980-2010 interval that match the observed values to a reasonable degree of accuracy. Although the GMP model per capita income results do not track short-term fluctuations, the long-term results are reasonably accurate. The model definitely reproduces the major features of the contemporary world economic situation: most richer nations are growing faster than most poorer nations, the absolute gap between the richest and poorest nations in the world is getting larger, and aggregate measures of world income inequality are gradually rising.

Following validation, two principal simulations of the GMP model were run for the 51-year interval 2010–2060. The "without-GMP" simulation sets the key parameter λ^{max} of the transfer allocation function to 0, so that no nation pays any proportion of its residual into the total transfer fund, and effectively there is no Global Marshall Plan in operation. The "with-GMP" simulation uses the same numerical parameter values with the single exception that λ^{max} is set to 0.2, indicating that the richest nation in the world pays 20 percent of its residual into the total transfer fund. The without-GMP simulation shows that while a handful of the poorer nations may achieve "takeoff" conditions during the 2010–2060 period, the basic observed trends during the 1980–2010 interval may be expected to continue through the 2010–2060 interval: most richer nations will grow faster than most poorer nations, the absolute gap between the richest and poorest nations in the world will get larger, and aggregate measures of world income inequality will continue to rise.

The with-GMP simulation shows a far more attractive possibility. This simulation is a hypothetical ("what-if") exercise that envisions that a Global Marshall Plan had been commenced in 2010 and continued on through 2060. It demonstrates a pattern of remarkable acceleration of the economic growth of the poor nations, at the cost of only a very slight retardation of the economic growth of the rich nations. To illustrate, consider the relative growth of Nigeria and the United States with the GMP in operation versus without the GMP in operation. In the absence of a GMP, Nigerian per capita income over the 2010–2060 period is projected to grow from $1,522 (in 2005 international PPP dollars) to $2,135, a 40.27 percent increase; while in the presence of a GMP, Nigerian per capita income over the same period is estimated to grow from $1,522 to $51,987, a 3315.7 percent increase. In the absence of a GMP, U.S. per capita income over the 2010–2060 period is projected to grow from $42,541 (in 2005 international PPP dollars) to $76,917, a 80.91 percent increase; while in the presence of a GMP, U.S. per capita income over the same period is estimated to grow from $42,541 to $75,840, a 78.27 percent increase. The Nigerian results are representative for the poor nations; the United States results are representative for the rich nations. The fundamental implication is that a tremendously expanded, worldwide economic development assistance effort might well be tremendously successful in terms of dramatically raising average living standards in poor nations while costing the rich nations only a modest retardation in the rate of growth of their own average living standards.

Another important indicator of the difference between the without-GMP and with-GMP scenarios is the projected change in the WMRatio (Weighted Mean Ratio) over the 2010-2060 period. The WMRatio, defined as the weighted mean over all nations of the ratio of the PCY of a specific nation to the PCY of the richest nation, is an "inverse" measure, meaning that the lower it is, the higher the level of inequality. The without-GMP simulation shows this coefficient, computed over the 146 nations in the dataset, starting at 0.1882 in 2010 and finishing at 0.2581 in 2060, while the with-GMP simulation shows it finishing at 0.6350 in 2060. This indicates a decline in inequality between 2010 and 2060 (–37.14 percent) without a GMP. but a much more substantial decline with a GMP (–237.41 percent).

Given the reigning pessimism with respect to the near-term economic prospects for the developing countries, the immediate reaction of many if not most contemporary economists to these results will be that they are "too good to be true," that they fall beyond the remotest bounds of plausibility, that they are simply not believable. But these results should not be categorically and peremptorily rejected. What is needed is calm and deliberate contemplation of the potential significance of these results. In the end, of course, it may be reasonable to ignore or reject them, but before that they deserve a "fair trial." Therefore, we proceed now to consider some of the objections that might be lodged against the fundamental implications of this research.

Over-Optimistic Parameter Values. The argument here is that the encouraging results shown by the benchmark with-GMP simulation are an invalid artifact stemming from over-optimistic parameter values. This argument might stipulate that the theoretical structure of the GMP model is reasonable, but maintains that the numerical parameter values used in the benchmark simulation are unrealistic. Perhaps the single most fundamentally unrealistic benchmark parameter value (continuing with the argument) is $\xi = 0$, which says that all observed differences in per capita income between nations are the result of differentials in generalized capital stocks K, and that none are the result of differentials in total factor productivity A. But an arguably plausible hypothesis is that owing to deeply entrenched political and cultural factors, total factor productivity varies widely across nations: it is low for poor nations and high for rich nations. Probably the second most fundamentally unrealistic benchmark parameter value is $\chi = 1$, which says that all foreign aid receipts of recipient nations will be successfully converted into generalized capital. But an arguably plausible hypothesis here is that owing to substantial administrative costs and substantial losses to graft and corruption, only a fraction of foreign aid receipts will in fact be successfully converted into generalized capital.[1] In addition to these obviously unrealistic parameter values, there may be other cases of inaccurate parameter values, for example in the production and/or consumption function, which combine to generate invalid results.

Of all the objections to this research, this is the only one capable of being explored within the context of the GMP model itself. This was done by means the "selected sensitivity analyses" reported in the concluding section of Chapter 4. Results are shown for variations in the numerical values of a variety of model parameters. Table 4.6 shows representative results for variations in α^*, ν, k_1, τ_0, a, b, ϕ, and γ. This table indicates that variation within reasonable numerical ranges for these parameters does not affect the qualitative conclusion that a very large amount of progress in the living standards of the poor nations may be achieved at the cost of a very minor retardation in the growth rates of living standards in the rich nations.

However, it must be conceded that the impact of the two parameters representing the two objections described above, ξ and χ, is just as predicted by skeptics. If either of these parameters departs sufficiently from its benchmark value, then the GMP model simulations demonstrate that the Global Marshall Plan would indeed be a complete failure. On the other hand, the model simulations run with less optimistic values of these parameters do bring to light two very important offsetting indications: (1) the departures from the benchmark value would have to be very large for the program to be fully ineffective; (2) even with these parameters at their extreme pessimistic values, showing little economic progress among the poor nations despite the GMP, the retarding effect on the rates of growth of per capita income in the rich nations would not be significantly increased. In other words, the worst-case scenario is that a GMP would simply not benefit the poor nations—not that a GMP would not benefit the poor nations *and* impose heavy costs on the rich nations.

A specialized variant of the "over-optimistic parameter values" argument focuses on ξ (the productivity differential source coefficient). According to this variant, there is much evidence that the key to economic performance is total factor productivity and not stocks of factors of production. This evidence suggests that to the extent that the GMP model can be taken seriously as a representation of economic reality, the actual value of the ξ parameter is close to or equal to 1, indicating that all or most of the current differences in per capita income among nations are attributable to differences in the total factor productivity coefficients rather than to differences in stocks of generalized capital. For example, Robert Solow's classic 1957 work on the sources of U.S. economic growth estimated that less than half of the total increase in national output could be attributed to increases in capital and labor.[2] Another example is the classic work of Abram Bergson (1978) comparing United States with Soviet Union economic performance, which indicated that the ratio of S.U. total factor productivity to U.S. total factor productivity was much less than the ratio of S.U. capital stock to U.S. capital stock.[3]

The crucial problem with this argument is that previous economic research demonstrating the greater dependence of economic performance on total factor productivity than on capital stock has used a narrow definition of capital stock based mostly on business physical capital. The value of social physical capital is rarely included, and the value of human capital (in terms of its cost of production, i.e., educational and training expenditures) is never included. In later work, Solow himself pointed out that "total factor productivity" in sources of growth research is in effect simply a terminological proxy for all factors affecting economic growth other than narrowly measured capital and labor.[4] In the case of sources of growth over time, one of these factors is technological progress. In the case of cross-national comparisons at a given point in time, technological progress is not relevant, but there are several other factors affecting economic performance, and many if not most of them are affected by past investments in costly commodities. The clearest example of this consists of expenditures on the commodities "education and training," these commodities in turn determining how much effective productive power is represented by a certain numerical population of laborers. In a word, what economists currently think of as "total factor productivity" is to a large extent dependent on prior investments in costly commodities other than what is currently thought of as "capital." These investments are included in the generalized capital concept. Since generalized capital has never been measured, there exists no evidence against differences in generalized capital stocks being the primary determinant of differences in per capita income.

Results Inconsistent with Past Experience. The argument here is that if it were true that extreme differentials in per capita income were the result of extreme differentials in generalized capital stocks, then the foreign aid programs of the past would have achieved a much higher level of success. After all, according to the underlying hypothesis being put forward in support of the proposed Global Marshall Plan, the generalized capital stocks of the poor nations are tiny and virtually microscopic relative to the generalized capital stocks of the rich nations. This explains the tremendously accelerated growth of the poor nations at the same time that the rich nations experience only a minor retardation of growth: the Marginal Products of the extremely small generalized capital stocks of the poor nations are huge in relation to the Marginal Products of the extremely large generalized capital stocks of the rich nations. But if this were actually the case, would we not have witnessed a much greater payoff to the foreign aid receipts of the poor nations during the last half century? True, the amounts of foreign aid provided to the poor nations were small in relation to those envisioned by the proposed Global Marshall Plan, but they were still fairly substantial in an absolute sense. For example, many LDCs at certain points in time have received amounts comparable to the amounts that were received by the Western European nations during the operation of the Marshall Plan from 1948 to 1951—but these LDCs did not emulate the explosive growth of the Western European recipient nations during that period.

The answer to this objection is that the foreign aid flows of the past, while they have been large in an absolute sense, were small in relation to the need, and for most of the LDCs did not constitute the necessary "critical mass" to initiate rapid economic progress. In nuclear physics, the critical mass is that quantity of uranium that when compacted will initiate a nuclear explosion. If you compact a quantity of uranium even slightly below the critical mass, nothing will happen. This basic concept has applications outside of nuclear physics. For example, in behavioral psychology, the "threshold of perception" refers to that minimum level of sensory stimulation required for the individual to become consciously aware of the stimulation. "Threshold of perception" could equally be termed the "critical mass" of sensory stimulation that will initiate conscious awareness of the stimulation.

I submit that the notion of a "critical mass" is fully relevant to the actual success or failure of economic development assistance efforts, and that the principal reason for the poor performance of the recipient nations in the past has been the fact that the resources provided fell short of the necessary critical mass. The argument that the resources provided actually exceeded what should have been a critical mass because they involved "billions and billions of dollars" is probably just faulty accounting, because the sums are not properly deflated. "Billions and billions of dollars" continues to be a lot of money to one individual or one household, but it may not be particularly impressive in terms of billions of people. When "billions and billions of dollars" is divided by "billions and billions of people," the result may not be too impressive.

For example, according to Table 2.2 above, in 2010 the members of the Development Assistance Committee of the OECD, and other providers of foreign aid, provided a total of $131,670,210,000 (almost 132 billion dollars) in Overseas Development Assistance (ODA). For the same year, the Gross National Incomes of all nations categorized by the World Bank as high-income nations was $45,678,296,324,881 (45 trillion, 678 billion, 296 million, 324 thousand, and 881 dollars). Thus the ODA dispensed by the high-income nations in 2010 amounted to 0.2883 percent of their combined income for that year (a little over one-fourth of 1 percent). At the same time, the combined population of the poor and middle-income nations (categorized as such by the World Bank) that are beneficiaries of ODA was 5,598,138,472 (approximately 5.6 billion). That works out to $23.52 per head.

This is probably not enough to get the job done. The global economic inequality problem is a massive, deeply entrenched problem. As such, it will probably require a massive, coordinated effort to overcome it. It will probably require a much larger effort than that of the Marshall Plan of 1948–1951. The Western European nations at that time were already economically advanced, industrialized nations—the purpose of the Marshall Plan was merely to assist them in recovering from the destruction of World War II, not to enable them to attain a qualitatively higher level of economic development.

Deficiencies of the GMP Model. The argument here is that the GMP model is too simplistic and unrealistic for the results derived from it to be taken seriously. For example, it ignores international trade and investment, it utilizes very simple mathematical forms for the production and consumption functions, and it takes no account of complicating factors within the national economies, such as different levels of domestic income inequality within different nations. There is at least one important indication that these various deficiencies generate results that are not to be trusted: the fact that the benchmark with-GMP simulation indicates dramatic improvements occurring within the first few years of initiation of the GMP. A model that is presumably invalid in one important respect is probably invalid in other respects as well.

To begin with, it must be frankly admitted that the extremely rapid improvement in the global economic inequality situation shown by the benchmark with-GMP simulation is not to be believed. Clearly, the model does not incorporate the lags that would surely apply in the real world. It would be a simple enough matter to add a lag structure in the application of the total transfer fund to generalized capital accumulation in the LDCs. Such a structure would evade the problem of an excessively rapid improvement in the first years of program operation. I did not do so for two reasons. First, specifying a precise structure of the lag would involve pure guesswork. Second and more importantly, I want to be professionally forthcoming in presenting this research, and not withhold important evidence from the reader, even if that evidence is not supportive of the GMP model's realism. At the stage of specifying the theoretical structure of the model, it did not occur to me that "excessively rapid improvement" could emerge as a problem in the numerical simulations. So be it, and this fact must indeed be considered a serious caveat in evaluating the significance of the research. My response to the problem is simply that the GMP model is designed to represent long-term development rather than short-term development. The long-term focus is manifested by the fact that the model does not allow for short-term fluctuations in economic variables but merely tracks their smoothed long-term evolution. The GMP model is clearly unrealistic in its failure to account for short-term fluctuations, but this particular unrealism is not a serious problem in view of the long-term focus of the model. I would argue that the same is true of the GMP model's failure to incorporate lags, which are a short-term rather than a long-term phenomenon.

As for the "simplicity" of the GMP model, this in itself is not a serious criticism of the research. Simplicity is relative. While the GMP model does not attain the scale and complexity of some of the largest general equilibrium models and macro-econometric models in use today, it is certainly not below the average scale and complexity of economic models routinely applied to economic policy issues. As all practitioners of economic policy analysis realize, there is a tradeoff between realism and practicality. Non-economists often sneer at economic models on grounds that they "assume away" many obviously important aspects of economic decision-making and interaction—while at the same time (somewhat inconsistently) they complain about the mathematical complexity of these same models. The fact remains, however, that only by "assuming away" many aspects of the problem is the analysis able to proceed, and to reach meaningful conclusions. True, the absence of complete realism means that the evidence derived from formal policy analysis is never conclusive, and is merely circumstantial evidence that has to be evaluated along with other evidence of a less formal nature, in arriving at a final judgment on a specific policy issue.

Another important point in this regard is that the "simplicity of the model," in and of itself, does not necessarily bias the results in one direction or the other. In our case specifically, the simplicity of the GMP model does not necessarily predispose it to showing that a real-world GMP would be highly successful. Or if it does in fact do this, it is not apparent how. To the contrary, there is one obvious counter-example that might be proposed to suggest that the simplicity of the GMP model might bias it *against* showing successful results from the proposed Global Marshall Plan. The GMP model does not incorporate trade among nations, and a strong consensus exists among contemporary economists that international trade is highly beneficial to all participants, and moreover, that increased participation in international trade is the chief remaining hope to those LDCs wishing to initiate rapid economic progress. Presumably, therefore, a model that incorporated the various "expansionary feedback effects" of international trade might indicate an even higher level of success of a massive, worldwide economic development assistance effort.

Two other examples of this sort may be cited. The benchmark GMP simulation does not assume any diminution in population growth rates among the nations, nor does it assume any reductions in the military expenditures of the nations, as percentages of their respective national incomes. Ever since the middle of the twentieth century, it has been widely recognized that rapid population growth operates as a serious drag on economic growth in terms of average living standards, and that the demographic transition to lower birth rates as the economic condition of a given population improves is humankind's best hope of avoiding an eventual Malthusian crunch. The fact that population growth rates in most nations are in fact declining at the present time is indeed a very optimistic indication. Throughout the Cold War, it was bemoaned that tremendous resources were being poured into military armaments and manpower that might otherwise have been invested in economic development projects. Since the Cold War ended in the early 1990s, military spending in most nations around the world has declined significantly, but it remains quite high in an absolute sense. Like rapid population growth, heavy military spending is widely acknowledged to constitute a drag on economic growth—especially in relatively poor developing countries.

Just as the benchmark GMP simulation does not depend on expansionary feedback effects from increased international trade, so too it does not depend on further reductions in population growth rates, nor on further reductions in the percentage of resources devoted to military purposes by the nations. If optimistic assumptions about further foreign trade expansion, further reductions in population growth rates, and further reductions in military spending had been incorporated into the benchmark simulation, the results would have been even stronger. Be that as it may, the level of success displayed by the benchmark with-GMP simulation of the GMP model is surely sufficient. As it is, these results are in grave danger of being dismissed out of hand because they are simply "too good to be true." It would not necessarily be advantageous to show results that are even more successful.

Ignores Distributional and Environmental Issues. Because of its utilization of per capita income as the sole measure of the economic condition of each nation, the GMP model utilized in this research does not take into account the distribution of income within nations. Two nations might have exactly the same per capita income, yet the first might have an extremely unequal distribution of income and the second a much less unequal distribution. It is widely agreed that all other things being equal, the less economic inequality within a nation, the better off are the people of that nation. By the same token, the GMP model takes no account of environmental conditions within nations. Once again, two nations might have exactly the same per capita income, yet the first might be laboring under a heavy burden of pollution and the second might have much cleaner air and water. It is also widely agreed that all other things being equal, the less pollution within a nation, the better off are the people of that nation.

These particular objections are not so much to the model itself, but to the desirability of economic growth in and of itself, especially very rapid economic growth. Obviously the central objective of a Global Marshall Plan would be to accelerate the economic growth of the recipient nations to very high levels. But clearly, very rapid economic growth might have a tendency to exacerbate economic inequality, and it might also tend to have severely adverse effects on the natural environment. While these problems are certainly very serious, it is questionable that they add up to a sensible case against rapid economic growth. They are more realistically regarded as unfortunate side effects that should be controlled insofar as possible, consistent with the overriding objective of reducing the global inequality problem within a reasonable period of time.

In fact, it might be regarded as rather hypocritical for people living in the richest nations to preach the virtues of slow growth (or no growth) to the impoverished populations of the developing nations, when the former are enjoying the highest living standards ever attained in the history of humanity. A modest level of economic inequality within a nation, and a high level of environmental cleanliness, are plausibly regarded as "superior" goods, meaning that they are more affordable to people who are already enjoying a high standard of living as measured by per capita income. While rapid economic growth will almost unavoidably entail serious disadvantages in the short run, it is to be hoped that in the long run these disadvantages will be brought under control, and the overall effects of growth will then be viewed in a more positive light.

In his seminal article "Economic Growth and Income Inequality," the economic historian Simon Kuznets hypothesized that income inequality tends to increase during the earlier stages of economic growth, but then tends to decrease during the later stages.[5] In graphical terms, the postulated relationship between per capita income and income inequality may be described as "an inverted-U" or a "dome-shaped curve." The graphical representation of the postulated relationship was soon dubbed the "Kuznets curve." Sometime later, during the 1990s, a substantial literature developed on the so-called "environmental Kuznets curve": a postulated dome-shaped relationship between per capita income and environmental degradation (pollution).

In general, a Kuznets curve (KC) represents a postulated relationship between per capita income, measured on the horizontal axis, and some dysfunctional socio-economic or technical condition, measured on the vertical axis. The original Kuznets curve pertained to distribution and is hence appropriately referred to as the distributional Kuznets curve (DKC). In the case of the original DKC, the dysfunctional variable is wealth and/or income inequality. In the case of the more recent environmental Kuznets curve (EKC), the dysfunctional variable is environmental pollution. Both dysfunctional variables (income inequality and environmental pollution) have in common that they are related in complicated ways to the overall economic prosperity of the nation. The fact that the relationships are complicated implies difficult questions as to other contributory factors, direction of causation, estimation methodology, and the degree to which a Kuznets curve is "exploitable" in the sense that real-world economic policy is sensibly guided by the relationship.

With respect to the DKC, even without any systematic and formal empirical evidence to confirm it, the hypothesis that income inequality first increases and then decreases as economic growth proceeds is quite plausible. One might consider, for example, the economic history of the United States. In the early days of the United States, from 1780 through approximately 1810, the economy was predominantly agrarian, with the primary productive activity (excluding the plantation economies of the Southern states) being carried on within a multitude of small farms. Even without hard data, it is a compelling intuition that in those days the distribution of income was quite egalitarian. But then the Industrial Revolution commenced, at a slower pace prior to the Civil War (1861-1865), and at an accelerating pace afterwards. By the end of the 1800s, the nature of the U.S. economy had changed drastically: production was largely concentrated in large-scale industrial corporations, and a class of super-wealthy capitalists had emerged: Vanderbilt, Carnegie, Rockefeller, J. P. Morgan—a class later described as the "robber barons."

There is an unmistakable intuition that the distribution of income at the end of the nineteenth century was far more unequal than it had been at the beginning of the century. But as the twentieth century progressed, the large fortunes were eroded as a result of the vicissitudes of war and depression, and also owing to increasing social policy aimed at equalizing the distribution of income and wealth: antitrust legislation introduced around the turn of the century, the progressive income tax inaugurated during World War I, the extensive social legislation promulgated during the Great Depression of the 1930s. By the time Kuznets wrote "Economic Growth and Income Inequality" in the 1950s, formal statistical evidence existed of a decline in income and wealth inequality within the

United States during the first half of the twentieth century. A similar situation had transpired within many if not most of the other economically advanced nations as of the mid-twentieth century. Thus even without formal statistical support, the hypothesis of an inverted-U relationship between average income and income inequality over time possesses considerable plausibility.

It should be mentioned, however, that more recently—over the last decades of the twentieth century—there has apparently occurred a marked increase in wealth and income inequality within most of the economically advanced nations. In fact, the phrase "the Great U-Turn" was coined in 1988 by the sociologists Bennett Harrison and Barry Bluestone to describe this recent development, and within the field of economics increasing interest is emerging in what is being termed the "uninverted-U curve" (Ram, 1997; Savvides and Stengos, 2000).[6] But this recent upturn in inequality is unrelated to the original Kuznets hypothesis, which pertains to the transition from a less developed, primarily agricultural economy to a more developed, primarily industrial economy. In any event, at this point it remains to be seen how long-lasting and numerically significant the recent "Great U-Turn" will be.

With respect to the EKC, just as a mental comparison of the United States at three points in time (1800, 1900, and 2000) provides strong, albeit informal, support for the distributional Kuznets curve, it does the same for the environmental Kuznets curve. In 1800, the U.S. economy was primarily agrarian, and aside from the transformation of woodland into farmland, the impact of human activity on the environment was minor. By 1900, however, the economy had evolved drastically from an agrarian to an industrial nature. We picture great clouds of noxious smoke belching forth from thousands of gigantic factories scattered thickly over much of the landscape. Raw materials for the factories were provided by the host of mines, drilling fields, and ore pits of the extractive industries. The impression is unavoidable that the environment was far more polluted as of 1900 than it had been in 1800.

But with the advent of Theodore Roosevelt in the U.S. presidency at the turn of the century, preservationist and environmental concerns began gaining ground. Polluting industries were subjected to an increasing amount of regulation aimed at reducing the flow of pollutants into the waterways and atmosphere. Perhaps even more important than government regulation was the gradual but persistent transformation of an inherently dirty extractive-industrial economy into a much cleaner service economy. Environmental cleanliness is generally deemed a superior good, and as per capita income increased, more of it was affordable. As a result, the U.S. environment was far less polluted in 2000 than it had been in 1900, despite a much larger population and a much higher per capita income.

It has been argued that this general pattern is common to many of the nations of the world. For example, Theodore Panayotou (1997) describes the process as follows: "At low levels of development both the quantity and intensity of environmental degradation is limited to the impacts of subsistence economic activity on the resource base and to limited quantities of biodegradable wastes. As economic development accelerates with the intensification of agriculture and other resource extraction, and the take-off into industrialization, the rates of resource depletion begin to exceed the rates of resource generation, and waste generation increases in quantity and toxicity. At higher levels of development, structural change towards information-intensive industries and services, coupled with increased environmental awareness, enforcement and environmental regulations, better technology and higher environment expenditures, result in the leveling off and gradual decline of environmental degradation."[7]

The empirical basis for the original distributional Kuznets curve (DKC), as set forth in Kuznets' seminal article, was quite sparse, consisting as it did of a few scraps of anecdotal evidence. The first systematic statistical investigation was reported in a 1976 paper by Montek S. Ahluwalia published in the *American Economic Review*. The dataset included 62 nations, including 14 developed nations and 6 socialist nations, over a range of years from the late 1960s through the mid-1970s. The author summarized the principal findings as follows (1976, p. 129): "There is a substantial confirmation of a statistically significant relationship between income shares of various percentile groups and the logarithm of per capita GNP. Furthermore, the relationship is clearly not monotonic since a significant relationship is identified only when the per capita GNP variable is entered in quadratic form. This formulation generates the familiar U-shaped pattern: the income share of the lower income groups (alternatively defined as the lowest 60 percent or the lowest 40 percent) first declines and then rises with increasing per capita GNP, while the share of the upper income group (top 20 percent) describes the opposite pattern." Shortly afterwards Ahluwalia published a more detailed exposition of his research in the *Journal of Development Economics* (1976).[8]

In evaluating the significance of this evidence, Ahluwalia candidly discussed the potential pitfalls of inferring a time-series relationship from cross-section data. The Kuznets hypothesis proposes that there exists an inverted-U relationship between per capita income and income inequality over time within a given nation. What Ahluwalia's results suggest is that there exists an inverted-U relationship between per capita income and income inequality over nations at a point in time. This would be sufficient to indicate a similar time-series relationship only under the assumption that all nations are following similar development patterns over time—quite a strong assumption. In skeptical commentaries on the distributional Kuznets curve, the dubiousness of using cross-section relationships to infer time-series relationships is always invoked.

A direct test of the Kuznets hypothesis would examine the relationship between per capita income and income inequality over time within a single nation. No such direct test is possible because there is no country in the world for which data on inequality extends sufficiently far back into the past. The most abundant data on inequality, of course, apply to the advanced industrial nations such as the United States and the nations of Western Europe. In some cases, reliable data on inequality in these nations extends back several decades—to around the turn of the twentieth century. But almost invariably, inequality measures for these types of nations show a secular decline throughout the first six decades of the twentieth century. In other words, all these nations apparently passed their Kuznets curve turning points (presuming the curve is a reality) prior to the collection of systematic data on inequality. But the fact remains that the publication of Ahluwalia's findings in a highly prestigious economic forum gave these results a great deal of exposure within the economics profession, and left a strong impression on many if not most economists that the Kuznets hypothesis regarding income distribution is a reasonable approximation to reality. More recent cross-section studies that are generally consistent with Ahluwalia include Eusufzai (1997), Fishlow (1996), and Ram (1988, 1995).[9]

Continuing on to the EKC, in point of fact one of the most interesting empirical regularities discovered by economists over the last few decades is a relationship that has come to be known as the environmental Kuznets curve. In contrast to the DKC, for which the statistical evidence has been somewhat thin, the statistical evidence supportive of the EKC—at least for certain measures of environmental pollution—has been quite strong and robust. The EKC for a particular pollution indicator is estimated by regressing that indicator on per capita income, per capita income squared, and (usually) various additional control variables that might plausibly affect the relationship between per capita income and pollution. If the estimated coefficient of per capita income is positive and statistically significant, and the estimated coefficient of per capita income squared is negative and statistically significant, this constitutes verification of the EKC in this particular data set. Such verification has been achieved over a wide range of pollution indicators, using many different control variables, using either levels or logarithms of the variables, at a very high level of statistical significance, over a range of estimation methodologies, and often with very high explanatory power of the multiple regression equation.[10]

The controversies among economists over the distributional Kuznets curve (DKC) and the environmental Kuznets curve (EKC) mainly have to do with the potential policy implications of the estimated relationships. Among those who are generally skeptical toward government intervention in economic processes, the principal policy implication of the DKC is that the government of a developing nation should not try to equalize the distribution of wealth and income because increasing inequality in these distributions is a natural concomitant of the early stages of economic growth, and that if economic growth proceeds long enough, the problem of economic inequality will tend to decline naturally, without need of interventionist policy. To this same school of thought, the principal policy implication of the EKC is that the government of a developing nation should not try to impose strict environmental restraints on business enterprise because an increasing level of environmental pollution is a natural concomitant of the early stages of economic growth, and if economic growth proceeds long enough, the problem of environmental pollution will tend to decline naturally, again without need of interventionist policy. In this view, economic equality and environmental cleanliness are "luxuries" that can be well afforded only by nations that have already achieved a high level of economic prosperity according to the "bottom line" indicator of per capita income.

To others, such analysis and prescription is invalid and unacceptable. They do not agree that dysfunctional conditions such as a high level of economic inequality or a high level of environmental pollution are either necessary or sufficient for the attainment of a satisfactory rate of economic growth. They point to the relative fragility of statistical findings of dome-shaped relationships between per capita income and dysfunctional conditions, and they also argue that an observed relationship in a cross-section sample of nations at a point in time might well be a poor guide to a time-series relationship within a given nation over a period of time. A certain amount of evidence has been adduced, also, that suggests that such dysfunctional conditions as economic inequality and environmental pollution can be impediments to economic growth rather than facilitators of economic growth. And finally, there is the question of exactly where the turning point lies. Turning point estimates from the DKC and EKC literatures are remarkably variable. It is not implausible, therefore, that most nations of the world, except for the minority of extremely poor nations, have indeed passed their turning points, and should be legitimately adopting policies that will reduce economic inequality and environmental pollution.

The overall implication of the Kuznets curve literature, whether on the distributional curve or the environmental curve, is that the problems and disadvantages of economic growth, in the sense of rising prosperity as measured by per capita income, are not permanent. This literature gives us reason to hope that the undesirable consequences of growth from the agrarian to the industrial stage will eventually be overcome. As nations become more prosperous, they will be able to afford more of such socially superior goods as greater economic equality and higher environmental quality. Thus concerns about these aspects of growth are not valid arguments against growth per se, and they should not be used as arguments against the implementation of a real-world Global Marshall Plan.

THE IMPLEMENTATION ISSUE

Another complaint about the research described in this book might be that it has nothing to say on the numerous applied policy questions in the area of foreign aid, questions that have intrigued and puzzled a generation of economists. But unless clear and cogent answers are provided to these questions, and these answers are duly incorporated into the actual operation of the Global Marshall Plan, the program would just be "throwing money at the problem" on a massive scale—the most probable consequence of which would be profligacy and waste on an equally massive scale.

There are a wide variety of difficult implementation questions, of which the following are merely representative:

- What would be the appropriate proportions, of the total amount of foreign aid provided to each recipient nation under the Global Marshall Plan, to be allocated to plant and equipment, education and training, and social infrastructure?
- How should specific projects be chosen? What principles of investment analysis should be applied to proposed business enterprises? How should proposed social infrastructure projects be evaluated? How should the monetary equivalents to non-specific social benefits be estimated?
- What proportion of assistance funds should be channeled through national governments, what proportion through local governments, what proportion through profit-making enterprises, what proportion

through non-profit organizations?

- What proportion of assistance should be provided in the form of grants, and what proportion in the form of interest-bearing loans? To what extent should debt relief be considered as foreign development assistance?
- To what extent should assistance be tied, that is, required to be spent by a specific recipient nation in a specific donor nation?
- Should foreign direct investment expenditures in recipient nations by corporations in a specific donor nation be considered as an offset to that nation's transfer fund expectations under the Global Marshall Plan?
- Should there be a special role for the OPEC nations, most of which are oil-rich but otherwise poor?
- What, if any, requirements should be placed on the recipient nations as a precondition for receiving aid? For example, should they be required to abolish certain tariffs or quotas, to privatize publicly owned enterprises or to operate publicly owned enterprises on a commercial basis, to curtail welfare entitlements, or to minimize regulation of privately owned businesses?
- Should aid receipts be influenced by population control policies or environmental safeguards implemented by the recipient nations?
- Should aid recipients be required to institute and enforce anti-corruption measures, and to be transparent in the use of funds?
- Should the aid disbursements to a specific nation be influenced by the extent to which authentically democratic political conditions exist within that nation?
- What sort of governance institutions should be set up? For example, should the United Nations be given primary authority, or should this authority be exercised by a quasi-independent agency? Should the ultimate authority be subject to some type of democratic accountability, both to the populations of the donor populations and the populations of the recipient populations?
- Should the severe existing restrictions on international migration be loosened immediately as part of the overall equalization effort, or should they be left in place until the rising prosperity of the developing nations eases pressures toward illegal migration?

It is quite true that this research has nothing directly to add to the discussion of these kinds of questions. But it is necessary to proceed one step at a time. The purpose of this research is to demonstrate the possibility that a sufficiently massive economic development assistance program might be dramatically successful, raising the living standards of poorer nations by a tremendous amount while at the same time only slightly reducing the growth rate of living standards in the richer nations. Once this possibility has been established and accepted, then would be the time to get into the details of program functioning. It is not necessary to resolve all the myriad implementation issues in advance of deciding whether or not to undertake the proposed Global Marshall Plan. Indeed, if resolution of all these issues were made a precondition for deciding the basic question of whether or not to initiate a GMP, then this latter decision would probably never be made. Specifics of foreign aid implementation have been debated for decades in the past, are being debated at the present time, and will no doubt continue to be debated into the indefinite future. Even if a real-world GMP were initiated and were soon in full swing, these issues would still be controversial.

The only fundamental implementation principle suggested by the GMP research presented here is that as much as humanly possible of the transfer fund contributions of the rich donor nations should find its way into augmenting the generalized capital stocks of the poor recipient nations. This suggests that the overwhelming emphasis of GMP expenditures ought to be on education and training in the human sphere, and in the capital sphere on what is generally known as "project assistance"—as opposed to other less effective aid forms such as technical assistance, food aid, debt relief, humanitarian aid, military aid, and so on. The core objective would be to get as much physical capital as possible into place (social capital and commercial capital), and to provide the labor force with the knowledge and skills necessary to make effective use of that physical capital. Obviously, there must be administrators in both the donor nations and the recipient nations, but equally obviously the purely administrative expenses of the program should be kept to a reasonable minimum.

As to the diversion and loss of resources through graft and corruption, I believe that it would be reasonable, in view of the overwhelming importance of the program to the future of humanity, to attempt to deter this by means of a draconic enforcement system. After all, a Global Marshall Plan may well represent humanity's last best chance to resolve the global economic inequality problem once and for all within a reasonable period of historical time. A GMP would be on a sufficient scale to hold out serious hope that success might be achieved. Individuals directly involved in the program could not readily rationalize graft and corruption on the basis that since the amounts involved are clearly insufficient to achieve measurable success anyway, they are not actually doing anyone any appreciable harm by taking bribes and extorting kickbacks. Aside from the inspirational aspects of the effort that might deter a certain amount of misbehavior, it would be reasonable to reinforce the positive psychic motivations by powerful negative sanctions, by means of establishing an extremely rigorous system of internal accountability and monitoring, and to implement extremely severe penalties for any sort of individual malfeasance that interferes with the success of the program.

Beyond these obvious points I would not be prepared to go at this point. The specifics of program operation are certainly important, and would have a significant effect on program performance. But they would not have a decisive and determinative effect. That is to say, whether or not the program would be successful depends critically on whether sufficiently large transfers take place, not on whether or not the transfers are utilized with maximum efficiency. It seems safe to say, in the light of more than 50 years of past experience with foreign aid, that egregious errors would be avoided. There is already an extensive prescriptive literature contributed by knowledgeable authorities, not all of them enthusiastic supporters of the principle of foreign aid.[11] Much has been learned, and continues to be learned, from this literature. Assuming that sufficient resources are committed to the program by the rich nations to reach the desired goal, the degree of operational efficiency attained by the program might affect the time taken to achieve the goal by a factor of plus or minus 20 percent. But the degree of operational efficiency, in and of itself, is not likely to determine the qualitative outcome, i.e., to determine whether or not success is achieved within a reasonable period of historical time.

WHY A GMP?

Well back in the nineteenth century, living standards in the industrializing nations of Western Europe and North America began climbing appreciably above living standards in the rest of the world. This trend continued on and on, throughout the twentieth century and into the twenty-first. As a result, an extremely large gap now exists between living standards in a handful of very rich nations and living standards throughout the rest of the world. This gap is not only a danger to world peace and tranquility, it is also an affront to equity and an offense to common decency. It is simply not fair that accidents of birthplace should have so much to do with the level of material welfare achieved by any given human being. People in the developing nations work just as long and hard as do people in the developed nations. In fairness, then, they should be enjoying similar living standards. No one with a proper appreciation of universal standards of morality and ethics should be indifferent to the present level of global economic inequality. It should be a source of discomfort and anxiety to all of us.

The general consensus today, especially in the rich nations, is that this situation, while lamentable and regrettable and all that, is nevertheless immutable and immovable. Or at least it will remain immutable and immovable throughout the lifetimes of all those persons now alive, and probably throughout the lifetimes of their children, and possibly throughout the lifetimes of their grandchildren, and their great-grandchildren, and so on and so forth unto the n'th generation. But by all that is positive and progressive in humanity—this consensus should be overturned. We should gather together our resources and our resolution, and commence a determined assault upon global economic inequality. We owe it to ourselves and to our descendants to eradicate this problem from the face of the earth once and for all.

Although the most direct and obvious benefit of a Global Marshall Plan would be to the huge populations of the poorer nations lifted once and for all out of poverty, the populations of the richer nations would garner significant benefits as well. To begin with, there is basic human compassion. It has always been a fundamental strength of the human species, throughout the evolutionary struggle, that we take care of our own, that if we are able to, we provide help and assistance to those in need, that we do not readily turn our backs on our fellow human beings. It is hard to imagine the pride and relief that would be felt throughout the world if by human action we were able to finally overcome the problem of world poverty.

Aside from that, economic prosperity among those nations today termed "LDCs" would impact favorably on the future economic prosperity of today's "advanced nations." International trade and investment would be strengthened, there would be further exploitation of economies of scale in the production of many commodities, the interrelated problems of excessive population growth and environmental degradation would be made subject to better control. Finally, there is the key political dimension. Worldwide prosperity would provide a more secure foundation for civil harmony and democratic institutions within nations, would reduce the economic motivations toward conflict that have historically been a major factor in the generation of international warfare, and would reduce the level of military expenditure that nations feel is necessary to maintain their security. In short, a Global Marshall Plan would be a solid investment in the future for all humanity—not just for the populations of the Less Developed Countries.

A start has already been made. Foreign development assistance programs have been an integral part of international relations for well over half a century. These programs have shifted a certain quantity of investment resources from the rich nations to the poor nations, and have quite likely been instrumental to the observed economic progress of the poor nations. But the rate of observed economic progress in most of the poor nations has been unsatisfactory, as manifested by the widening economic gap between the richest and poorest nations. Foreign aid programs should be dramatically increased and expanded. Policy changes (e.g., trade liberalization, privatization of public enterprises) might be desirable because they improve the efficiency with which any given amount of foreign aid is invested—but they are unlikely to be decisive in and of themselves. Without a major increase in the *quantity* of foreign aid, improvements in quality will probably have only a minor effect. Roughly what is needed is an expansion of the foreign aid contributions of the richest nations from well under 1 percent of GNI to somewhere between 2 and 4 percent of GNI. This increase could be easily afforded by most of the rich nations.

In all likelihood, the success probability of a real-world GMP is being seriously underestimated at the present time. Computer simulations of a model of the proposed Global Marshall Plan show the possibility of a tremendous rise in the living standards of the poor nations, while at the same time the living standards of the rich nations continue to rise at rates comparable to the rates observed throughout the last few decades. A diminution in the projected growth rates of living standards in the rich nations does in fact occur, but it is a very minor diminution—arguably a virtually unnoticeable diminution. The program is therefore based on the concept of "common progress": that the living standards in all nations of the world will continue to advance (progress would be common to all nations), but the living standards in the rich nations will rise at a very slightly diminished rate in order that the living standards in the poor nations rise at a tremendously accelerated rate. The results of these simulations pose a direct challenge to the commonly expressed opinion that "there exists no meaningful evidence" that any foreign aid program within reasonable limits could overcome the world inequality problem within a reasonable period of time.

But what guarantees, it might be asked, are there that results obtained from computer simulations of a theoretical model of a Global Marshall Plan will have any bearing whatever on real-world outcomes? Are these results not merely wishful thinking? Would not the more likely outcome of a real-world GMP on the scale proposed be the generation of waste, graft, and corruption on an unimaginable scale, of the enrichment of a handful of bureaucrats and businessmen while the economic status of the great masses of poor people in the LDCs is only marginally improved, if at all?

It must be conceded, of course, that there are no firm guarantees that a real-world GMP would not be a colossal failure. Even in terms of the GMP model developed in this research, not all of the computer simulations show good results. Good results—in fact, spectacularly good results—are obtained for the benchmark numerical values of the model parameters. A case may be made that the benchmark parameter values are inherently plausible, but the case is hardly conclusive. Furthermore, the model is developed in such a way as to encompass the viewpoints of those who maintain that foreign aid is of little or no value in promoting the economic growth of recipient nations.

One familiar allegation is that differences in economic productivity between nations are based mostly on different political circumstances or cultural conditions, and that differences in capital stocks, however "capital" is defined, have little or nothing to do with economic productivity differences. This allegation is encompassed by the GMP model parameter ξ. Another familiar allegation is that foreign aid resources are mostly consumed by administrative costs and graft, and that very few of these resources are actually put to the intended purposes. This allegation is encompassed by the GMP model parameter χ. It is shown, by means of running GMP computer simulations with these parameters set to sufficiently adverse values, that the program might well have little or no reducing effect on world economic inequality.

The fact of the matter is, however, that *no* social policy decision (even if that social policy decision be that there be *no* active social policy to ameliorate a particular problem) can ever be based on fully conclusive evidence. Despite our best efforts at modeling and forecasting, the future remains obscure, and the consequences that any particular policy will bring about in the future remain equally obscure. Decision-making under uncertainty—that is, making decisions now that will impact on future outcomes in unpredictable ways—is an inevitable feature of all human existence, whether it be at the individual level, the organizational level, or the social level. Although there is no guarantee that a real-world GMP would be a success, there is equally no compelling or conclusive evidence that it would be a failure. It would be unreasonable to reject a Global Marshall Plan out of hand, on the basis of the mere *possibility* that it would be a failure.

The benchmark with-GMP policy simulation described earlier clearly establishes the alternative possibility that a real-world Global Marshall Plan might well be dramatically successful. The benchmark simulation also indicates that the cost to the rich nations of financing the program would not be excessive either in terms of forgone growth or of foreign aid contributions as a percentage of national income. And it is worth noting that these results are obtained from a benchmark simulation which in some ways is biased against progress. This simulation does not allow for positive effects from increased international trade, nor for positive effects from further exploitation of economies of large-scale production. It does not presume that population increase will slow down, nor that military spending will diminish.

There is a traditional proverb that is most apt: "The proof of the pudding is in the eating." You cannot resolve the question of whether a certain pudding tastes good by lengthy theoretical disputations about the human sense of taste and the relative proportions of ingredients in the pudding. Rather you have to eat the pudding—or at least taste it. In the same way, you cannot resolve the question of the potential performance of a Global Marshall Plan by lengthy theoretical disputations based on the inconclusive evidence of our past experiences with economic development assistance. Rather you must initiate such a program and observe the results. There is simply no substitute for experiment.

Another fundamental point deserves reiteration here: Owing to the unavoidable fact that there is a non-negligible probability that an actual Global Marshall Plan would be extremely *in*effective in attaining its goals, the proposal of this book is that such a program be initiated *on a provisional and experimental basis*. This does not mean that it would be initiated on a small basis. For a worthwhile test, it must be initiated on a large basis—a *very* large basis. What it means, rather, is that the program should be initiated with a clear understanding on the part of all participants, including both rich donor nations and poor recipient nations, that continuation of the program beyond an experimental period of 10 to 15 years will depend on the achievement of tangible, dramatic progress in terms of rising living standards within all parts of the populations of the poorer nations. If tangible, dramatic progress is *not* being made after a reasonable interval has elapsed, then the program would be very quickly either scaled down or phased out altogether. The proposal is most definitely *not* that a Global Marshall Plan be pursued indefinitely, for decade after decade, even if results continue to be disappointing. The proposal, rather, is that highly successful results in the early going (the first 10 to 15 years of GMP operation) be a precondition for continuation of the GMP.

If there is one thing that humanity should have learned by now from the sciences, it is that much if not most worthwhile knowledge is obtained not through a priori reasoning and abstract debate, but rather through empirical investigation and experimentation. In translating the fruits of scientific inquiry into useful artifacts, successful engineering designs are developed using trial and error, not hypothetical disputations. What holds true in the physical sciences and engineering also holds true in the social sciences: little useful knowledge will be gained in the absence of empirical experimentation. The experimental method is universally accepted within all science—although its applications are far more abundant in the physical and biological sciences than they are in the social sciences. It would greatly benefit the future prospects of humanity were this method to be more widely understood and accepted within the realm of social policy.

I recognize full well the limitations of the previously discussed GMP model research with respect to the actual real-world potentialities that may (or may not) be resident in a Global Marshall Plan. Such a program might indeed be a dismal failure, despite the indications from the benchmark GMP model simulation that it could be a dazzling success. What needs equally strong emphasis, on the other hand, is the extreme dubiousness of blindly rejecting these results on grounds that it is "well known" or "obvious to any reasonable person" that anything on the scale of the proposed Global Marshall Plan must inevitably be a dismal failure. The fact that this latter viewpoint is currently very widespread does not necessarily make it a correct viewpoint.

Some cynics and pessimists maintain that objective information is powerless against certain deeply rooted prejudices and preconceptions. Specifically in this case, they would allege that it would not matter how strong an objective case could be made for initiating a GMP, no such program will ever be initiated in the real world owing to the ingrained prejudice among the populations of the would-be donor nations against "unworthy foreigners" in the would-be recipient nations, and to the entrenched preconception in these same populations that such a program would be doomed to abject failure.

I oppose this viewpoint most strenuously. It seems inconsistent with the great achievements of humanity in the past and the gradual but steady progress of human civilization throughout all recorded history. There is no denying the fact that humanity has inflicted upon itself an abundance of evils and disasters, and that many of these may be attributed to the intellectual and emotional shortcomings of individual human beings. But setbacks, dramatic though they may be, should not blind us to the overall trend of progress. The typical human being possesses high qualities, and the positive side of our nature often wins out. Otherwise global human society would not have come as far as it has.

But it might be asked, Is the world ready for a Global Marshall Plan?

After all, at the present time the large majority of people in the rich nations are highly resistant to proposals for increasing foreign aid. On the other hand, there are a few widely respected authorities who do advocate substantially expanded foreign aid. Probably foremost among them is Jeffrey D. Sachs, labeled a "celebrity economist" by *Time* in the cover story ("How to End Poverty") of its March 14, 2005, issue. The cover story consisted mainly of excerpts from Sachs' bestselling 2005 book *The End of Poverty: Economic Possibilities for Our Time*. Recently published books in a similar vein to Sachs' *The End of Poverty* include *The Bottom Billion* by Paul Collier, *One Economics, Many Recipes* by Dani Rodrik, *The Peace-Keeping Economy* by Lloyd J. Dumas, and *The Quest for Prosperity* by Justin Yifu Lin.[12]

These books have in common with the present book that they are generally in favor of increasing the foreign development assistance expenditures of the wealthy nations. However, there are two principal differences between those books and this book. First, this book offers hard numerical evidence, derived from computer simulations of a comprehensive economic model, that a Global Marshall Plan could make major inroads against the global economic inequality problem within a 50-year planning period—without this program significantly slowing down the economic growth of the rich nations. Second, this book offers a far more ambitious proposal, envisioning contributions by the wealthy nations into the GMP ranging between 2 and 4 percent of their Gross National Incomes. In contrast, Sachs' program for "ending world poverty" envisions raising foreign aid contributions of the wealthy nations to the long-standing United Nations goal of 0.7 percent (seven-tenths of 1 percent), and the aid would target mainly the poorest elements within the recipient nations. In the nearly 10 years since *The End of Poverty* was published, there has been no discernible progress toward this goal. The reason for this is that the large majority of people in the rich nations believe that it wouldn't do any good to raise foreign aid to 0.7 percent of GNI, or to 1 percent, or to any other percent. All this would do is raise the tax burden on the people of the rich nations without doing any appreciable good for the people of the poor nations. This book offers hard evidence that challenges this tragic misconception.

In my view, therefore, the present lack of support among humanity for an expansion of the economic development assistance effort to the level envisioned by the proposed Global Marshall Plan, especially among the people of the rich nations, is not the result of ineradicable prejudices and preconceptions. Rather it is the result of a miscalculation of the relative benefits and costs of such a program. The benefits are underestimated, and more importantly, the costs are overestimated. But these miscalculations are by no means inevitable. They are definitely capable of rectification.

Predictably, skeptics will complain that if a Global Marshall Plan were actually undertaken in the real world, it would constitute nothing more than a "giant pork barrel" for the personal enrichment of corrupt bureaucrats and venal businessmen. Sad to say, they might be right. But should the possibility of failure—a possibility which is of course inevitable where any important undertaking is concerned—be allowed to forestall even an attempt at success? According to the poet, "It is better to have loved and lost, than never to have loved at all." The same principle holds with respect to a GMP. If we are doomed to disappointment, then so be it—we will be made aware of the futility of the effort in short order. But surely we ought not be deterred by cynical skeptics and petty-minded pessimists who disparage even the mere aspiration toward a better world.

Notes

CHAPTER 1

1. A few illustrative references in the general literature on world economic inequality, economic development, and related policy issues, in chronological order, are as follows: Peter T. Bauer and Basil S. Yamey, *The Economics of Under-Developed Countries* (Chicago: University of Chicago Press, 1957); Gunnar Myrdal, *The Challenge of World Poverty: A World Anti-Poverty Program in Outline* (New York: Pantheon, 1970); Gustav Ranis, editor, *The Gap between Rich and Poor Nations* (New York: St. Martin's Press, 1972); Paul Alpert, *Partnership or Confrontation? Poor Lands and Rich* (New York: Free Press, 1973); Keith B. Griffin, *International Inequality and World Poverty* (New York: Holmes and Meier, 1978); Jacques Loup, *Can the Third World Survive?* (Baltimore, Md.: Johns Hopkins University Press, 1983); William Ryrie, *First World, Third World* (New York: St. Martin's Press, 1995); John Dixon and David MacArov, editors, *Poverty: A Persistent Global Reality* (New York: Routledge, 1998); Klaus Nurnberger, *Prosperity, Poverty and Pollution: The Emergence of a Global Economic Responsibility* (New York: St. Martin's Press, 1999); Jeffrey D. Sachs, *The End of Poverty: Economic Possibilities for Our Time* (New York: Penguin, 2005); David Held and Ayse Kaya, eds., *Global Inequality: Patterns and Explanations* (New York: Polity Press, 2006); K. S. Jomo and Jacques Baudot, eds., *Flat World, Big Gaps: Economic Liberalization, Globalization, Poverty and Inequality* (New York: Palgrave Macmillan, 2007); Paul Collier, *The Bottom Billion: Why the Poorest Countries are Failing and What Can Be Done About It* (New York: Oxford University Press, 2007); Dani Rodrik, *One Economics, Many Recipes: Globalization, Institutions and Economic Growth* (Princeton, NJ: Princeton University Press, 2008); Jeffrey D. Sachs, *Common Wealth: Economics for a Crowded Planet* (New York: Penguin, 2009); David Hulme, *Global Poverty: How Global Governance Is Failing the Poor* (New York: Routledge, 2010); Lloyd J. Dumas, *The Peace-Keeping Economy: Using Economic Relationships to Build a More Peaceful, Prosperous, and Secure World* (New Haven: Yale Univ. Press, 2011); Justin Yifu Lin, *The Quest for Prosperity: How Developing Economies Can Take Off* (Princeton, NJ: Princeton Univ. Press, 2012); Justin Yifu Lin, *Against the Consensus: Reflections on the Great Recession* (Cambridge, UK: Cambridge Univ. Press, 2013).

2. See, for example, William Easterly, *The White Man's Burden: Why the West's Efforts to Aid the Rest Have Done So Much Ill and So Little Good* (New York: Penguin Press, 2006); Robert Calderisi, *The Trouble with Africa; Why Foreign Aid Isn't Working* (New York: Palgrave Macmillan, 2006); Dambisa Moyo, *Dead Aid: Why Aid Is Not Working and How There Is Another Way for Africa* (Farrar, Straus and Giroux, 2009). As may be noted from these examples, the best ammunition for the "aid doesn't work" school is provided by sub-Saharan Africa. For a balanced commentary on *The White Man's Burden*, see Nicholas D. Kristof, "Aid: Can It Work?" (*New York Review of Books* 53(15), October 5, 2006).

3. Although the prevalence of poverty is closely associated with the degree of inequality, they are conceptually distinct. Poverty is normally thought of in terms of absolute deprivation: for example, as having an income less than that required to support a "decent standard of living." But if the entire distribution of income, graphically represented, were to shift to the right (i.e., the income of every household in the economy were to rise by the same proportion), this would reduce the prevalence of poverty but it would not necessarily reduce the degree of inequality. There are several widely utilized measures of inequality in economics: the coefficient of variation, the proportion of income received or wealth owned by the wealthiest 10 percent, 5 percent, or 1 percent of the population, the Gini coefficient, the decile ratio, the 20-20 ratio, the Palma ratio, the Hoover index, the Atkinson index, the Theil entropy measure. Each of them has various subtle advantages and disadvantages relative to the others. For technical work on the measurement of inequality, see the following: Amartya Sen, *On Economic Inequality* (Oxford: Oxford University Press, 1973); Anthony B. Atkinson, *The Economics of Inequality*, second edition (Oxford: Clarendon Press, 1983); Frank A. Cowell, *Measuring Inequality*, second edition (New York: Prentice-Hall, 1995); David G. Champernowne and Frank A. Cowell, *Economic Inequality and Income Distribution* (Cambridge: Cambridge University Press, 1998); Jacques Silber, *Handbook of Income Inequality Measurement* (Boston: Kluwer Academic Publishers, 1999); Frank A. Cowell, "Measurement of Inequality," in Anthony B. Atkinson and Francois Bourguignon, editors, *Handbook of Income Distribution* (New York: Elsevier, 2000).

4. Almost without exception, authorities on the world economy agree that widespread poverty in the LDCs constitutes a "threat to peace." The following early statement from Paul Alpert (*Partnership or Confrontation? Poor Lands and Rich*, New York: Free Press, 1973, p. ix) is typical: "A conflict of far greater scope is emerging as the major threat to peace, continued progress, and the very survival of our civilization. This is the conflict between the rich minority and the vast, rapidly growing majority of the underdeveloped poor in Asia, Africa, and Latin America, the proletariat of humanity." For the most part, however, analysis of the threat is brief and superficial, as for example in Goran Ohlin ("Interna-

tional Politics of Underdevelopment," in Gustav Ranis, editor, *The Gap between Rich and Poor Nations,* New York: St. Martin's Press, 1972, p. 63): "The argument that the gap is a threat to international security is sometimes taken to suggest that the rich countries, as small islands of prosperity, will find themselves attacked by the populous underprivileged nations around them. This appeal to the fears of the prosperous does not have much warrant in history. Technology may of course change that and many other things. A more down-to-earth argument is that many developing countries represent international danger spots where political instability threatens to involve the great powers in escalating conflicts." For a comparatively rare full-scale analysis of these kinds of possibilities, see Mario'n Mushkat, *The Third World and Peace: Some Aspects of the Interrelationship of Underdevelopment and International Security* (New York: St. Martin's Press, 1982). The rich political science literature on the relationship between economic inequality and political instability/conflict (often referred to as the "EI-PI" or "EI-PC" nexus) was surveyed and analyzed by Mark I. Lichbach in "An Evaluation of 'Does Economic Inequality Breed Political Conflict?' Studies" (*World Politics* 41(4): 431-470, July 1989). The overwhelming majority of the literature looks at the EI-PC relationship within nations, but presumably an analogous situation holds at the international level. Lichbach describes the conventional viewpoint as follows (p. 431): "Does economic inequality breed political conflict? In other words, are nations with a more unequal distribution of income and wealth more subject to phenomena like revolution, rebellion, terrorism, demonstrations, and coups than those with a more equal distribution. Most students of conflict would answer yes. All major theorists of conflict believe that economic inequality is, at least, a potentially important cause of dissent." This is also the basic conclusion from a later survey: Eric Thorbecke and Chutatong Charumilind, "Economic Inequality and Its Socioeconomic Impact" (*World Development* 30(9): 1477-1495, September 2002).

CHAPTER 2

1. For example, in early 2014, inputting the query "Foreign Aid in Title" to the EconLit database resulted in 9,982 results.

2. The following are some illustrative references, in chronological order, to the extensive theoretical and empirical literature on the nature, purposes, and potential effects of foreign aid: Seung Hee Kim, *Foreign Capital for Economic Development: A Korean Case Study* (New York: Praeger, 1970); Teresa Hayter, *Aid as Imperialism* (New York: Penguin, 1971); John R. Parkinson, editor, *Poverty and Aid* (Oxford: Basil Blackwell, 1983); Raymond F. Mikesell, *The Economics of Foreign Aid and Self-Sustaining Development* (Boulder, CO: Westview, 1983); Roger C. Riddell, *Foreign Aid Reconsidered* (Baltimore: Johns Hopkins University Press, 1987); Paul Mosley, *Foreign Aid: Its Defense and Reform* (Lexington, KY: University Press of Kentucky, 1987); Stephen

Browne, *Foreign Aid in Practice* (New York: New York University Press, 1990); Paul Mosley, Jane Harrigan, and John Toye, *Aid and Power: The World Bank and Policy-Based Lending, Vol. 1: Analysis and Policy Proposals, Vol. 2: Case Studies* (New York: Routledge, 1991); Robert H. Cassen, *Does Aid Work? Report to An Intergovernmental Task Force,* second edition (New York: Oxford University Press, 1994); Murray C. Kemp, *The Gains from Trade and the Gains from Aid* (New York: Routledge, 1995): Claus C. Rebien, *Evaluating Development Assistance in Theory and Practice* (Brookfield, VT: Ashgate, 1996); David Dollar and Lant Pritchett, *Assessing Aid: What Works, What Doesn't, and Why* (New York: Oxford University Press for the World Bank, 1998); Kanhaya L. Gupta, ed., *Foreign Aid: New Perspectives* (Kluwer Academic Publishers, 1999); William Easterly, *The White Man's Burden: Why the West's Efforts to Aid the Rest Have Done So Much Ill and So Little Good* (New York: Oxford University Press, 2006); Roger C. Riddell, *Does Foreign Aid Really Work?* (New York: UK: Oxford University Press, 2007); Dambisa Moyo, *Dead Aid: Why Aid Is Not Working and How There Is a Better Way for Africa* (New York: Penguin, 2009).

3. On the history, politics, and economics of the Marshall Plan, see Harry Bayard Price, *The Marshall Plan and Its Meaning* (Ithaca, NY: Cornell University Press, 1955); Herbert Carleton Mayer, *German Recovery and the Marshall Plan, 1948-1952* (Bonn and New York: Edition Atlantic Forum, 1969); Hadley Arkes, *Bureaucracy, the Marshall Plan, and the National Interest* (Princeton, NJ: Princeton University Press, 1972); John Gimbel, *The Origins of the Marshall Plan* (Stanford, CA: Stanford University Press, 1976); Immanuel Wexler, *The Marshall Plan Revisited: The European Recovery Program in Economic Perspective* (Westport, CT: Greenwood, 1983); Charles L. Mee, *The Marshall Plan: The Launching of the Pax Americana* (New York: Simon & Schuster, 1984); Michael J. Hogan, *The Marshall Plan: America, Britain, and the Reconstruction of Western Europe, 1947-1952* (New York: Cambridge University Press, 1987); Robert J. Donovan, *The Second Victory: The Marshall Plan and the Postwar Revival of Europe* (New York: Madison Books, 1987); Henry Pelling, *Britain and the Marshall Plan* (New York: St. Martin's Press, 1988); Charles S. Maier, editor, *The Marshall Plan and Germany: West German Development within the Framework of the European Recovery Program* (Oxford: Berg Publishers, 1991); Gregory A. Fossedal, *Our Finest Hour: Will Clayton, the Marshall Plan, and the Triumph of Democracy* (Stanford, CA: Hoover Institution Press, 1993); Greg Behrman, *The Most Noble Adventure: The Marshall Plan and How America Helped Rebuild Europe* (New York: Simon & Schuster, 2008).

4. Walt Whitman Rostow, *The Stages of Economic Growth: A Non-Communist Manifesto* (Cambridge: Cambridge University Press, 1960). Second edition: 1971; third edition: 1990. Antecedents by Rostow to this profoundly influential

book include the following: *The Process of Economic Growth* (New York: Norton, 1952); with Max F. Millikan, *A Proposal: Key to an Effective Foreign Policy* (New York: Harper and Brothers, 1957); "The Take-Off into Self-Sustaining Growth" (*Economic Journal* 66: 25-48, March 1958); "The Stages of Economic Growth" (*Economic History Review* II(12): 1-16, August 1959). The impact of the work was such that it was soon the subject of a large-scale IEA conference: Walt Whitman Rostow, editor, *The Economics of Take-Off into Sustained Growth: Proceedings of a Conference Held by the International Economic Association* (New York: St. Martin's Press, 1963). During the Vietnam era, Rostow was a leading advisor to U.S. Secretary of Defense Robert McNamara. Other major economic works by W. W. Rostow include: *How It All Began: Origins of the Modern Economy* (New York: McGraw-Hill, 1975); *Why the Poor Get Richer and the Rich Slow Down: Essays in the Marshallian Long Period* (Austin: University of Texas Press, 1980); *Eisenhower, Kennedy, and Foreign Aid* (Austin: University of Texas Press, 1985); *Rich Countries and Poor Countries: Reflections on the Past, Lessons for the Future* (Boulder, CO.: Westview Press, 1987).

5. Befitting the importance of the United States as the primary source of foreign aid throughout most of the second half of the twentieth century, there is an abundant literature focused specifically on U.S. foreign aid, from which the following are representative examples: William A. Brown and Redvers Opie, *American Foreign Assistance* (Washington: Brookings Institution, 1953); Charles Wolf, Jr., *Foreign Aid: Theory and Practice in Southeast Asia* (Princeton, NJ: Princeton University Press, 1960); John D. Montgomery, *The Politics of Foreign Aid: American Experience in Southeast Asia* (New York: Praeger, 1962); Robert A. Goldwin, editor, *Why Foreign Aid?* (Chicago: Rand McNally, 1963); Jacob Rubin, *Your Hundred Billion Dollars: The Complete Story of American Foreign Aid* (Philadelphia: Chilton, 1964); David A. Baldwin, *Foreign Aid and American Foreign Policy: A Documentary Analysis* (New York: Praeger, 1966); Harry G. Johnson, *Economic Policies toward Less Developed Countries* (Washington: Brookings Institution, 1968); Goran Ohlin, "The Evolution of United States Aid Doctrine," in Benjamin J. Cohen, editor, *American Foreign Economic Policy* (New York: Harper and Row, 1968); John A. White, *The Politics of Foreign Aid* (New York: St. Martin's Press, 1974); Elliott R. Morss and Victoria A. Morss, *U.S. Foreign Aid: An Assessment of New and Traditional Development Strategies* (Boulder, CO: Westview, 1982); Alfred Maizels and Machiko Missanke, "Motivations for Aid to Developing Countries" (*World Development* 12(9): 879-900, 1984); John Wilhelm and Gerry Feinstein, *U.S. Foreign Assistance: Investment or Folly?* (New York: Praeger, 1984); R. D. McKinlay and A. Mughan, *Aid and Arms to the Third World: An Analysis of the Distribution and Impact of U.S. Official Transfers* (New York: St. Martin's Press, 1984); Walt Whitman Rostow, *Eisenhower, Kennedy, and Foreign Aid* (Austin: University of Texas Press, 1985); Robert E. Wood, *From Marshall*

Plan to Debt Crisis: Foreign Aid and Development Choices in the World Economy (Berkeley: University of California Press, 1986); Robert J. Berg and David F. Gordon, editors, *Cooperation for International Development: The United States and the Third World in the 1990s* (Boulder, CO: Lynne Rienner, 1989); David Porter, "United States Bilateral Foreign Aid and Multilateral Aid: A Comparison," in Mekki Mtewa, editor, *International Science and Technology: Philosophy, Theory and Policy* (New York: St. Martin's Press, 1990); John W. Sewell, "Foreign Aid for a New World Order," in Brad Roberts, editor, *U.S. Foreign Policy after the Cold War* (Cambridge, Mass.: MIT Press, 1992); Henry J. Bruton, "Foreign Aid to the Less Developed Countries," in Joseph A. Pechman, editor, *Fulfilling America's Promise: Social Policies for the 1990s* (Ithaca, NY: Cornell University Press, 1992); David H. Lumsdaine, *Moral Vision in International Politics: The Foreign Aid Regime, 1949-1989* (Princeton, NJ: Princeton University Press, 1993); Manlio L. De Angelis, *U. S. Foreign Aid Programs* (Boulder, CO: Westview, 1996); Vernon W. Ruttan, *United States Development Assistance Policy: The Domestic Politics of Foreign Economic Aid* (Baltimore: Johns Hopkins University Press, 1996): Carol Lancaster, *Transforming Foreign Aid: United States Assistance in the 21st Century* (Washington: Institute for International Economics, 2000); George M. Guess, *The Politics of United States Foreign Aid* (New York: Routledge, 2007); Curt Tarnoff and Marian Lawson, *Foreign Aid: An Introduction to U.S. Programs and Policy* (Washington: Congressional Research Service, 2009).

6. Some illustrative references to the large statistical literature on the effectiveness (or lack thereof) of foreign aid are as follows: Keith B. Griffin, "Foreign Capital, Domestic Savings and Economic Development" (*Oxford Bulletin of Economics and Statistics* 32(2): 99-112, February 1970); Gustav S. Papanek, "Aid, Foreign Private Investment, Saving and Growth in Less Developed Countries" (*Journal of Political Economy* 81(1): 120-130, January-February 1973); Volker Bornschier, Christopher Chase-Dunn, and Richard Robinson, "Cross-National Evidence of the Effects of Foreign Investment and Aid on Economic Growth and Inequality: A Survey of Findings and Re-Analysis" (*American Journal of Sociology* 84(3): 658-683, November 1978); Paul Mosley, John Hudson, and Sara Horrell, "Aid, the Public Sector and the Market in Less Developed Countries" (*Economic Journal* 97(387): 616-641, September 1987); Constantine Michalopoulos and Vasant Sukhatme, "The Impact of Development Assistance: A Review of the Quantitative Evidence" (in Anne O. Krueger, Constantine Michalopoulos, and Vernan W. Ruttan, eds., *Aid and Development*, Baltimore, Md.: Johns Hopkins Press, 1989); Nasir M. Khilji and Ernest M. Zampelli, "The Fungibility of U.S. Military and Non-Military Assistance and the Impacts of Expenditures of Major Aid Recipients" (*Journal of Development Economics* 43(2): 345-363, April 1994); Craig Burnside and David Dollar, "Aid, Policies and Growth" (*American Economic Review* 90(4): 847-868, September 2000); William Easterly, "Can Foreign Aid Buy Growth?" (*Journal of Economic Per-*

spectives 17(1): 23-48, Summer 2003); Carl-Johan Dalgaard, Henrik Hansen, and Finn Tarp, "On the Empirics of Foreign Aid and Growth" (*Economic Journal* 114(496): F191-216, June 2004); Raghuran G. Rajan and Arvind Subramanian, "Aid and Growth: What Does the Cross-Country Evidence Really Show?" (*Review of Economics and Statistics* 90(4): 643-665, November 2008); Tseday Jemaneh Mekasha and Finn Tarp, "Aid and Growth: What Meta-Analysis Reveals" (UNU-WIDER Working Paper, 2011/22).

7. Gustav S. Papanek, "Aid, Foreign Private Investment, Saving and Growth in Less Developed Countries" (*Journal of Political Economy* 81(1): 120-130, January-February 1973).

8. Paul Mosley, John Hudson, and Sara Horrell, "Aid, the Public Sector and the Market in Less Developed Countries" (*Economic Journal* 97(387): 616-641, September 1987).

9. Craig Burnside and David Dollar, "Aid, Policies and Growth" (*American Economic Review* 90(4): 847-868, September 2000).

10. The term "Washington consensus" was coined by John Williamson, a senior fellow with the Institute for International Economics (IIE), in a background paper prepared for a November 1989 IIE conference, published as "The Progress of Policy Reform in Latin America," in John Williamson, editor, *Latin American Adjustment: How Much Has Happened?* (Washington D.C.: Institute for International Economics, 1990). According to Williamson's later discussions of his famous phrase, he intended it to be a list of policy directions on which most economic policy analysts of the conservative Reagan and Bush administrations (1981-1993) would be in general agreement, and that it certainly did not represent his own personal opinions on proper development policy. Almost immediately, however, the term took on a life of its own as a "neoliberal manifesto" of the high road to growth and prosperity as perceived and advocated by political conservatives. Accordingly, it was quickly assailed by political liberals as a program that, if implemented too enthusiastically, would result in unacceptably high economic inequality, social unrest, and political instability, with consequent adverse effects on long-term economic growth. The following is a selection of later writing on the Washington consensus: Lance Taylor, "Polonius Lectures Again: The World Development Report, the Washington Consensus, and How Neoliberal Sermons Won't Solve the Economic Problems of the Developing World" (*Bangladesh Development Studies* 20(2-3): 23-53, June-September 1992); John Williamson, "Democracy and the Washington Consensus" (*World Development* 21(8): 1329-1336, August 1993); John Williamson, "Lowest Common Denominator or Neoliberal Manifesto? The Polemics of the Washington Consensus," in Richard M. Auty and John Toye, editors, *Challenging the Orthodoxies* (New York: St. Martin's Press, 1996); John Williamson, "The Washington Consensus Revisited," in Louis Emmerij, editor, *Economic and*

Social Development in the Twenty-first Century (Baltimore: Johns Hopkins University Press, 1997); E. Wayne Nafziger, "Liberalism, Structural Adjustment, and the Washington Consensus: The Debt Crisis in Africa," in Nahid Aslanbeigui and Young-Back Choi, editors, *Borderlands of Economics: Essays in Honor of Daniel R. Fusfeld* (New York: Routledge, 1997); Jose Antonio Ocampo, "Beyond the Washington Consensus: An ECLAC Perspective" (*CEPAL Review* 66: 7-28, December 1998); Joseph E. Stiglitz, "More Instruments and Broader Goals: Moving toward the Post-Washington Consensus" (*Revista de Economia Politica* 19(1): 94-120, January-March 1999); Moises Naim, "Washington Consensus or Washington Confusion?" (*Foreign Policy* 118: 87-103, Spring 2000); Charles Gore, "The Rise and Fall of the Washington Consensus as a Paradigm for Developing Countries" (*World Development* 28(5): 789-804, May 2000); John Williamson, "What Should the World Bank Think about the Washington Consensus?" (*World Bank Research Observer* 15(2): 251-264, August 2000); T. N. Srinivasan, "The Washington Consensus a Decade Later: Ideology and the Art and Science of Policy Advice" (*World Bank Research Observer* 15(2): 265-280, August 2000).

11. William Easterly, "Can Foreign Aid Buy Growth?" (*Journal of Economic Perspectives* 17(1): 23-48, Summer 2003).

12. William Easterly, Ross Levine, and David Roodman, "Aid, Policies, and Growth: Comment" (*American Economic Review* 94(3): 774-780, June 2004); Craig Burnside and David Dollar, "Aid, Policies, and Growth: Reply" (*American Economic Review* 94(3): 781-784, June 2004).

13. Jakob Svensson, "Foreign Aid and Rent-Seeking" (*Journal of International Economics* 51(2): 437-461, August 2000); Stephen Knack, "Aid Dependence and the Quality of Governance: A Cross-Country Empirical Analysis" (*Southern Economic Journal* 68(2): 310-329, October 2001); Alberto Alesina and Beatrice Weder, "Do Corrupt Governments Receive Less Foreign Aid?" (*American Economic Review* 92(4): 1126-1137, September 2002); José Taveres, "Does Foreign Aid Corrupt?" (*Economics Letters* 79(1): 99-106, April 2003); Paolo Mauro, "The Persistence of Corruption and Slow Economic Growth" (*IMF Staff Papers*, 51(1): 1-18, 2004); Stephen Knack and Deborah A. Bräutigam, "Foreign Aid, Institutions, and Governance in Sub-Saharan Africa" (*Economic Development and Cultural Change* 52(2): 255-285, January 2004); Stephen Knack, "Does Foreign Aid Promote Democracy?" (*International Studies Quarterly* 48(1): 251-266, March 2004); Naci Mocan, "What Determines Corruption? International Evidence from Microdata" (*Economic Inquiry* 467(4): 493-510, October 2008); Mattia Busse and Steffan Gröning, "Does Foreign Aid Improve Governance?" (*Economics Letters* 104(2): 76-78, August 2009); Hannes Öhler and Peter Nunnenkamp, "Needs-Based Targeting or Favoritism? The Regional Allocation of Multilateral Aid within Recipient Countries" (Kiel Working Paper 1838, March 2013); Roland Hodler and Paul A. Raschky, "Regional Favoritism"

(*Quarterly Journal of Economics* 129(2), May 2014).

14. Peter Bauer, *Economic Analysis and Policy in Underdeveloped Countries* (Durham, NC: Duke University Press, 1957); *Indian Economic Policy and Development* (London: George Allen and Unwin, 1961); *Dissent on Development* (Cambridge, MA: Harvard University Press, 1972); *Equality, the Third World, and Economic Delusion* (Cambridge, MA: Harvard University Press, 1981); *Reality and Rhetoric: Studies in the Economics of Development* (Cambridge, UK: Cambridge University Press, 1984), *The Development Frontier: Essays in Applied Economics* (Cambridge, MA: Harvard University Press, 1991). Bauer's viewpoint might perhaps be best understood as a manifestation of the wounded pride of the British Colonial Office following the dissolution of the British Empire in response to agitations of ungrateful natives. See the commentary by Meghnad Desai in "Homilies of a Victorian Sage: A Review Article on Peter Bauer," in Meghnad Desai, *The Selected Essays of Meghnad Desai,* Vol. 2: *Poverty, Famine, and Economic Development* (Brookfield, VT: Ashgate, 1995). The negativity of Bauer's position was relatively unpopular in the 1950s and 1960s, but as the general ideological pendulum in the West swung inexorably toward conservatism in the 1970s and 1980s, Bauer became something of a darling of the increasingly influential conservative movement. See, for example, the festschrift in Bauer's honor sponsored by the Cato Institute (James A. Dorn, editor, *Cato Journal*, Spring/Summer, 1987).

15. A low-level equilibrium trap comes about through the interaction of two functions: (1) a function relating the growth rate of total output to the level of per capita output; (2) a function relating the growth rate of population to the level of per capita output. Starting from a very low level of per capita output, both functions are assumed be positively related to per capita output. A low-level equilibrium trap is created if the population growth rate function cuts the total output growth rate function from below. In this case, rises in per capita income above the intersection level cause the population growth rate to rise faster than the output growth rate. Since by definition the growth rate in per capita output is the difference between the total output growth rate and the population growth rate, this causes the per capita output growth rate to become negative and per capita output to subside to the initial low level at which the two functions intersect. This low level is a stable equilibrium. The objective is to get the economy past another higher intersection point between the two functions at which the population growth rate function intersects the total output growth rate function from above. In this case, increases in per capita output beyond this level would increase the total output growth rate more than they increase (or even possibly decrease) the population growth rate—which leads to a further increase in per capita output. The seminal contributions on this theory were Harvey Leibenstein, *A Theory of Economic Development* (Princeton, NJ: Princeton University Press, 1954), and Richard Nelson, "The Theory of the Low-Level Equi-

librium Trap in Underdeveloped Economies" (*American Economic Review* 46(5): 894-908, December 1956). Leibenstein's elaborate development of the concept was carried forward in his book *Economic Backwardness and Economic Growth: Studies in the Theory of Economic Development* (New York: Wiley, 1957), and in numerous papers later collected into the compendium *The Collected Essays of Harvey Leibenstein*, Volume 1: *Population, Development and Welfare* (New York: New York University Press, 1989). The low-level equilibrium trap is standard material in economic development textbooks, but it does not often appear in the professional literature, perhaps because the basic idea is too simple, or perhaps because it is politically incorrect to suggest that low-income nations are entrapped. However, the trap is an essential component in a selection of more recent professional contributions, for example: Holger Strulik, "Demographic Transition, Stagnation and Demoeconomic Cycles in a Model of the Less Developed Economy" (*Journal of Macroeconomics* 21(2): 397-413, Spring 1999); John M. Litwack and Yingi Qian, "Balanced or Unbalanced Development: Special Economic Zones as Catalysts for Transition" (*Journal of Comparative Economics* 26(1): 117-141, March 1998); Manash R. Gupta, "North-South Trade, Economic Backwardness and the Population Problem" (*Keio Economic Studies* 33(1): 51-62, 1996).

16. The full reference to the 1943 Rosenstein-Rodan article is Paul N. Rosenstein-Rodan, "Problems of Industrialization of Eastern and Southeastern Europe" (*Economic Journal* 53: 202-211, June-September 1943). Some later references in the professional economics literature on the "big push" concept are as follows: Kevin M. Murphy, Andrei Shleifer, and Robert W. Vishny, "Industrialization and the Big Push" (*Journal of Political Economy* 97(5): 1003-1026, October 1989); Kevin M. Murphy, Andrei Shleifer, and Robert W. Vishny, "Income Distribution, Market Size, and Industrialization" (*Quarterly Journal of Economics* 104(3): 537-564, August 1989); Paul Krugman, "Increasing Returns and Economic Geography" (*Journal of Political Economy* 99(3): 483-499, June 1991); Paul Krugman, "History versus Expectations" (*Quarterly Journal of Economics* 106(2): 651-667, May 1991); Paul Krugman, "The Fall and Rise of Development Economics," in Paul Krugman, *Development, Geography, and Economic Theory* (Cambridge: MIT Press, 1995); Anthony J. Venables, "Trade Policy, Cumulative Causation, and Industrial Development" (*Journal of Development Economics* 49(1): 179-197, April 1996); Peter Skott and Jaime Ros, "The Big Push in an Open Economy with Nontradable Inputs" (*Journal of Post-Keynesian Economics* 20(1): 149-162, Fall 1997); Jeffrey D. Sachs and Andrew M. Warner, "The Big Push, Natural Resource Booms and Growth" (*Journal of Development Economics* 59(1): 43-76, June 1999).

17. Albert O. Hirschman worked as a financial and economic advisor to the government of Colombia in the 1950s, following which he held academic positions at Yale, Columbia, Harvard, and the Institute for Advanced Study at

Princeton University. His best-known work is *The Strategy of Economic Development* (New Haven: Yale University Press, 1958). Other major works include *Development Projects Observed* (Washington: Brookings Institution, 1967); *Exit, Voice, and Loyalty: Responses to Decline in Firms, Organization, and States* (Cambridge, MA.: Harvard University Press, 1970); and *A Bias for Hope: Essays on Development and Latin America* (New Haven: Yale University Press, 1971).

18. Stringfellow Barr, *Citizens of the World* (New York: Doubleday, 1952).

19. Seymour Melman, *The Peace Race* (New York: Ballentine, 1961).

20. Al Gore, *Earth in the Balance: Ecology and the Human Spirit* (Boston: Houghton Mifflin, 1992).

21. Franz-Josef Radermacher, *Global Marshall Plan: A Planetary Contract* (Global Marshall Plan Initiative, 2004); Florian J. Huber, *Global Governance and the Global Marshall Plan* (Saarbrücken, 2007). Since the time of the original Marshall Plan, other discussions of possible innovative policy directions for ameliorating global economic inequality have sometimes invoked the term "Marshall Plan," for example in Angelos T. Angelopoulos, *A Global Plan for Employment: A New Marshall Plan* (New York: Praeger, 1983), and Charles A. Cerami, *A Marshall Plan for the 1990s: An International Roundtable in World Economic Development* (New York: Praeger, 1989). However, the policy directions under consideration in such works tend to focus on alternatives to direct foreign aid such as employment promotion and debt relief. And there is little effort to quantify what would be necessary to make significant inroads into global economic inequality by means of such measures.

CHAPTER 3

1. The GMP model described herein is in the general tradition of several other international models such as the Link Project (J. L. Waelbroeck, *The Models of Project Link*, Amsterdam: North-Holland, 1976; B. G. Hickman, ed., *Global International Economic Models*. Amsterdam: North-Holland, 1983; M. Dutta, ed., *Economics, Econometrics and the LINK: Essays in Honor of Lawrence R. Klein*, New York: North-Holland, 1995); the Globus model (S. A. Bremer, ed., *The Globus Model: Computer Simulation of Worldwide Political and Economic Development*, Boulder, Co.: Westview Press, 1987); the Duchin-Lange model (F. Duchin and G.-M. Lange, *The Future of the Environment: Ecological Economics and Technological Change*, New York: Oxford University Press, 1994); the WorldScan model (R. Nahuis, "Global Integration and Wages in a General Equilibrium World Model: Contributions of WorldScan," in P. Brenton and J. Pelkmans, eds., *Global Trade and European Workers*, New York: St. Martin's Press, 1999); the Mercosur model (X. Diao and A. Somwaru, "An Inquiry on

General Equilibrium Effects of Mercosur, An Intertemporal World Model," *Journal of Policy Modeling,* 22(5): 557-588, 2000); and the Ingenue model (M. Aglietta et al., "Economic Consequences of Pension Reforms in Europe: An Investigation with the Ingenue World Model," Centre d'Etudes Prospectives et d'Informations Internationales (CEPII) working paper 2001/17, 2001). To the author's knowledge, however, none of these models have been designed specifically to examine foreign development assistance, nor have they ever been applied to this issue. For example, the Globus model focuses on political institutions and international trade, the Duchin-Lange model focuses on environmental issues, the Ingenue model examines the effect of differentials in demographic aging among nations, the Mercosur model analyzes the effects of the Southern Common Market on member nations and non-member nations. And so on. None of these models have considered the concept of a Global Marshall Plan.

2. This book represents an expansion and updating of the research reported in James A. Yunker, "Could a Global Marshall Plan Be Successful? An Investigation Using the WEEP Simulation Model" (*World Development* 32(7): 1109-1137, 2004).

CHAPTER 5

1. An extreme variant of this hypothesis is that owing to its dysfunctional effects on social cohesion and morale (fostering corruption, inequality, and so on), foreign aid actually *reduces* the total factor productivity coefficients of the recipient nations. In terms of the GMP model, this hypothesis could be formalized by specifying that each nation's A coefficient is a negative function of its absolute share S. This specification was not added to the model because to this author it appears highly implausible. Aside from the odor of sanctimonious rationalization that hangs about the hypothesis (the corollary being that halting foreign aid "would be for their own good," referring to the recipient nations), it would seem that if there were any significant amount of validity in it, then there should be a statistically significant and numerically appreciable *negative* relationship between foreign aid receipts and economic growth. The statistical literature on the effects of foreign aid is mostly divided between studies that find a positive effect and studies that find no effect. Only a small minority of studies have found a negative effect.

2. Robert M. Solow, "Technical Change and the Aggregate Production Function" (*Review of Economics and Statistics,* 39(3): 312-320, August 1957).

3. Abram Bergson, *Productivity and the Social System—the USSR and the West* (Cambridge, Ma.: Harvard University Press, 1978).

4. Robert M. Solow, *Growth Theory: An Exposition* (New York: Oxford University Press, 2000).

5. Simon Kuznets, "Economic Growth and Income Inequality" (*American Economic Review* 45(1): 1028, March 1955).

6. Bennett Harrison and Barry Bluestone, *The Great U-Turn: Corporate Restructuring and the Polarizing of America* (New York: Basic Books, 1988); Rati Ram, "Level of Economic Development and Income Inequality: Evidence from the Postwar Developed World" (*Southern Economic Journal* 64(2): 575-583, October 1997); Andreas Savvides and Thanasis Stengos, "Nonlinearities in the Inequality-Development Relationship: Examining the Kuznets Hypothesis with the Threshold Regression Model," in Christos C. Paraskevopoulos, Theodore Georgakopoulos, and Leo Michelis, eds., *The Asymmetric Global Economy: Growth, Investment and Public Policy* (Toronto: APF Press, 2000).

7. Theodore Panayotou, "Demystifying the Environmental Kuznets Curve: Turn a Black Box into a Policy Tool" (*Environment and Development Economics* 2(4): 465-484, October 1997).

8. Montek S. Ahluwalia, "Income Distribution and Development: Some Stylized Facts" (*American Economic Review* 66(2): 128-135, May 1976); "Inequality, Poverty and Development" (*Journal of Development Economics* 3(4): 307-42, December 1976).

9. Rati Ram, "Economic Development and Income Inequality: Further Evidence on the U-Curve Hypothesis" (*World Development* 16(11): 1371-1376, November 1988); "Economic Development and Income Inequality: An Overlooked Regression Constraint" (*Economic Development and Cultural Change* 43(2): 425-434, January 1995); Zaki Eusufzai, "The Kuznets Hypothesis: An Indirect Test" (*Economics Letters* 54(1): 81-85, January 1997); Albert Fishlow, "Inequality, Poverty and Growth: Where Do We Stand?" in M. Bruno and B. Pleskovic, eds., *Annual World Bank Conference on Development Economics* (Washington D.C.: The World Bank, 1996).

10. Maureen Cropper and Charles Griffiths, "The Interactions of Populations, Growth and Environmental Quality" (*American Economic Review* 84(2): 250-254, May 1994); Gene M. Grossman and Alan B. Krueger, "Economic Growth and the Environment" (*Quarterly Journal of Economics* 110(2): 353-377, May 1995); Thomas M. Selden, "Environmental Quality and Development: Is There a Kuznets Curve for Air Pollution Emissions?" (*Journal of Environmental Economics and Management* 27(2): 147-162, September 1994); Thomas M. Selden and Daqing Song, "Neoclassical Growth, The J Curve for Abatement, and the Inverted U Curve for Pollution" (*Journal of Environmental Economics and Management* 29(2): 162-169, September 1995); David I. Stern, "Progress on the Environmental Kuznets Curve?" (*Environment and Development Economics* 3(3): 173-196, May 1998); David I. Stern, Michael S. Common, and Edward B. Barbier, "Economic Growth and Environmental Degradation: The Environmental Kuznets Curve and Sustainable Development" (*World Development* 24(7):

1151-1160, July 1996); Vivek Suri and Duane Chapman, "Economic Growth, Trade and Energy: Implications for the Environmental Kuznets Curve" (*Ecological Economics* 25(2): 195-208, May 1998); Dale S. Rothman and Sander M. De Bruyn, "Probing into the Environmental Kuznets Curve" (*Ecological Economics* 25(2): 143-145, May 1998); Sander M. De Bruyn and Roebijn J. Heintz, "The Environmental Kuznets Curve Hypothesis," in Jeroen C. J. M. van den Burgh, *Handbook of Environmental and Resource Economics* (Northampton, Mass.: Edward Elgar, 1999); Sander M. De Bruyn, J. C. J. M. van den Burgh, and J. B. Opschoor, "Economic Growth and Emissions: Reconsidering the Empirical Basis of the Environmental Kuznets Curves" (*Ecological Economics* 25(2): 161-175, May 1998); F. G. Hank Hilton and Arik Levinson, "Factoring the Environmental Kuznets Curve: Evidence from Automotive Lead Emissions" (*Journal of Environmental Economics and Management* 35(2): 126-141, March 1998); David I. Stern and Michael S. Common, "Is There an Environmental Kuznets Curve for Sulphur?" (*Journal of Environmental Economics and Management* 41(2): 162-178, March 2001).

11. For example, William Easterly, author of *The White Man's Burden: Why the West's Efforts to Aid the Rest Have Done So Much Ill and So Little Good* (New York: Penguin Press, 2006) and perhaps the most prominent critic today of foreign aid, collaborated with Tobias Pfutze on an article entitled "Where Does the Money Go? Best and Worst Practices in Foreign Aid," published in a prestigious American Economic Association journal (*Journal of Economic Perspectives* 22(2): 29-52, Spring 2008). The purpose of this article is not to question or condemn the principle of foreign aid, but rather to inquire how aid might be applied most effectively, or perhaps, least *in*effectively. The tone of the article is suggested by the following quote: "This paper begins with a discussion of best practice for an ideal aid agency, and with the difficulties that aid agencies face because they are typically not accountable to their intended beneficiaries. Perhaps the foremost best practice is transparency, since without transparency, all other evaluations of best practice are impossible. We then consider four dimensions of best practice: *Specialization* measures the degree to which aid is not fragmented among too many donors, too many countries, and too many sectors for each donor. *Selectivity* measures the extent to which aid avoids corrupt autocrats and goes to the poorest countries. *Ineffective aid channels* measures the extent to which aid is tied to political objectives or consists of food aid or technical assistance. *Overhead costs* measures an agency's administrative costs relative to the amount of aid it gives."

12. Jeffrey D. Sachs, *The End of Poverty: Economic Possibilities for Our Time* (New York: Penguin, 2005); Paul Collier, *The Bottom Billion: Why the Poorest Countries are Failing and What Can Be Done About It* (New York: Oxford University Press, 2007); Dani Rodrik, *One Economics, Many Recipes: Globalization, Institutions and Economic Growth* (Princeton, NJ: Princeton University

Press, 2008); Lloyd J. Dumas, *The Peace-Keeping Economy: Using Economic Relationships to Build a More Peaceful, Prosperous, and Secure World* (New Haven: Yale University Press, 2011); Justin Yifu Lin, *The Quest for Prosperity: How Developing Economies Can Take Off* (Princeton, New Jersey: Princeton University Press, 2012).

INDEX

About the Author

James A. Yunker received his PhD in economics from Northwestern University in 1971, and is currently professor of economics at Western Illinois University in Macomb, Illinois. Author of ten books and approximately ninety journal articles, Yunker's contributions cover a wide spectrum from economic theory to contemporary policy issues. In addition to a large body of work appearing in economics journals, he has published in professional journals in education, library administration, criminology, political science, and international relations. Yunker is no stranger to controversy, and although his conclusions are sometimes directly contrary to prevailing conventional wisdom, his work is always characterized by careful and judicious appraisal of the existing evidence relevant to the issue under investigation. In his writing on controversial policy issues, Yunker's objective is to clarify and illuminate these issues in such a way that judgments on them may be based on focused and informed reasoning rather than unconscious prejudices and preconceptions.

Lightning Source UK Ltd.
Milton Keynes UK
UKOW04n1827150216

268083UK00010BB/301/P